Hollis Read

The Coming Crisis of the World

The Great Battle And the Golden Age

Hollis Read

The Coming Crisis of the World
The Great Battle And the Golden Age

ISBN/EAN: 9783744724289

Printed in Europe, USA, Canada, Australia, Japan

Cover: Foto ©ninafisch / pixelio.de

More available books at **www.hansebooks.com**

THE

COMING CRISIS OF THE WORLD:

OR,

THE GREAT BATTLE AND THE GOLDEN AGE.

THE SIGNS OF THE TIMES INDICATING THE APPROACH
OF THE GREAT CRISIS, AND

THE DUTY OF THE CHURCH.

BY

REV. HOLLIS READ,

AUTHOR OF "GOD IN HISTORY," "INDIA AND ITS PEOPLE," "PALACE OF THE GREAT
KING," ETC.

WITH AN INTRODUCTORY NOTE,

BY REV. S. H. TYNG, D.D.

———•◦•◦•———

COLUMBUS:

FOLLETT, FOSTER AND COMPANY.

M DCCC LXI.

PREFACE.

We arrogate nothing when we say we are living in a very remarkable period of the world's history. A very general impression obtains in all reflecting minds, that we are on the confines of another of those signal crises which mark the history of our race, and indicate human advancement. The signs of the times are strangely significant. Events in Italy, in Turkey, in China, and especially at the present moment in the United States of America, all indicate the coming of a crisis of surpassing interest. In the Papal, in the Pagan, and in the Mohammedan world, we see signs of coming catastrophes which shall shake terribly the earth, and which presage the no distant approach of the great Battle and the golden age of the Church.

The rebellion in China is becoming more and more formidable. At the moment when England and France from without are bringing their thunders to bear on that mighty Empire, fearful rumblings of the earthquake are heard within. The "Rebels" are making fearful strides, and creating ominous forebodings in the minds of the Celestials that the days of the Imperial Dynasty draw near their end. In the downfall of this Dynasty we behold the dying struggle of the last great *Pagan* power.

In like manner the waning of the Crescent—the decay and the dying out of the Moslem power in Turkey, is a sure presage of the no distant extinction of the dominion of Mecca. And the stirring events of the present moment in Italy, and the civil commotions—the volcanoes over which every Catholic nation in Europe trembles, give no doubtful tokens that great Babylon is toppling to her fall. But in the yet more stirring and startling events now transpiring in our land, we seem at the present moment to lose sight of the commotions that agitate the other nations of the earth, and the mighty elements that are, whether above or beneath the surface, there working out the final destiny of man. It is now in America that the great battle rages. It is the battle for *human freedom*—for self-government—for universal emancipation. The Enemy to be assailed and vanquished is generally the same. In India and China it finds its embodiment in a Pagan Priestcraft. In Europe it is despotism of Rome. In America it is met in the system of African Slavery. Now in turn has this monster form of sin come up in remembrance before Heaven and awaits its final doom. A fearful crisis approaches. Light has broken upon this dark domain of sin. The grim monster writhes in anguish and rouses all his ire for the last conflict. It is *our* division of the great and final battle, which shall soon caluminate in the universal triumph of civil and social freedom, and of a pure Religion.

It is not the design of the following chapters to advocate any *theory* on the subject of the Millennium, but to present some of the features, and the signs of the coming of a generally looked for, and a much desired event. It does not so much concern us *when* the Millennium shall commence—whether before or after the judgment, or how long it shall continue—whether literally a thousand years, or for an indefinitely long period, as it does to know what shall be the signs of its coming; what its character; what is doing as a providential agency, and what the Church has to do, as a matter of human agency, to bring about this happy period? It is designed to take that kind of practical view of the subject in which it is believed the great majority of evangelical Christians harmonize.

It seems to the writer much to be deplored that that happy age, —that "golden age" of Christianity, on which prophets have loved to dwell, and sacred poets to sing, and the great teachers in Israel to expatiate; and of which saints of all ages have delighted to talk and write, to hope and pray, should, in some quarters, be so treated as to prejudice the minds of pious, sober men against the discussion of it. Because it has been made the theme of strange speculations and wild vagaries, it is not the less a theme suited to raise the hopes, and wing the faith, and fill with holy joy the hearts of all God's people. Discard the idea of a yet to come golden age of the Church, and how can we vindicate the ways of God in the dispensations of his grace among men? Only the scanty first fruits shall be gathered in during the present dispensation. During "these times of the Gentiles," the gospel is to be *preached* to all nations as a "witness;" and a

Gentile Church shall be gathered in—a great company of believers shall be taken out of all nations, who, during this dispensation, shall stand as the representative of the Church of God, more conspicuous, more glorious than the Church had ever been before, but of no glory compared with that which shall follow. The great harvest age of the Church is yet to come; and shall we not contemplate it as one of the great FACTS of our blessed Religion? It is eminently fitted to fire the zeal and quicken the diligence of the people of God.

The writer's object will be gained if he shall contribute some humble share to guide the minds of his readers to a serious contemplation of these great events which seem to be hastening on apace, and prepare them to meet a consummation so devoutly to be wished.

The world is, at the present moment, in a singularly expectant posture—waiting the next grand climacteric in human affairs. Again, *the great heart of the world yearns for a Deliverer.* The whole creation groaneth beneath burdens too burdensome to be borne. There is a feeling in the human breast that despotism, bloodshed, fraud, oppression and unbridled lust, have, in defiance of heaven, rioted long enough, and that a righteous God will soon rise in his wrath and make a short work. This prophetic yearning for deliverance—this instinctive prophecy of the human heart, is not peculiar to the Christian. The Hindoo, the Mohammedan, the Papist feels it. The world waits the coming change.

INTRODUCTORY NOTE.

THE sheets of this work have been submitted to my perusal, by the great kindness of its author. He has with equal friendship and humility asked the expression of my opinion concerning it. I hardly feel it becoming in me to assume a compliance with such a request. I certainly have no power to add any value to the author's well-earned and established reputation given him by his previous works. The world of readers have expressed their continued and unqualified admiration of the knowledge of facts, and the wisdom of the conclusions, which these books have displayed. The present publication will certainly increase this extended confidence and respect, and gain for its author even a higher reputation than he has before possessed.

In the midst of overwhelming duties, I have read it with great delight. I should not hold myself responsible for an agreement in all its details of opinion. I should feel compelled to carry some of its conclusions much farther. I should adopt as necessary deductions, or even as indispensable elements of argument and expectation, some great facts from which the author relucts in doubt. But it is impossible not to admire the whole line of argument and conclusion which is here laid out,—nor will it be easy, with reason, to reject the general results which are deduced. The interest of the argument and arrangement is maintained without flagging ; and the intelligent Christian reader will find himself unwilling to lay down the book until he has completed its perusal.

The closing chapters upon the destiny of the earth are vastly important. They involve a truth, rarely mentioned, perhaps not often considered, and yet I am persuaded, the very revelation of the Holy Scriptures upon the subject. A restored earth, the future everlasting dwelling-place of the redeemed of God, has long been to my mind, the clear promise and testimony of the word of God upon this subject. "We, according to his promise, are looking for a new earth, wherein dwelleth righteousness." The author of this volume brings out this triumphant prospect, succinctly but clearly. He might have enlarged it with multiplied details, and fortified it with many divine authorities. What he has done, he has done wisely and well. I cannot doubt his book will be the means of awakening far more general attention to this great subject, and extending an inquiry and study which cannot but result in the conviction of increasing numbers of Christians of the truth and justice of his conclusions.

With proper diffidence of my right to the position implied in a commendation of this work,—but with very great sincerity of pleasure in my own perusal of it, I very cheerfully accept the honor offered me in the author's request for this approving introductory note.

S. H. T.

New York, *January* 23, 1861.

CONTENTS.

CHAPTER I.

(xiii)

CHAPTER VI.

CHAPTER XV.

CHAPTER XVI.

CHAPTER XVII.

CHAPTER XVIII.

CHAPTER XIX.

CHAPTER XX.

CHAPTER XXI.

CHAPTER XXII.

THE COMING CRISIS OF THE WORLD.

CHAPTER I.

The hope of a Golden Age—John's vision—The three Tabernacles—The Temple, the New Jerusalem, or the Perfect Temple, types of the Church, Militant, Triumphant or Millennial, and the Church Perfect and Glorified—Our Plan—Nature and character of the Millennium.

HOPE has ever pictured to the human mind the idea of some future golden age. Poets have sung the good time coming. Philosophers have portrayed their Utopias; in which all the social and domestic relations of man shall be blessed — laws and civil institutions shall realize all their beneficent designs —in which man in all his relations and positions shall expand into a perfect manhood; in which his mental and moral capabilities shall meet their full development, and he flourish in all his primeval glory—in which renovated nature, disenthralled from the curse of six thousand years, shall glow again in all her pristine loveliness and beauty: "beautiful meadows alternated with pleasant groves; a serene and cloudless sky spread over them, and a soft, celestial light sheds a magical brilliancy over every object. The heroes there renew their favorite sports"—Orpheus discourses enchanting music. Perpetual spring reigns: the earth teems with bounty thrice a year; and all cares, pains and infirmities are banished from those happy abodes.

But the longing desire and the cherished expectation of a return to earth of the beauty and glory of Paradise, is by no means a notion but dimly and doubtfully traced through heathen Mythologies or systems of ancient Philosophy; or faintly imaged forth in early dispensations of the true Faith. We ever and anon meet in these systems and dispensations, as might be expected, reflections — scattered rays, of these animating truths, more or less vivid and just; yet the idea of earth's emancipation from the curse, and the inauguration of the reign of peace and righteousness among men, lives with the best religious instincts of the human heart, and is associated with the most ecstatic hopes of the people of God in all ages of the world.

Weary and heavy laden, struggling against life's burdens, and but too often overcome by its temptations and sins, the hopeful, waiting children of the promise are reaching forward to the halcyon days when the beauties and glories of Eden shall again return, and the voice of God shall again walk among the trees of the garden. Angels shall mingle with men, and heaven and earth enjoy sweet communion. Seers of old have predicted such a period; ancient bards have sung it—patriarchs, and saints in every age of the Church, have prayed for, hoped and waited for these golden days—when all shall be righteous, when the New Jerusalem shall be came down from heaven—when the glory of the Lord shall be revealed and all eyes shall see it—when the kingdoms of this world shall become the kingdom of our Lord, and his will shall be done on earth as it is in heaven; when sickness and sorrow shall no more intrude; when all tears shall be wiped away:

> "Disease was none; the voice of war forgot,
> The sword, a share; a pruning-hook, the spear:
> Men grew and multiplied upon the earth,
> And filled the city and the waste; and Death
> Stood waiting for the lapse of tardy age,
> That mocked him long."

This was the beatific vision which the beloved disciple saw on the Isle of Patmos. A vista was opened to him through the clouds that should darken the pathway of the Church in her onward career through the world, and he saw, as if painted on canvas, the future glories of the Millennial day.

" And I heard a great voice out of heaven, saying, Behold, the tabernacle of God is with men, and he will dwell with them, and they shall be his people, and God himself shall be with them, and be their God. And God shall wipe away all tears from their eyes; and there shall be no more death, neither sorrow nor crying, neither shall there be any more pain: for the former things are passed away." This is the glorious consummation of all so devoutly wished for, prayed for and waited for, by all whose names are written in the Lamb's Book of Life. They are the Temple of the living God—living stones in the true Tabernacle, the New Jerusalem, descended out of heaven from God.

Mention is made of three tabernacles erected by the children of Israel, and used as their great central places of worship *before* the building of the Temple by Solomon. The first was erected by Moses in the early period of the journey through the desert; the *second* was the one of which we have a very particular account in the last half of the book of Exodus; which is by distinction called, *the* tabernacle; the *third* was the tabernacle built by David on the reception of the ark from the house of Obed-edom. It is the second, the one known as *the* tabernacle, the one made after the " pattern shown in the mount," which I shall take occasion to use to illustrate an important idea in the history of the Christian Church.

This Tabernacle was designed to be a stiking *type of the true Church.* The apostle Paul speaks of the gospel Church as the true tabernacle, *which God hath pitched and not man.* And again he speaks of the Tabernacle and the things pertaining thereto *as the patterns of things in the heavens.* He calls the tabernacle the "holy things made with hands, but which are *figures* of the true;" or the spiritual tabernacle made without hands—the kingdom that cometh without observation—that is not of this world. It is called a "worldly sanctuary," in distinction from the heavenly, or that which is signified by the typical one. The CHURCH is called a Temple—a living Temple. The Tabernacle was a type—a sort of miniature representation of the Church—a "figure of the true tabernacle."

The design of the Tabernacle is further suggested by the *manner* in which it was built. First, it was made after a *heavenly model.* God charged Moses that he should see to it that he made all things "after the pattern shown him in the mount." The various materials of which every several part should be made; its form, dimensions, curtains, coverings; every tenon, socket, loop and tache; every minute particular was specified. No less than fifteen chapters are taken up in the details of the directions how the tabernacle should be constructed, together with its furniture, the officiating priests, their vestments and duties.

The Tabernacle, too, was built by the *voluntary contributions of the people.* They brought their silver and their gold, their jewels, their precious stones, fine linen, wood, brass, and skins—a great variety of materials of the richest kind. Judging from the immense amount of wealth which appears to have been expended in the construction of the Tabernacle, in connection with the fact that the Israelites were at this time sojourners, or wanderers in the wilderness, we may believe that it was a selection, if not an accumulation of most of the precious things of the nation.

The cost and elegance of the Tabernacle is a matter which deserves a passing notice. We have data from which we may calculate at least a *part* of the expense of this structure. Simply the gold and the silver, used in the construction, amounted to more than $800,000 ($810,600); and if we add to this the brass and copper, and shittim wood; the rich embroidered curtains and canopies; the jewels set in the High Priest's ephod and breastplate; the furniture of the Tabernacle, and the skillful workmanship of the whole, the value must be immense. A million of our money would not cover it. This sum was raised partly by voluntary contributions and presents, and partly by a poll-tax of half a shekel a head for every male Israelite above 20 years old. The sum raised by this tax was 100 talents, and 1775 shekels, that is, £35,354 7s. 6d., or $157,000. The beauty, elegance, expensiveness, and the peculiar construction of the Tabernacle, indicate a design in its construction, much beyond the mere convenience of affording the wandering Israelites a place of worship. It was a figure of things to come—a type of the true gospel Church.

But we have another representation of the Church—or a metaphorical description of the true Tabernacle, or heaven. After the vision of the general judgment, "John saw the holy city, new Jerusalem, coming down from heaven, prepared as a bride adorned for her husband. And I heard a great voice out of heaven saying, Behold, the Tabernacle of God is with men, and he will dwell with them, and they shall be his people, and God himself shall be with them, and be their God." And in this condition of things it is added, there shall be no "tears"—no "death" —nor "sorrow nor crying," nor "pain,"—"*for the former things are passed away.*" This is of course the perfect, consummated, the glorified state of the Church—not only an advanced condition of the Church, but the final and perfect condition. This is the true Tabernacle itself, for which every former building has been preparing the way, and for which each has been preparing stones with which to build.

The *tabernacle* well represented the *Church in the wilderness*—the Church migratory—the Church altogether militant. During this condition, the Church has no rest—no habitation—she is the camp of the great Captain—the host of the Lord dwelling in a *tent*. The final and glorified state of the Church shall be a state of rest and habitation—unchangeable—and is very appropriately represented by a CITY—a city that hath "foundations," not to be undermined or in any way subject to the decay of time—a city of "habitation;" those who dwell in it shall be at *rest*, shall fear no change—whose streets are of *gold*—whose walls are of precious stones—whose gates are of pearl—and whose light is the Temple of the Lord; and whose gates, on every side, are open night and day.

This we may call the New Jerusalem state of the Church, or the Church triumphant. But between the Tabernacle state of the Church and the New Jerusalem state, there appears to be an intermediate dispensation, which we may, with propriety, call the *Temple* state of the Church. After the migratory state of God's people was ended and they changed their tents for the substantial dwellings of Palestine, they finally exchanged the Tabernacle, which was the symbol of their *wilderness state*, for the yet more substantial, permanent, beautiful, and costly *Temple.* This we may take to represent an *advanced* state of the Church and a state *intermediate*, between the Tabernacle of the wilderness and the New Jerusalem from heaven. The Temple was more than the Tabernacle, yet much less than a *city*, the New Jerusalem from heaven. The Tabernacle was built after the pattern shown in the Mount; the Temple was built after the similitude of the Tabernacle, yet a higher order of structure; and the New Jerusalem is the true Spiritual Tabernacle itself. They are all of the same pattern, and are symbols, or representations, of the same reality, each, however, an advanced step on the preceding.

If, then, we may take the Tabernacle as a type of the true gospel Church in her *wilderness state*, and the New Jerusalem, of her glorified state, may we not take the Temple as a symbol of her Millennial state?—a state of greater glory than ever before, and yet not of perfect glory; a state of more rest, peace and purity than ever before, and yet not of perfect rest, peace or purity.

An illustration of this kind indicates perhaps better than we could otherwise do, the comparative perfection of the different dispensations of grace through which the Church of God has from age to age been conducted. The Church is a *growth*—from the weakest, rudest infancy to a beautiful, perfect manhood. Or it is a structure, from an altar of unhewn stone, to the "golden altar" that stands before the throne of God above. It is the concentration and the summation of the Divine Wisdom, Goodness and Mercy. It is in the moral Universe—the Palace of the Great King—the Temple of the living God, where we behold, in all the perfection of beauty, the moral workmanship of our God.

Allowing these preliminary remarks to contribute what they may to the better understanding of what shall follow, I propose in the present volume to pursue the following inquiries:

I.   What are we to expect as the Millennial state of the Church?

II. How is such a state to be brought about? Means—instruments—divine mode of operation?

III. The signs of the approach of such a period.

IV. Are there indications already—do we find these signs so verified in our own age as to betoken its near approach?

V. May we expect this reign of peace and righteousness in our world without a great conflict? And what shall this conflict be?

VI. What is the duty of the Christian Church in reference to the approach of the Millennium?

There is a very general expectation among pious people that the Church is yet to enjoy a Millennium, or a thousand years of high spiritual prosperity — that this long desired and happy period shall be preceded and indeed induced by wars, commotions and divine judgments, as well as by an extensive prevalence of the gospel; and that it shall be followed by an unusually bold and virulent outburst of iniquity—the long suppressed energies of sin and the restrained violence and hatred of Satan being let loose —which shall seem for a time to be about to overwhelm and crush the Church, but which shall after a little while and in a most remarkable way, be overruled to the complete discomfiture of the Enemy and to the final dismay of all the foes of the Church.

I. Our first inquiry relates to the *nature and character* of the *Millennium.*

But we meet at the very threshold an objection against the views held concerning the Millennium, by the Church at large. A class, and perhaps a growing class of Christians, do not believe in any intermediate state between the present confused, unbelieving condition of the Church, and the glorified and perfect condition. They believe in the speedy coming of the Lord Jesus Christ to set up his personal reign on the earth—in the resurrection and judgment *before* the Millennium, and in the eternal and universal reign of Christ on this earth. Their views of the Millennium are, that it is a perfect and glorified state—that probation shall have closed— sin be completely eradicated from the earth, and unalloyed holiness have exclusive possession.   The view I take of the Millennium is this :   It is in the progress of Redemption *the next signal dispensation of God's grace to man.*   It is the *third* and the last dispensation under the Abrahamic covenant.   I say under the Abrahamic covenant, for we seem, only from the call of Abraham, to be able to make out, historically, a regular and onward progress of the work of grace.   Before Abraham, the Sun of Righteousness, which rose so bright on Eden and shone for a little season, cast only a confused light over this dark world—shining only ever and anon through the bright example of some Patriarch or Prophet, some Job or Melchisedech.   But after this interesting epoch, the confused light became more and more concentrated, and from this period we are able to trace the regular gradation of human salvation.   The first grand step of advancement, we call the *Mosaic Dispensation,* a dispensation limited in its range, confined to the people of one small nation, and none the less limited in its developments of spiritual light and life.   It was a carnal dispensation—little more than a Religion of *form*—at most a Religion of ordinances.   It did not address itself strongly to the *moral* sentiments of our natures, but stood rather in meats and drinks, and diverse washings.   The washing of regeneration, the doctrine of atonement, the spiritual life of the soul, the duties of universal Benevolence, and the retributions of futurity, were but dimly shadowed forth.   This was the *legal* Dispensation—the Dispensation in which God *vindicated his unity and propagated his law.*   But the light of this dispensation was soon extinguished— or rather its light was swallowed up in the transcendently greater light of the gospel Dispensation.   It was as the extinguishing of a twinkling star-light by the rising of the full-orbed sun.   The narrow boundaries of Jerusalem were broken down—the whole world now became an arena for the full development of God's grace to man through the gospel—the gospel should now be preached to *all* nations—the invitation to life and immortality should be extended to every son and daughter of Adam.

"The plan of God, in revealing his will to man, is in accordance with the great law of his providence :—first, the blade ; then the ear ; then the full corn in the ear :—first, the blushing dawn ; then the rising sun ; then its meridian effulgence.   In the revelation of his will, it was, first, the promise as to the seed of the woman ; then the typical economy of Moses ; then came prophets who gradually unfolded the coming of a brighter day, when the Lord would make a 'new covenant with the house of Israel, and with the house of Judah.'   And, then, at the point of time where the lines of history and prophesy met and blended, called 'the fulness of time,' 'the Word was made flesh.'   And in the person of Christ we see again the law of development ; he was first the babe of Bethlehem ; soon we see him confounding the doctors in the temple ; thence onward, to his baptism by John and by the Holy Ghost, he grew in favor with God and with man.   And having taught the way of life as it was never taught before, and having given the most convincing proofs of the divinity of his mission, by the most astonishing manifestation of miraculous power, having finished the work which was given to him to do, having revealed the great principles, and laid the foundation of the new covenant, he went up to enter upon the glory which he had with the Father before the world was.   And before he ascended on high he gave a ministry to the Church, some to be prophets, some apostles, some evangelists, some pastors and teachers, for the perfecting of the saints, for the edifying of the body of Christ." *

Christianity was an *advance* on the former Dispensation, so extraordinary that even the apostles formed no adequate concep-

---

* Kirwan, in N. Y. Observer.

tion of it. Nothing short of a miracle could convince Peter, and through him, the other apostles, that they might go and preach to the Gentiles—and that the Gentiles should be gathered into the same fold and under the same shepherd with the Jews. This was the "mystery hidden from the foundation of the world," but now made known to the apostles. The gospel should be preached to all, and a selection—or *election* should be made out of all nations. But this dispensation gives signs of coming to a close without having accomplished what were announced should be the final consummations of the gospel. We expect that such promises as these will be fulfilled: "In thee shall all the families of the earth be blessed." "The meek shall inherit the earth, and delight themselves in the abundance of peace." "All the ends of the earth shall fear him." "He shall have dominion from sea to sea, and from the rivers to the ends of the earth." "All kings shall fall down before him; all nations shall call him blessed." "The whole earth shall be filled with his glory."

Such promises have not yet been fulfilled; and indeed, we have no reason to expect their fulfilment under the present order of things. We look therefore for the opening of new scenes— for the ushering in of a new order of things, which shall be at least as signal an advance on the present gospel dispensation, as that is on the Mosaic. The kingdom of Christ shall yet be *universal on this earth*—righteousness shall prevail—sin shall be in subjection—Rulers, people—Kings and nations shall acknowledge the Messiah as a Prince and Saviour.

We think therefore that we may affirm the following things of the Millennium:

1. It will not be a *sinless* state. It is not the final, perfect, glorified state of the Church. Man will still be on probation. Temptations to sin will still exist. All this is very evident from the fact that at the *close* of the thousand years, there shall be found

still on earth such a multitude who shall raise the standard of revolt and make war against the saints. Yet, though it shall not be a sinless state, it shall be a state in which sin shall not *reign.* During the present dispensation Satan still remains the "*god* of this world." At the commencement of it, he was vanquished, but not *dispossessed.* During the whole of this period sin has *reigned unto death.* During the happy period looked for, righteousness shall reign unto eternal life. Righteousness shall be in the ascendant—shall be all-prevalent. Sin shall be a reproach and a byword. It shall be the reign of peace—of purity—of holiness. It shall be a period as remarkable at least for the preponderance of righteousness, as the past eighteen hundred years has been for the preponderance of sin—as remarkable for the reign of Christ in the hearts of men, as the past period has been for the reign of Satan.

2. We may take the following as some of the characteristics of that blessed period : *God will be glorified on earth.* Atheism, infidelity, irreligion will be unknown, except as they exist in cringing subordination to the righteous. Talent, time, wealth will be made to honor and beautify the sanctuary of the Lord. The kings of the earth, the great, the rich, the wise, the exalted, will bring their honor and riches into the house of the Lord. They will consecrate them to the service of God. It will be a time, too, when the great multitude of the earth's inhabitants shall be saved. It will be especially a time of the *reign of the Spirit.* "I will pour my spirit upon thy seed and my blessing upon thy offspring." "All thy children shall be taught of God." "This is my covenant in those days, saith the Lord ; my spirit which is upon thee, and my words which I have put in thy mouth, shall not depart out of thy mouth, nor out of the mouth of thy seed, nor out of the mouth of thy seed's seed, saith the Lord, from henceforth and forever." There shall be a succession of pious families from gen-

eration to generation. Piety shall descend from father to son, not by natural generation, but by a promised effusion of the Holy Spirit, and as a blessing on pious, parental instruction and believing prayer.

Another characteristic of that period shall be, that the Devil, who now goes up and down in the earth like a roaring lion, seeking whom we may devour, *shall be bound.* Men shall then be delivered from his wiles and temptations. The invisible powers of darkness shall no more assail them—spiritual wickedness in high places no more harm them. What a deliverance to be shielded from the fiery darts of the wicked one!

Again, it will be a time of *universal peace.* War is confessedly one of the greatest curses humanity is heir to—the vilest progeny of sin. The war-spirit, rioting in blood and carnage which is incidental to a wholesale human butchery, may claim a nearer kindred to the spirit of the pit than any thing to be found on earth. But this shall be no more: " He maketh wars to cease unto the ends of the earth; he breaketh the bow; he cutteth the spear in sunder; he burneth the chariot in fire" " They shall beat their swords into ploughshares and their spears into pruning-hooks." The *occasions* of war shall be removed. The rights of man being no longer invaded, each doing as he would that another should do to him, all shall be peace. What a contrast from the present clashing, contending, belligerent state of the world!

Health and long life, again, will bless the race of man. How much of life at the present time is but mere *endurance!* Life now is not *lived* and enjoyed, but *groaned* out in anguish and woe! How many meet the " evil days," in which they say, " I have no pleasure in them!" How many walk in bitterness all their life, languishing under weakness and pain! How many are cut off in the very morning of life, and see their hopes blasted ere they were realized! But in that day it shall not be so. " The inhabitants shall no more say, *I am sick.*" " As the days of a tree, shall be the days of my people, and my elect shall *long enjoy* the work of their hands." They shall build houses and inhabit them—plant vineyards and eat the fruit of them. Death is the wages of sin—and no small share of the sicknesses and diseases to which we are subject, is but the legitimate fruit of our own transgressions.

The virtuous habits which will then prevail, will vastly prolong the term of human life, and of consequence greatly increase the population of the globe; and the blessing of the Lord on the ground and *the increased industry* and skill of man, will fill the earth with an overflowing abundance. Long life, and health and plenty shall then be the heritage of man.

Another feature of that age relates to the happy change which shall characterize *civil governments* in their relation to the Church. If not openly hostile, they have been generally and really opposed to the free growth and prosperity of the Church. It shall not be so in the day of Zion's prosperity. " Kings shall be thy nursing fathers." " I will make all thine officers peace, and thine exactors righteousness." " Thou shalt suck the breasts of kings." The righteous being in authority, the people shall rejoice. " Kings shall minister unto thee." " They shall bring their riches and glory unto thee."

It will be, too, a time of extraordinary *knowledge.* Health, leisure, piety, and superabounding plenty will make study easy and successful. The high state of civilization and refinement which shall obtain in those days; the increased opportunities for gaining knowledge; the protracted term of human existence; the increased aspirations of the pious mind after all true knowledge, all imply that knowledge will be pursued with a zeal and success not now known.

But of all the characteristics which shall distinguish that

blessed period, *holiness* shall be the most prominent. "All the people shall be righteous." Abounding righteousness shall distinguish that period. All shall now be "righteousness and peace and joy in the Holy Ghost." That is, the *prevailing* feeling of the world shall be holy. Sin shall be kept in subjection—wicked men shall be held in merited reprobation and contempt—good men alone shall be exalted—and true worth, genuine goodness, unostentatious, sincere piety be honored among men.

That shall be a good day to Zion—it shall be the triumph of Christianity in our world—the righteous shall see and be glad.

But how shall this good time, so long waited for by patriarchs and prophets, and prayed for by all saints, be brought about? What means, what instruments, what divine interpositions and agencies shall be employed to realize the many and precious promises of its coming? We reserve these considerations for the next chapter.

In the mean time let us reflect, 1st, what motives we have to the cultivation of holiness. The kingdom of heaven is within us. The Millennium is simply an increase of personal holiness.

2d. The Millennium is the triumph of Christianity. The Church is now in her wilderness state. She shall come forth in all her beauty and majesty, put on her strength and appear in her glory. She shall take possession of the earth. As we trace this rising kingdom from the humiliation of the cross to its triumph in the conquest of the world, we shall have occasion to rejoice in the strength of the Lord our Saviour.

CHAPTER II.

Duration of the Millennium—How it is to be brought about—The means and instrumentalities—The mode of the Divine operation.

> " And it shall come to pass in the last days that the mountain of the Lord's house shall be established in the top of the mountains, and shall be exalted above the hills; and all nations shall flow into it."—*Isa.* ii. 2.

ISAIAH is the far-seeing, the evangelical prophet. No one speaks more freely of the defections and sins of the Church. No one rebukes more severely, yet opens so freely, unfailing sources of encouragement. As in the motto to this chapter, he often refers to the future glory of the Church—to that more exalted and advanced state of Zion which we call the Millennium, or the highest earthly condition of the Church; and also to her final and glorified state.

" The mountain of the Lord's house" is a term which the Jews were accustomed to apply to the Temple, or rather to the hill on which the Temple stood. The meaning of the prediction is that ZION, the true Church—the living Tabernacle—that which is represented by the term Zion, or the true Temple of the Lord, *is destined to hold a position yet on this earth which she has never yet held.* She is to be exalted above all the principalities and powers of this world—she is to be " established" in honor and riches and moral power far above all the towering hills of human pretension —far above the loftiest mountains of earthly power and magnificence.

II. In the prosecution of the theme announced, I proceed to a consideration of our SECOND INQUIRY: How is the state of things alluded to to be brought about?

I have not deemed it necessary to consume time to establish the *fact* that the CHURCH is yet to enjoy her golden age on this earth. No fact seems to be more clearly and abundantly established in the word of God, and none more fully responded to by reason.. Strange, indeed, if this earth, so admirably fitted up for a habitation of man, should be given up to waste and spoiling— to the dominion of Satan, the god of this world. How soon was the beauty of Eden faded! How soon the peace and purity of the primeval morning changed into the violence and corruption of a disastrous day! Sin changed Eden into a wilderness. The earth has since been full of violence. Carnage and bloodshed and moral corruption have principally made up its history. But shall it always be so? Shall not the bloom and beauty of Eden again return? Shall not the tree of life again scatter its leaves for the healing of the nations? Shall not the tree of knowledge again flourish in the midst of the garden? Shall not earth's primeval beauty and fragrance return? Shall not peace and purity, and long life, and plenty and health, like the plentiful and perennial streams from some exhaustless fountain, bless the now smitten, suffering race of man? We look for such a period. Reason, as well as the sure word of prophecy, allows us to look for such a period.

Precisely *how long* a period this shall be, we may not find it easy to determine. Satan shall be bound a thousand years. *Literally*, a thousand years shall we suppose? This seems not to preserve the proportion of things, and therefore militates against reason—nor does it better accord with the Scripture representations of this period. Six thousand years are allowed to *prepare* for this period—two thousand in preparations so incipient and indefinite as to leave it doubtful from any historical records which we have, whether the work of redemption were really advancing or retrograding. From Adam to Abraham it was doubtless a period of effective preparation ; but it was that kind of preparation which goes on in the forest—*hewing the wood and quarrying the marble.*   The next two thousand years passed away principally in the collection of the materials for, and in the laying of the foundation of, the living Temple. During this period (from Abraham to Christ) the superstructure began to be raised, but so incomplete that a general outline of the finished Temple could scarcely be discerned. Now Christ came, and from that time the ostensible progress of the work has been much hastened, yet nothing is brought to its completion. The Church has only been preparing to take possession of the earth—the Temple has been being made ready to be reared. There has been no such acknowledged possession, no such Temple fully erected. Is it reasonable that the *preparation* should occupy six thousand years, and the actual realization and enjoyment of the complete building but a thousand years?

The Scriptures, I think, represent the Millennium to be an indefinitely long period—I do not know how long. The number, a thousand, in Scripture, as also in conversation, is often put for an indefinitely great number, without intending to define how great. We find the Millennium spoken of in such terms as these: "Yet a little while and the wicked shall not be ; but the meek shall *inherit the earth*, and shall delight themselves in the abundance of peace." The reign of the wicked, which was at least six thousand years, is spoken of as a *little while.* The reign of the righteous on the earth is spoken of as a permanent *habitation.* "Blessed are the meek for they shall inherit the earth." "In his days shall the righteous *flourish*." Abundant are the expressions which speak of the earthly kingdom as a *long period*—long in reality, and long in comparison with the period when sin has had dominion.

But our position at this time is, that the expected Millennium of the Church shall be an *exalted condition*—a civil, social, domestic, individual, and especially, a *moral* or *religious* exaltation. The human apostasy was a signal and melancholy *depression of humanity*— a debasement. The newly-created man was a noble creature—godlike, heavenly ; and the newly-created earth was a beautiful globe, redolent with the Divine goodness, and radiant with the Divine glory. The holy, happy, beautiful pair of Eden found as beautiful a counterpart in that ever-blooming, smiling, fertile earth. But sin came as a poison to mar the face of man, to send disease and pain into his bones and death into his soul— as the thunder-bolt, the earthquake and the deluge, to mar the beauty of the earth ; and as the demon of war, the famine and pestilence, to send terror and desolation into the habitations of man.

Man's condition has heretofore been a suffering and degraded condition. Despotism, Infidelity, Barbarism, have been so many harpies preying on the vitals of man's well-being on earth. The better condition of which we speak, is to be a deliverance from these manifold evils. The physical condition of the earth shall be changed. Barrenness shall give place to fertility—deformity to beauty. The improved moral character of man—the vastly increased industry, enterprise and public spirit—an improvement of taste, knowledge and skill, will do wonders to overcome the physical ruins of the fall, and to renovate, beautify and fertilize the whole face of the earth. *Civil governments* will then exist in their perfection. The oppressions, abuses and unwarrantable usurpations of despotism will be unknown. Wars shall cease.

Even the weapons of war shall be converted into the implements of husbandry—and none shall *learn* war any more. The *social* condition of man too shall then be as remarkably changed and elevated. The causes of all social, domestic and individual strifes, animosities and evils will be removed, and of consequence man in all these relations become happy. Nor need I say how effectually the removal of such evils will tend to the further progress of the race. In nothing will the Millennium be more remarkable than in rapid progress in all that is good and really worthy of human pursuit—in holiness and true goodness; in the pursuits of knowledge; in progress in all useful and ornamental arts; in the sciences; in all the peaceful avocations of life; and in all improvements, inventions, and discoveries; and in whatever can contribute to the true elevation, dignity, enjoyment and usefulness of man.

As the basis and substratum of all this, lies man's *moral* improvement. This is the great distinctive characteristic of the Millennium. The cause that has brought man into his present confused and suffering condition, is not, as some suppose, simply that his *civil and social* relations are disordered, and consequently all that is needed is the reorganization of society. The cause is a *moral* one. It is because *man is a sinner*. When therefore, as in the Millennium, men shall "all be righteous"—shall all be "taught of God"—"shall delight themselves in the abundance of peace," all these natural evils shall be removed.

In the prevalence of holiness, therefore, we shall meet all the varied prosperity so abundantly foretold of the latter-day glory of Zion.

But it is time that I proceed more directly to our Second Inquiry, viz.:

How the Millennium shall be brought about? or the mode of its introduction and of what, as A RESULT, it shall consist? First, we may pursue the inquiry in relation to the *materials* of which it is composed; and secondly, as to the *means and instruments*. In pursuing the inquiry, I shall use the emblem of a *Temple* as a convenient representation of the Millennial Church.

1. How shall this Temple be constructed as to its *materials?* The Tabernacle, the figure of the Church in its first type, was built of a great variety of choice materials brought by the people as their free-will offerings—their jewels and most valued treasures.   And the Temple, a structure not differing essentially from the Tabernacle, except as a magnificent durable edifice differs from a frail tent, was built of materials prepared with great care and expense in a *previous reign.*   David prepared the materials, and of these Solomon built the Temple.   I mean that the Millennium shall be a natural, and, under God's hand, a necessary *result*, drawn from all that is good and godlike in all the past ages of the Church.   The Millennium shall be a concentration, an accumulation of the good and right of all past ages.   It shall be a resurrection (as it is called) of all that is approved of God in the past history of the Church.   The past may be regarded in the light of a series of *experiments.*   Under all possible circumstances—under all the gone-by forms of government—by the aid of all sorts of institutions, systems, associations, and by a great variety of forms under which the Church has existed, God has been developing the good and right.   Under all possible circumstances the *net has been cast*, gathering the good and the bad; the bad has been rejected and the good carefully gathered up and preserved.   Truth, justice, right—all that is godlike—approved of God, is *eternal.*   It is perhaps not too much to believe that every truth which has been practically illustrated in the past history of our world is immortal, whether it be in the form of a political principle or precept, or a religious maxim or truth, or a social, domestic or personal virtue.   Though it shall seem to share

the fate of mortals, yet it shall rise again. It shall have part in the first resurrection, and shall reign with Christ a thousand years. Here God will garner the wheat, while the chaff he will burn with unquenchable fire.

Perhaps there has never been a *form of government*, in which, with all the rubbish of despotism and wrong, which has often burnt like an oven and often burnt itself to annihilation, there has not been gathered up some sound maxims of political economy—the pure gold of political truth. Republics, Monarchies, Despotisms, have each contributed (though by no means equally) to form the perfect Temple of political wisdom which the nations in the days of the Messiah shall enjoy. Under no existing form is the *patriarchal* form of government so beautifully illustrated as in the present Chinese Government. Nor do I know that any other makes *merit* so exclusively and essentially the only qualification for an office of state.

Other forms of government are incidentally and, as by mistake, furnishing other fragments of the right and true, which the great Architect is carefully guarding, and which will finally go to make up the sum total of a perfect system. The political economy of the Millennium shall be constructed of pre-existing materials—shall be a summation of the results of all former experiences. No existing form will answer the demands of that period.

And so I may say, perhaps with equal truth, there has never been a form of Religion—a Church organization, which has not contributed some living stone to the true Temple. As I suppose no existing form of civil government shall be the prevailing form in the Millennium, so I suppose that no present form of the Christian Church is the Millennial form. Yet no form of the Church has been so deformed—no condition been so corrupt, as not to illustrate some of the true beauties and excellencies of the Church—

though the worst forms of Christianity illustrate the truth rather by way of *contrast* and *perversion*. We may take the Romish Church for an example. As an organization, this Church is not a system of absolute error, but of perverted Truth. It is a frightful skeleton of the true Body, every bone and joint hung and saturated with corruption. Its soul is gone, and its flesh and sinews are decayed—its strength and beauty departed. The virgin daughter of Zion has become an harlot She has a soul, but it is the soul of a devil. Yet no other professed body of Christ has retained so much of the *framework* of the true Church. A counterfeit coin may have more of the proper form of a dollar than a poor, bruised, deformed coin of the genuine metal. So with the Romish Church. It has retained the best skeleton of the true Body; but, oh! what a filling up—what distorted muscles! What a life heaves its lungs! what a soul animates its frame!

The leading features of the Romish Church are, the *Supremacy of the Pope*, or *Headship in her chief Bishop; Infallibility* of the Church; *Unity* of the Church; *Consecration* of the whole man to the good of the Church; *Absolution* by the priest, and *Indulgences*. These are all, in their relation to Christ and his Church, great Truths—though by the Romanizers, shamefully perverted. Not one is an absolute falsehood. The chief Bishop *is* the Supreme Head of the Church. Christ is this Bishop, and not the Pope. No Church communion has more distinctly held up before the world the idea of *Headship* in the Church than the Romish. Again, the Romish Church (like no other) has kept before the world the idea of the *Infallibility of the true Church* —absolute infallibility in her Head, and relative infallibility in herself. Rome attributes Infallibility to a corrupt Church. A pure, holy, godlike Church is, in the same proportion as she is godlike, infallible. "Ye shall judge the world." "Ye shall judge angels." The Church of the living God is *the pillar and ground* of the truth. As founded on the truth, as a practical illustration of the truth, the judgments of the Church must so far be *according to the truth*. And of course all the decisions of a perfect Church would be infallible.

Nor is the *unity* of the Roman Church a false boast. To say nothing of the false bonds which have kept Rome together, or of the base purposes of her union, the two hundred millions of Romanists which are scattered over the earth, are held together as no other organization has been in our world. And there has, too, been a *consecration* of its members to this communion which has been known in no other. Nothing more accords with truth than the entire consecration of its members to the true Church. And so also the offensive doctrine of *Absolution* by the priest, contains a truth (of which it is the perversion) of great value. Christ does allow his people to use his name, to proclaim pardon through his blood—to propound the *terms* of forgiveness and the means of sanctification—and through faith and prayer to make *effectual* these means. A pure, holy Church is a repository of vast powers for the renovation of the world. The ministry of the Church are the authoritatively constituted dispensers of these powers. And I have no doubt, if the Church were that high, holy, Christ-like body she *should* be, and in the day of her glory *will* be, that such will be her *identity* with Christ, such her *power* of *faith* and *prayer*, and intimate communion with Christ, that the distorted Romish doctrine referred to will more nearly represent the relation of the Church to the forgiveness of sin than the present groveling, crippled state of the Reformed Church now does.

Even then, from the abominations that make desolate, from the ruins of Rome, the great King may select important materials with which to construct the framework of the new Building. And in like manner it might be shown how the Divine Hand, by a similar mode of selection, may make every system, organization and institution that has been, contribute its choicest materials—contribute all that is of any value to exalt the mountain of the Lord's house above the tops of the mountains. They shall bring all their glory and honor into it. The present advanced condition of the world is made up of the results of past experiences. That yet higher condition of which I speak, shall be the result of a yet longer train of experiences. Every new invention, discovery and improvement—every advancement in knowledge, freedom, civilization and science—every new conquest over some new element, power or substance in nature—every new facility for increased intercourse and communication with other parts of the world, and, more especially, every increase of Divine knowledge and of holy principle and of pious living, are not only hastening on, but furnishing the materials of which the Millennium is made up.

2. Our second inquiry under the present head, relates to the *means* and *instruments* by which the Millennium shall be brought in. The most essential means is the bringing the mind of the world under the tuition and influence of Divine Truth. This shall be done by preaching a pure gospel, circulating the Bible, promoting religious education, and increasing and extending the power of the religious Press. Before this day shall come, and as contributing to its realization, "many shall go to and fro, and knowledge shall increase." By these means man is made a nobler being and a fitter material for such a state of things, and a fitter instrument to advance it.

But there are other means of bringing about this period of a more extraordinary character, which we may speak of either as *means* or as *signs*, for they are both. I shall therefore do little more than to mention them here. They more properly belong to another part of the general subject, viz., *the signs of* the coming of the Millennium. I refer to the *wars* and *great commotions*, to the *judgments*, *famines* and *pestilences* which shall precede the peaceful reign of righteousness. God is known by the *judgments* he executes. In no way does God more clearly and dreadfully vindicate his claims to sovereignty than by his judgments. Men must not only be prepared with right hearts and right characters for the Millennium, but there are formidable *obstacles* to be removed out of the way. Satan's empire is to be broken up —mighty dynasties to be dissolved—systems as old as the world —institutions as old as sin—manners, customs, maxims and practices interwoven with every fibre of life, and cherished by the strongest feelings of a perverted heart, and fed by the worst passions humanity is heir to, are all to be annihilated. Mighty revolutions are to be effected before the empire of peace and righteousness can be established on this earth. Something may be done by gradual, peaceful means—by instruction in righteousness— preaching, teaching, moral suasion. Other obstacles can only be broken to pieces by the sledge-hammer of WAR, or be starved out by gaunt *Famine*, or be burnt out by the devouring flame, or perish under the withering blast of the Pestilence. As the King of kings goeth forth conquering and to conquer, preparing the way to set up his kingdom on the earth, the *Pestilence goeth before him*—a *sword* proceedeth out of his mouth, and he is red as one that treadeth the wine-press. Whatever opposeth is taken out of the way; valleys are exalted, mountains made low, rough places smooth, and the way of the Lord prepared before him.

But without pursuing the subject further at present, we are brought again to the conclusion that God worketh all things *after the counsel of his own will.* He worketh by one set of means and then by another—by all sorts of instruments, by all sorts of systems and institutions, by all sorts of men and measures, educing good from all and rejecting the evil—and then preserving all these fragments of good and erecting them at last into one beautiful, perfect Temple—the perfect from the imperfect, good extracted from evil, order and beauty and perfection brought together, and the Temple constructed out of the most confused medley of deformity and confusion. What an idea does this give us of the wisdom, power and goodness of God! All events, all systems, all things are at his command. It is his purpose to glorify his Church on this earth—to establish the mountain of the Lord's house in the top of the mountains, and to exalt it above the hills. He will overturn, and overturn, and overturn, till all that hindereth shall be taken out of the way, and on the ruins of Satan's empire shall arise the beautiful Temple of Christ's Millennial glory on earth.

CHAPTER III.

"Tell us, when shall these things be? and what shall be the sign of thy coming,
and of the end of the world?"—*Matt.* xxiv. 8.

HERE are three distinct questions: 1st. *When* shall these things
be? 2d. What shall be the sign of thy coming? and 3d. What
shall be the signs of the end of the world? There was a propriety in blending these questions, as there also was in our Saviour's blending the answers he gave to them. The particular
"coming" of Christ here spoken of, is his coming at the destruction of Jerusalem. But the destruction of Jerusalem is used as
a type of the destruction of the world and the ushering in of the
last Judgment. The premonitions, preparations and signs of
the one are essentially the same as those of the other. And it
was to be expected that Christ would speak of the two in similar terms—so much so that we should not always be able to determine *which* he is speaking of. The one seems to be used as
the *type* of the other. Or the one is the primary and the lesser
fulfilment, and the other the great and the ultimate fulfilment.

And it will not be out of place to remark, that it is a peculiarity of Scripture prophecy that the same prediction may have more fulfilments than one. It may be applicable to one or more events, and has a succession and gradation in its fulfilments. The 72d Psalm is primarily a prediction of the glory of Solomon's reign, but ultimately, and in a higher sense, applicable to the glories of the kingdom of the Messiah. So, in like manner, the prediction of the coming of the Son of Man finds its fulfilment in his coming to be avenged on his crucifiers—to destroy Jerusalem, and to put out of the way an old and useless dispensation and to bring in a new one; and then, in his coming, to set up his earthly kingdom and to begin his Millennial reign; and finally, in his coming, to judge the world, to take vengeance on his enemies, and to be glorified in his saints. Each preceding event is not only a type of, but is preparatory to the following. All are parts of the same great scheme—an ascending series, reaching onward to the final end.

Analogous to this, we find any great confederated enemies of God's people designated as *Gog* and *Magog*, and the great battle-field on which they confront the followers of the Lamb, is called *Armageddon*. Such prophecies have, in the subordinate sense, been already more than once fulfilled. Yet we find that a still more formidable Gog and Magog than have ever yet appeared are to meet in dreadful combat, the representatives of Christ's people, and to contend for the dominion of the earth, when Christ shall be about to begin his reign of a thousand years—and a yet more dreadful encounter shall await the Church of Christ from the Gog and Magog that shall appear at the close of Christ's reign of a thousand years on earth. The *last* shall be *the* fulfilment, of which the preceding were but emblematical and preparatory, all forwarding the same great scheme, and the last consummating it.

Understanding the *coming of Christ*, spoken of in the passage at the head of this chapter, as referring to Christ's coming to close the present order of things, and, amidst the commotions incident to such a change, to open a new dispensation of his grace under the Millennial Empire, we will make the second inquiry of our motto the subject of our present discussion, viz.:

"WHAT SHALL BE THE SIGN OF THY COMING?"

III.   I therefore propose to point out some of the events that shall precede or accompany the ushering in of the Millennium. Many of these are mentioned or alluded to in this same 24th chapter of Matthew, and in the parallel passage in Luke.

1. The Millennium shall be preceded by terrible *Judgments*—wars and rumors of wars—famines, pestilences, earthquakes. The "year of the redeemed" has always been a "day of vengeance" to the wicked.   Great changes have usually been brought about by great commotions. An old order of things—old systems are not broken up and made to give place to others except through the storms of revolution.   And the great moral changes by which God has from time to time advanced the work of redemption, have not been achieved except by convulsions which have shaken terribly the earth.   The deliverance of the righteous has been the signal for the inflicting of judgments on the wicked.   It was so when God visited his people in Egypt.   Pharaoh's kingdom was desolated by ten plagues, and Pharaoh and his host were overwhelmed in the Red Sea.   The settlement of Israel in the land of Canaan was accompanied by the extermination, by various signal judgments, of the original inhabitants of Canaan.   The return of the Jews from the Babylonish captivity was preceded by the fall of the Assyrian Empire.   The bringing of the Gentiles into the Christian Church, in the place of the Jews who were rejected, was connected with the destruction of Jerusalem under circumstances so awful as to make it a fit emblem of

the judgments of the last days. If these preliminary changes and advances in the kingdom of Christ have been accompanied by the signal judgments of heaven, much more may we expect the yet greater change—the breaking up of the present order of things and the introduction of a new order, shall be brought about amidst yet greater commotions, and yet severer judgments. It shall be *a day of great tribulation such as was not since the beginning of the world to this time; no, nor ever shall be.* The dreadful wars, pestilences, famines, earthquakes, internal dissensions, massacres, and carnage that came on the Jews at the siege and destruction of Jerusalem by the Romans, stand as a mere figure, type or representative of those awful and far more extensive tribulations which shall fall on the enemies of God when Christ shall come to set up his earthly kingdom.

When, in the destruction of Jerusalem, Christ came to take out of the way the Jewish State and Church that he might bring in a more perfect dispensation, his way was heralded by judgments. Nation rose against nation—there were wars and rumors of wars—famines, pestilences and earthquakes in diverse places. The ushering in of a new system has always been by thunderings and lightnings—hail and fire mingled with blood—on earth distress of nations with perplexity, the sea and the waves roaring, and men's hearts failing them for fear, and for looking after those things which are coming on the earth; for the powers of the heavens shall be shaken.

The great movements of Providence are not so much *reformations as revolutions*—not a new vamping and repairing old systems, but a breaking up of the old material and a *recasting* it. The hammer of Revolution—wars, pestilences and famines, are the terrific agencies by which the things that have waxed old and are ready to perish, are broken to pieces and cast into the great crucible of the Almighty hand and recast, as it shall better please the great Architect.

Among the judgments that shall go *before* the Lord, as he comes to revolutionize the world, to destroy the wicked and to set up his Kingdom, is the Pestilence. The Bible account of the Pestilence is, that it is a scourge inflicted by God on the rebellious and disobedient—was inflicted on Israel when they worshipped Baal Peor—when they despised the manna, and made the golden calf; inflicted on the subjects of David when he numbered Israel; and on the Egyptians when they oppressed the people of God. It was sudden—desolating—fatal—noisome—and especially fatal in cities: a destroying angel stalking over the length and breadth of the land; walking as the Pestilence by night, and as the Destruction that wasteth by noonday.

2. As somewhat akin to what has been said, we find the Millennium shall be preceded by extraordinary *civil revolutions* and the complete overthrow of Despotism. The very beginning of troubles is the great commotions which shall arise among the nations: "wars and rumors of wars"—"nation shall rise against nation and kingdom against kingdom." Towards the close of the remarkable vision which was revealed to John, a scene was presented to him "*great* and marvellous," he says: "seven angels having the seven last plagues," the seven last series of judgments which should be inflicted on the nations; "for in them," he says, "is *filled* up"—completed or finished—"the wrath of God." The "fifth of these vials of the wrath of God was poured out *upon the seat of the beast;* and his kingdom was full of darkness; and they gnawed their tongues for pain." This is the "scarlet Beast" which we find in another place supporting the "woman arrayed in purple and scarlet, and decked with gold and precious stones and pearls, having a golden cup in her hand full of abominations and filthiness of her fornication: and upon her forehead was a

name written, MYSTERY, BABYLON THE GREAT, THE MOTHER OF HARLOTS AND ABOMINATIONS OF THE EARTH." This "woman"—this mystic Babylon—this Romish apostasy, is supported by the Beast—the civil power of the Papal nations. And it should be further remarked that these Papal nations, symbolized by the Beast, are the ten kingdoms—the "ten toes" of the great Roman Image which Daniel saw. These ten European kingdoms, into which the Western Roman Empire was broken up (a Beast with "ten horns"), still support the great Harlot, the mystic Babylon. The sure word of prophecy instructs us that these kingdoms shall be thrown into hopeless confusion, and come to utter ruin, before the Son of man comes to set up his kingdom. Of these kingdoms it is said that they "have one mind and shall give their power and strength unto the Beast;" "for God hath put into their hearts to fulfil his will, and to agree and give their kingdoms unto the beast, until the words of God be fulfilled;" and then he will put into their hands the cup of trembling and confusion and will bring them to an end.

We have in many passages of the ancient Prophets awful descriptions of the civil commotions which shall shake the earth before the reign of the saints—be severely felt by the ten kingdoms, yet by no means confined to them. All antichristian powers —all that oppose or have opposed the advancement and prosperity of the true Church, shall now come up in remembrance before God and be made to drink of the cup of his wrath. We may take as a specimen the 24th chapter of Isaiah: "Behold, the Lord maketh the earth empty, and maketh it waste, and turneth it upside down, and scattereth abroad the inhabitants thereof. The earth mourneth, and fadeth away; the world languisheth, and fadeth away; the haughty people of the earth do languish. The curse hath devoured the earth, and they that dwell therein are desolate: therefore the inhabitants of the earth are burned and few men left. The city is left desolate and the gate is smitten with destruction. Fear, and the pit, and the snare, are upon thee, O inhabitant of the earth. The earth is utterly broken down, the earth is clean dissolved, the earth is moved exceedingly;" and in like terms to the end of the chapter, there is described a dreadful, most inevitable and complete overthrow of the enemies of God. And all this at that identical time when the Lord shall come to be glorified in his saints. For it is added here: " From the uttermost parts of the earth we have heard *songs*, even glory to the righteous." In the midst of all these commotions and overturnings, " Lift up your heads, ye saints, and rejoice, for your redemption draweth near." It is the Lord come to avenge himself on his foes and to be glorified in his saints.

And in confirmation of this idea we cannot but remark, that in all these awful judgments on the nations, as described in this chapter, there is a great multitude who so distinctly discern the Hand of God in all these overturnings, and see in them so evident triumphs of the Redeemer's kingdom, that, as in the song of Miriam, when God had triumphed at the Red Sea, " They lift up their voice, they sing for the majesty of the Lord, they cry aloud. Wherefore glorify ye the Lord in the fires, even the name of the Lord God of Israel in the isles of the sea."

The *time* when this dreadful commotion among the nations shall be, is designated in the last verse: " Then the moon shall be confounded, and the sun ashamed, when the Lord of hosts shall reign in mount Zion, and in Jerusalem, and before his ancients gloriously." Nothing is more common in prophetic language than to represent any great civil catastrophe, as the overturning of kingdoms or cities, or the dethroning of kings and princes, by the darkening of the sun and moon and the fall of the stars, or some such terrible convulsion in the heavens. Hence, in the awful description we have of the events that are to herald the near approach of the Millennium, it is said: "Immediately after the tribulation of those days [that is, following on close upon the terrible judgments which are to scorch the earth as with fire] shall the sun be darkened," etc.; "the powers of the heavens shall be shaken." Or, in the words of another Evangelist, "There should be distress of nations, with perplexity, the sea and the waves roaring; men's hearts failing them for fear, and for looking after those things which are coming on the earth." All these are figures denoting terrible calamities. Waters denote peoples. The roaring of the sea and the dashing of waves, denote awful tumults among the nations.

We have before us here not only a great tumult and distress of nations, but the total wreck of governments—a complete overthrow of the present order of things—a destruction of all tyranny and despotism.

Two classes of nations are particularly designated as the subjects of these civil commotions, and of final annihilation in their present form. These are the ten Papal kingdoms—the ten that give support to the scarlet Beast, and are thereby partakers in the mysteries of iniquity and the abominations of the mystic Babylon; and all those nations that have persecuted the *Jews:* or, to include all in *one* class, we should say, all who have lifted their hand against God's people, whether it be his ancient covenant people, or the people and Church which he has chosen out from among the Gentiles. It has never been well with a nation or people that have evil-entreated the Church of God. Though this Church be for the time in a lapsed condition, yet God charges the wicked —even kings, to beware that they "touch not his anointed, and do his prophets no harm." Hence, we need not be surprised to hear God, while speaking comfortably to Israel and promising to visit them in kindness and to restore them to their native land, say, "Though I make *a full end of all the nations* whither I have scattered thee, yet will I not make a full end of thee; but I will correct thee in measure, and will not leave thee altogether unpunished." Israel should be chastened and reformed; the nations that have afflicted him shall be utterly destroyed.

3. Another sign of the near approach of the Millennium is *the increase of knowledge*, freedom and civilization—and especially *the universal spread of the Gospel*. "Many shall go to and fro, and knowledge shall be increased." "The gospel must first be published among all nations." Many have supposed that because the gospel should be *preached* to all nations, therefore all nations shall be *converted*. This appears to be a mistake. Matthew states the object of this universal publication of the gospel. It is not that it shall secure the conversion of all men, but "*for a witness* unto all nations." When Christ came at the destruction of Jerusalem, the gospel had been *preached* to all the known world as a witness to them of God's grace and of their guilt. And yet but a small number had savingly received the gospel. The same gospel shall again be preached to all the nations of the earth before the coming of Christ to set up his kingdom, yet it does not appear that men shall generally have embraced the gospel. He is to come in the midst of great abounding wickedness, of fatal apostasies. When he shall come, shall "he find faith on the earth?" The question implies that there shall be a melancholy want of piety on the earth at that period. Hence, I may name—

4. *Apostasies* and the *revelation of the Man of Sin, the rise of false teachers* and *false prophets* and *false Christs*, as the next sign of the approaching Millennium. "That day shall not come except there come a falling away first, and that man of sin be revealed, the son of perdition." "Many false prophets shall rise and shall deceive many." And so subtle shall these false teachers be—so much like the real friends of Christ—such signs and wonders shall they show, that, if it were possible, they would de-

ceive the very elect. The Son of man shall come as a thief in the night. Few shall be prepared—few watching. It shall be as it was in the days of Noah. While men were least suspecting it the dreadful day burst upon them. It would seem, as we shall see by and by, that at the coming of Christ to make an end of sin and to establish righteousness, he shall find the world in a state of unusual confusion, open sin and unblushing rebellion. And as he came in the days of Noah, to rescue the righteous from the hands of the wicked and to destroy an enemy already too bold and daring to be longer tolerated, so shall the coming of the Son of man be. Iniquity shall *abound*—and amidst this abounding wickedness and general corruption of public sentiment and the public taste and morals, the love, the allegiance and attachment of many who profess godliness, shall wax cold. In the Church it would seem there shall be much lukewarmness and apathy, yea, much bitterness, and wrath, and strife, and hatred : " Many shall be offended, and shall betray one another, and shall hate one another." " The brother shall betray the brother to death, and the father the son, and children shall rise up against their parents and shall cause them to be put to death." And in the world there shall rise up " scoffers, walking after their own lusts and saying, Where is the promise of his coming? and they shall eat and drink with the drunken."

That " day shall not come except there come a falling away first, and that man of sin be revealed, who opposeth and exalteth himself above all that is called God, or that is worshipped :" in other words, there shall be a great shaking and sifting of the Church, and a great and fearful rallying, and a temporary triumph of the wicked.

5. Dreadful *persecutions* shall precede the coming of the Millennium. " Then shall they deliver you up to be afflicted, and shall kill you ; and ye shall be hated of all nations for my sake."

" They shall lay their hands on you and persecute you, delivering you up to the synagogues, and into prisons, being brought before kings and rulers for my name's sake."

The great increase of religious knowledge—the general prevalence of truth—the general expectation of the approach of Christianity's triumph on the earth, and the many promises of the coming of this spiritual kingdom, will no doubt do much to provoke the hatred and opposition of ungodly men, and stir them up to a virulent persecution.

There are several other events which are to precede the establishment of the Millennial kingdom—events of much greater magnitude than any I have yet named, but which I must defer till the next chapter. I refer to the destruction of the Romish Beast or Papal Rome; the destruction of Mohammedanism; the downfall of the Dragon or the Eastern Roman Empire; the return of the Jews and the awfully magnificent circumstances which shall accompany that event; the drying up of the great river Euphrates, or the severance of the connection of religion and civil government, or of the union of Church and State; the sealing of God's servants; the " slaying of the witnesses," and the great and final battle of Armageddon. All these things must come to pass before the end of the present dispensation and the beginning of a better one. I will, however, speak of one more of the events that must precede this gracious reign of the Messiah.

6. It is the *sealing* of the servants of God. Precisely what this sealing is we do not know. It is represented as some remarkable act or protest, or some distinctive and prominent mark, whereby the servants of God should be known in the midst of a wicked and perverse generation. It seems to have reference to some public and decided withdrawment from the Romish Church, and from all those churches that have an alliance

with the state.   These sealed ones are described as they who have
not been defiled with women, for they are pure—they have not been
guilty of the great spiritual adultery of which so much is said by
John, the Revelator.   The great spiritual Babylon is represented
as an *Harlot*, gorgeously arrayed and seated on a scarlet Beast,
and all they that have communion with her as guilty of spiritual adultery.   The sealing here spoken of, therefore, has some
near connection with the coming out from the impurities and abominations of the Romish communion, and from every professedly
Christian communion which has an unholy alliance with the state.
Forasmuch as the world hath for a long time gone " wandering
after the Beast;" and "all nations have drunk of the wine of
the wrath of her fornication, and the kings of the earth have
committed fornication with her, and the merchants of the earth
have waxed rich through the abundance of her delicacies, few
events will become more prominent or attach to themselves more
importance in the eyes of the whole world, than a separation from
those great and corrupt communions, which have so long usurped
the place of Christ's Church on earth.   Such a transaction shall
undoubtedly take place.   " I heard another voice from heaven
saying, Come out of her, my people, that ye be not partakers
of her sins, and that ye receive not of her plagues.   For her
sins have reached up unto heaven, and God hath remembered her
iniquities."   " Therefore shall her plagues come in one day,
death and mourning and famine; and she shall be utterly burned
with fire; for strong is the Lord who judgeth her."

The separation from such a communion shall be a notable
event—a marked event, and they that separate themselves shall
do it in so conspicuous a manner, and shall so distinguish themselves and their principles in the act, that they shall hold up before the world a token of their decision as prominent as if it
were written on their foreheads.

In conclusion, we are led to raise the practical inquiry, What is the *duty* of God's people in the day of general tribulation ? Many and weighty indeed are the duties of God's people when the Lord is pouring out his wrath upon the earth. God is *known* by the judgments he executeth. When he speaks in his wrath, he would have men hear—be humble—watchful—obedient—prayerful. He would have them at such times repent and turn to God. When his judgments are abroad in the earth, he would have them " learn righteousness." Seeing in these fearful displays of God's displeasure against sin, the evil of sin and God's awful purpose to punish it, and having in these exhibitions of his displeasure some fearful premonition of the coming wrath, how careful should it make the people of God that they should not provoke him to more wrath, and to longer continuation of his just indignation against man.

But there are not wanting intimations that a period shall precede the Millennium, so disastrous—the judgments of heaven will at length become so heavy—the persecutions of the wicked so virulent—the times so tempestuous, that the people of God will be obliged to flee before it. If it shall not be so, what means such a passage as this ? " Come, my people, enter thou into thy chambers, and shut thy doors about thee ; hide thyself as it were for a little moment, until the indignation be overpast. For behold, the Lord cometh out of his place to punish the inhabitants of the earth for their iniquity : the earth also shall disclose her blood, and shall no more cover her slain."

The spirit of the martyrs shall rise again. It may yet cost a man as much to be a Christian as it ever did in the days of the cruelest, bloodiest persecution.

CHAPTER IV.

" What shall be the signs of thy coming, and of the end of the world ? "

I HAVE already named six of the great and prominent events
that shall precede the Millennium and be signs of its approach,
viz., *sore judgments—civil convulsions—*the *increase of knowledge,* and the universal spread of the gospel—*apostasies* and the
rise of false teachers—*grievous persecutions,* and *the sealing of the
servants of God.* I shall now proceed to name six other events
which shall be yet more far-reaching in their influence, and revolutionary and terrible, than those I have named.

But before I proceed to point out these signs, I shall make a
few general remarks on the main subject of our discussion. These
shall refer to the Scripture evidence that Christ shall yet set up
his kingdom on the earth and destroy his enemies. And 1st, the
petition in the Lord's Prayer: " Thy kingdom come, thy will be
done on earth as it is done in heaven." This I may call *the*
prayer of the present dispensation—to be used, no doubt, to the
very close of it. If this be so, and if this present dispensation

be final—be the closing up of the earthly kingdom of Christ, then we find ourselves praying (as the Lord himself commanded) for the coming of a kingdom which has *already come*. But no such kingdom as the one here prayed for has come—a kingdom in which God's will is done on earth as it is in heaven. The present Christian dispensation is not such a state. We may therefore expect such a condition of the Church—a time when all shall know the Lord—all shall be righteous—all do the will of God on earth *as it is done in heaven*. Again, the parable of the tares and wheat teaches the same thing. The righteous and the wicked are to exist together until the end of the world, as it is in our English translation, but in the original, the end of the *age* or *dispensation*. *Then* the Son of man will send his *angels* (these may be war, and the pestilence, fire and famine—including the angel having the everlasting gospel to preach) and gather out of his kingdom all things that offend, and all that do iniquity, and shall cast them into a furnace of fire, and then shall the *righteous shine forth as the sun in the kingdom of the Father*. After this present mixed condition of the world, when God's will is done but imperfectly, there shall follow a reign of the righteous. The enemies of the Lord shall be removed, and the dominion under the whole heaven be given to the saints of the Most High.

And the parable in which our Saviour is represented as a nobleman, going into a far country to receive a kingdom and *to return*, conveys the same truth. Having received the kingdom, he takes account of, receives, honors and rewards his servants, and punishes his enemies. "Those mine enemies, which would not that I should reign over them, bring hither and slay them before me." When he comes to be glorified in his saints, he comes to be avenged on his enemies. He is revealed in " flaming fire, with his *angels*"—which may mean his *judgments*. " The wicked shall perish, and the enemies of the Lord shall be as the fat of lambs.

They shall consume; into smoke shall they consume away." "All the kingdoms of the earth shall be destroyed." That is, as David says, " God will pour out his wrath upon the heathen that have not known him, and upon the kingdoms that have not called on his name"—upon all who will not acknowledge his name. The 2d Psalm seems written expressly to give a prominent utterance to this dreadful idea. This Psalm predicts the establishment of the Messiah's kingdom over the nations of the earth—the " heathen" being given him for an " inheritance," and the " uttermost parts of the earth for a possession; " and the centre of this kingdom shall be mount Zion. " I have set my king on my holy hill of Zion." In view of this, the heathen rage and the people imagine a vain thing, the kings of the earth set themselves, and the rulers take counsel together against the Lord and against his anointed, saying, "Let us break their bonds asunder and cast away their cords from us." This describes to the life even the present feeling of most of the kings and rulers of the earth against religious liberty and a pure religion. And when the light of Divine truth and the progress of religious liberty shall be such as severely to rebuke their despotism and to throw the reins of restraint on their passions, they will break out in open hostility. This will bring on the great conflict. The King who is to come and reign in righteousness, *shall break them with a rod of iron : he shall dash them in pieces like a potter's vessel.* This is a very different thing from converting them, and bringing them into a *willing* subjection. But without pursuing further this strain of remark, we may conclude that a fearful breaking up of the kingdoms of the earth, and the complete destruction of the strongest combinations of wicked men shall precede the establishment on earth of the Redeemer's kingdom, spoken of in the Scriptures as the reign of Christ a thousand years; or as the *world to come ;* or the appearing of the Lord; the *new earth ;* the *Regeneration;* the *restitution of all things.*

While we earnestly look and pray for the coming of such a period, we are moved to inquire *when* these things shall be? This inquiry is answered by another, viz.: What shall be the *signs* of the near approach of such a day? Besides those already pointed out, I shall mention other events, which, as signs, shall precede and open the way to the coming of the Millennium. And,

7. The next in order which we shall name is the destruction of the Man of sin—the Mystery of iniquity—the spiritual Babylon—the Mother of harlots—more familiarily known as Popery, that great system, political and ecclesiastical, which puts its chief Bishop, or Pope, in the place of Christ, or whose presiding, protecting deity is the Virgin Mary, and which has put the ordinances and traditions of men in the place of the living oracles of God. This great apostasy was foretold by the prophets, especially by Daniel, and the Apostle John in the Apocalypse, and is often referred to by the Apostle Paul, especially in his 2d Epistle to the Thessalonians. It is spoken of as a corrupt Christian Church—as a great persecuting power, claiming and exercising an extensive temporal as well as spiritual dominion—whose period of existence is limited to twelve hundred and sixty years, reaching down to the commencement of the Millennium, and which should be destroyed by the *brightness of Christ's coming.*

Were we able to fix precisely on the year in which Popery took its rise, we could fix with the same exactness on the year of its close, and consequently on the time of the beginning of the Millennium. But as Popery had many beginnings, or came to its growth by degrees, so we may expect its end will be. One and another of its hydra heads shall be cut off before its last terrific struggle for life, and its final death.

Nothing seems to be more clearly predicted than the destruction of this power before the establishment of the Redeemer's kingdom on the earth. Indeed, as this kingdom of antichrist is so extensive and monopolizing over the whole world, it is but reason that Christ and antichrist should not reign at the same time. The one must be put out of the way before the other can be set up. Daniel saw the Romish Hierarchy rise under the symbol of the *little horn*, having the eyes of a man, and a mouth speaking great things. And Daniel's attention was kept directed towards this little horn which he had seen come up among the ten horns or kingdoms, into which the Roman Empire had been divided, till he saw the end of this persecuting power: "I beheld till the thrones were cast down and the Ancient of days did sit;" and "one like the Son of man came to the Ancient of days, and there was given to him dominion, and glory, and a kingdom; and all people and nations and languages should serve him." But mark well what precedes the establishment of this kingdom. The Son of man comes—but a "fiery stream" went before him, and he rode as a mighty conqueror, taking vengeance on his enemies; and "I beheld then," says Daniel, "till the beast was slain and his body destroyed and given to the burning flame." The same little horn made war with the saints and overcame them; the Son of man then appears to judge the beast, and to take away his dominion, and to destroy him. "And the kingdom and dominion, and the greatness of the kingdom under the whole heaven, shall be given to the people of the saints of the Most High, whose kingdom is an everlasting kingdom, and all dominions shall serve and obey him."

Paul, in his 2d Epistle to the Thessalonians, very distinctly points out the Romish apostasy as a great usurping, persecuting power, that should rise and flourish and come to its end between his time and the coming of Christ's earthly kingdom. When this power shall be fully revealed, *the Lord shall consume it with the spirit of his mouth, and shall destroy it with the brightness of his coming.* In what way precisely we cannot tell, but in a way, as I shall hereafter point out, very extraordinary, and with a power the most signal and overwhelming, and perhaps miraculous, the Lord will render unto this mystic Babylon as she hath rendered to others, and "double to her according to her works; in the cup which he hath filled, he will fill to her double; because her sins have reached unto heaven, and God hath remembered her iniquities."

8. An eighth great event which we look for as to happen before the reign of a thousand years shall commence, is the *destruction of the Mohammedan* power.   This rose about the same time as the great Romish defection, and its duration is limited to the same period as Romanism, viz., 42 months, or 1260 years.   Precisely how this great colossal system of religious fanaticism and of political power shall come to an end, I do not know.   It has been generally supposed that its extinction is represented by the *drying up of the Euphrates.*   But I apprehend that is a misapprehension of the prophecy.   Yet we have reason to believe, as nothing particular is said of its end, that it shall not come to its death by violence, but shall die a natural death.   It is a great power raised up by the hand of God to curb the otherwise unendurable persecutions of the Romish Beast; the persecuting Beast being dead, it will, likely, die away, its terrific mission being finished.

9. Prophecy leads us to expect, before the latter-day glory of the Church, the reappearance on the great theatre of human affairs of the symbolic *dragon* (which we understand to represent the Eastern Roman Empire), and the destruction of this great power. This is the Greek Church, having one soul and spirit with the Romish Church, and which is at present embodied in the Russian Empire, the great Gog and Magog of the North. The dragon shall now appear in alliance with the Beast and the false Prophet. Russia shall now join arms with the civil powers that uphold the great

Babylon, and with Babylon herself, in persecuting the true Church. After the pouring out of the sixth vial on the river Euphrates and the drying up of its waters, "three unclean spirits like frogs came out of the mouth of the dragon, and out of the mouth of the beast, and out of the mouth of the false prophet." These are said to be the spirits of devils, working miracles, and going forth to the kings of the whole earth and of the world, to gather them to the battle of that great day of God Almighty. And when all these united antichristian and infidel powers have assembled in their wrath to crush forever the hated powers of Truth and Light, the Messiah, the King and Conqueror, shall suddenly appear and avenge his elect, and execute his wrath on his enemies.

This mad rallying of so fearful a coalition of the great powers of antichrist and of sin against evangelical Christianity, is to be a consequence of the great event symbolized by the drying up of the great river Euphrates. And if this be intended to represent, as has generally been supposed, the extinction of the Turkish Empire and of Mohammedanism, it is difficult to see how this event should produce such a panic among the aliens, and drive to such a frenzy the Beast, the Dragon, and the false Prophet, i. e. the Romish Hierarchy, and the civil states that support this Hierarchy, the empire of Russia, or the representative of the Greek Church, and the decaying interests of Islam. But if we take it to represent, as I suppose it does, the alienation and withdrawment of Christian men from State Churches—a coming out from Babylon, and leaving her to her own fate—an abandoning State religions for the religion of Christ, we shall see cause for this panic.

10. Another precursor of the Millennium, therefore, is *the severance of Church and State.* This unholy and unhappy alliance —a union of temporal and spiritual power—which has been a chief cause of the corruption of the Church and of the miseries

that have followed, shall be dissolved. As the spirit of liberty shall work, and men shall disenthrall themselves from this yoke, the despotic powers, both in the Church and in the State, will combine to suppress this rising spirit of liberty, and thus hasten on the great conflict, called the battle of the great day of God Almighty.

11. The *return* to their native land of *the Jews,* is another event which must precede the coming of the Messiah to set up the Millennial kingdom. It must here be borne in mind that, in the original grant of Canaan to Israel—in the covenant made with Abraham—the land was given to the promised seed for an *everlasting possession,* i. e. as long as the world stands. Though for a time the fulfilment of this promise is suspended on account of Israel's sins, yet the promise is not annulled. Israel shall yet be more glorious in the promised land than he ever yet has been. The promise is unconditional. "Thus saith the Lord God, When I shall have gathered the house of Israel from the people among whom they are scattered, I shall be sanctified in them in the sight of the heathen, then shall they dwell in *their land* that I have given to my servant Jacob. And they shall dwell safely therein."

I shall not multiply quotations to prove the *fact* of the return of the Jews to Palestine. No fact seems more abundantly established. They shall return *before* the Millennium, and their restoration and conversion to Christianity shall be so important and efficient means of the conversion of the world to Christ and the establishment of the Messiah's kingdom, that it said to be as "*life from the dead.*"

A few quotations here, showing the *position* of the Jewish Church and nation in the renovated kingdom, will neither appear out of place nor void of interest. They will show, too, by implication, that that kingdom shall not come till there shall be a gathering together of God's ancient covenant people. They shall constitute an important part of that kingdom. A cloud has come over the Jews for a time. Now is the times of the *Gentiles*. God is now visiting the Gentiles to take out a people for his name, and then, he says, *he will return and build up the tabernacle of David, which is thrown down.* "Thus saith the Lord, If heaven above can be measured and the foundation of the earth searched out beneath, I will also cast off the seed of Israel, for all they have done, saith the Lord." "For, as the new heavens and the new earth which I will make shall remain before me, so shall your seed and your name remain." "The zeal of the Lord of hosts will perform this." In the kingdom of which we speak, Jerusalem is again to become an important spot, and Judea a land of renown, and the people of Israel a beloved and honored people. And we shall see by and by that their return is intimately connected with scenes of the deepest interest which shall take place before the coming of the Messiah's kingdom.

Did our limits permit we might speak of other events, and social and moral conditions, which shall precede the coming of the Son of man; such as the *stupidity* and *listlessness* of the *wicked* —the *want of reverence*, of loyalty, of respect for authority; together with *the purification* of the Church from intemperance and various other forms of evil; and lastly, but not the least, the extensive revivals of religion which so delightfully characterize the present period. All these things indicate, no less than those before named, that a great revolution is at hand; and admonish us to watch and to wait the speedy coming of our ascended Lord. We pass these to notice but one other of the predicted signs which shall precede the great day of the Lord.

12. The only other events which I shall name, are, the "*slaying of the witnesses,*" and the final great battle of Gog and Magog—the "battle of the great day of God Almighty." But these two particulars, or rather this *twofold* particular (for they seem to

be intimately connected), involves too many things to be disposed
of in a summary manner.

We merely affirm that these things—this overthrow—must
come to pass *before* the Son of man come to set up his kingdom
on the earth.   It shall be a dreadful rebuff and a seeming overthrow of the Church, an awful precursor of the full dawn of the
Millennial Morn.

It may relieve the minds of some if I say another word here,
before I close, on the term, *the coming of Christ.*   I have already
used the term, and shall hereafter use it, as implying a *personal*
coming.   I would therefore here say, that, though I do not see
good evidence for the belief that Christ will *continue* a *personal*
reign on the earth, as King of Jerusalem and Prince and Potentate
of the whole earth, yet I find myself quite unable to dispose of
a great variety of very prominent passages of Scripture, without
believing that Christ will at least appear personally at the last
great battle, and personally vindicate his cause and take the most
signal vengeance on his enemies at a time when, in dreadful and
most formidable confederacy, they shall be gathered together
against him ; and that he will personally commence his reign in
Jerusalem.   How else can we understand the 14th chapter of
Zechariah, especially the following passages? "Behold, the day
of the Lord cometh, and the spoil shall be divided in the midst
of thee.   For I will gather all nations together against Jerusalem to battle ; and the city shall be taken, and the houses rifled,
and the women ravished ; and half of the city shall go forth in
captivity, and the residue shall not be cut off from the city.   Then
shall the Lord go forth and fight against those nations, as when
he fought in the day of battle.   And his feet shall stand in that
day on *the mount of Olives*, which is before Jerusalem on the
east ; and the mount of Olives shall cleave in the midst thereof
toward the east and toward the west, and there shall be a very

great valley: and half of the mountain shall remove toward the north, and half toward the south." — "And the Lord my God shall come, and all the saints with thee." "And the Lord shall be King over all the earth. In that day shall there be one Lord, and his name one."

It is further declared that, after the great conflict shall have passed, and the King shall establish his throne in Jerusalem, the people of all nations shall "even go up from year to year to worship the King, the Lord of hosts, and to keep the feast of tabernacles." "And it shall be, that whoso will not come up of all the families of the earth unto Jerusalem to worship the King, the Lord of hosts, even upon them shall be no rain."

Christ was born King of the Jews—he died as King of the Jews. When reproached as a usurper of the throne of David, he did not deny the charge. It is difficult for any plain reader of the declarations above quoted, to understand less than that Christ, when he shall set up his Millennial kingdom, shall make Jerusalem, in some special sense, the centre of his great spiritual empire. The Temple at Jerusalem shall be, as it were, the palace of the great King, where shall be seen his glory, and where shall be his more especial presence, and whither, representatively at least, all people, and tribes, and nations shall go up to worship, and keep the "feast of tabernacles." *

Christ's triumphal entrance into Jerusalem, riding on the colt of an ass, may be taken as an emblem of his future entrance as

---

* The feast of tabernacles was the great thanksgiving occasion of the Jewish economy —observed at the close of harvest, and hence often called the *feast* of *ingathering.* It was observed in commemoration of the wanderings of Israel in the wilderness, when they dwelt in tents or tabernacles. This occasion, when *evangelized* and observed in the golden age of the Millennium, will commemorate the now present *wilderness* state of the Christian Church (Rev. xii. 6), and, as such, there will be great beauty and propriety in its observance during that long and happy period. It shall commemorate that great *ingathering* into the new Jerusalem which shall then be come down from heaven.

King.   If it were not on the occasion of the feast of tabernacles,
yet it had a striking allusion to that feast.

Finally, we cannot be too solemnly impressed with the great
things which God is doing in our world. Undoubtedly, all things
are hastening to a grand and awful crisis.   All things seem to say,
" Be ye also ready; watch unto prayer, for ye know not in what
hour the Son of man cometh."

CHAPTER V.

"When ye shall see all these things, know that it is near."—*Matt.* xxiv. 33.

HAVING pointed out what are the signs—what the events and conditions of the world and of human affairs—which shall *precede* the coming of the Millennium, I pass to our next general topic, viz., that *the characteristics of the present age answer to the signs already named.* Our inquiry, therefore, now becomes :

IV. Are there special indications at the present time of the near approach of the Millennium?

We can return a satisfactory answer to this inquiry only by retracing our steps—though not exactly in the same order—and examining, as to each particular mentioned, whether present appearances justify any such expectation.

1. *Divine judgments*—wars, famines, pestilences, earthquakes in diverse places—do we find these so to characterize our times as to give sign that they are the predicted precursors of the Millennium? I think we do. We have wars, but more rumors of wars. So inflammable is the present state of the nations that but a spark would set them all in a blaze.

We retain a vivid recollection of the terrible upheavings of Europe by the devastating hand of war in 1848. And we shall not soon forget the wholesale carnage in the Crimea and about the walls of Sebastopol. And yet more recently have we been horrified at the unheard-of atrocities and butcheries of the late Sepoy war. And now again is the blast of the war-trumpet heard in the Italian war, and all Europe seemed about to rush to the battle. Nation may any day be dashed against nation, and the great decisive battle be but a step before us. The present position of the nations of Europe; the state of irritation which exists; the formidable preparations which have been made and are still making, and above all the *necessity* there seems to be for an extensive, exterminating war, to remove out of the way some of the most formidable obstacles to the final and universal establishment of Immanuel's kingdom, all prognosticate the approach of carnage and desolation, such as the world has not before seen. It may be delayed, but shall not fail till its dread mission be fulfilled.

And the first half of the present century has been signalized, too, by the prevalence of a pestilence of a most malignant character; almost unknown in the world till within the last fifty years. And here it will be not out of place, nor void of interest, I trust, to glance for a few moments at the strange history of the pestilence which has but so recently visited our land, in its devastating progress round the world. In its singular history we shall recognize the *pestilence that goeth before Him*, who is about to wrest from the usurper the empire of this world and to establish his kingdom on its ruins: and on this account it deserves some particular attention in this connection. I speak of the Asiatic cholera, which, as a matter of recent history and of Heaven's judgments on men, should not be allowed to pass out of mind.

With a single exception, the cholera seems to have been unknown in the world till 1817. But this exception was a terrible one, such as dreadfully to indicate what a fearful instrument of destruction this angel of death was now commissioned to wield. It was in 1782–3, while a noble struggle was making in North America to establish liberty on some permanent foundation, and thereby contribute much to hasten the day of the world's Millennium—it was while all things were preparing in *Europe* for one of those civil convulsions which precede some real civil and moral advancement—it was while the English in India were in the zenith of their glory, adding province to province in their already stupendous empire, consolidating there a power which is very justly the wonder of the world, and a stupendous scheme of Providence for the elevation and renovation of the degraded nations of the East—it was, I say, in 1782–3, that another angel came out of the Temple, having one of the seven last plagues. This was one of those terrific agencies which the conqueror on the white horse would employ to subjugate the world to himself. This angel appeared—not now finally to fulfil his dread mission, but to indicate his *power*—and having spread his wings upon the blast and dropped thick about him the spoils of death, he disappeared for a third of a century.

His appearance was on this wise : A body of 5000 troops, stationed at Ganjam in India, was suddenly attacked with a new disease of such incredible malignity that men in perfect health dropped down dead by dozens. Besides those who were thus smitten instantaneously, 500 sickened in one day, and for the most part died in the space of an hour. The next day the distemper still raged with unabated fury, and on the third day more than half the army had either perished or were in the hospital. The next year (1783) the army, under Sir John Burgoyne, was attacked, and 1000 perished within a month, some not surviving the attack more than an hour. The year after the same strange malady broke out among the pilgrims at Hurdwar, and slew 20,000. After some such dreadful displays of power and malignity, this destroying angel took his flight and left the earth for thirty-four years.

In 1817 the cholera reappeared in Bengal with extraordinary malignity. It now appeared no longer *local*, but migratory; for, in a few weeks, it had ravaged every town and village from the mouth of the Ganges up to its confluence with the Jumna.

From this central district the Pestilence went forth by three general routes on its mission of death around the world. To the south-west its track was marked with anguish and death in the direction of Madras and Ceylon; to the south-east, along the opposite coast of the Bay of Bengal, to Arracan and the Malays; and by a western route it traversed the whole peninsula of Hindostan, overtaking in its course the British army, and cutting down 9000 in the course of a week; it traveled towards Europe by the way of the Persian gulf; 10,000 perished in Muscat—18,000 in Bassora (one-third of its population) died in eleven days. It passed along the Tigris to Aleppo, and along the Euphrates to Erzeroum in Armenia; and thence it came to the confines of Europe, where it strangely paused from 1823 to 1829. In 1830 we find the pestilence ascending the Volga, where in one month it numbers 2367 victims, and rapidly approaching Moscow. In 1831, it is found threading all the chief European rivers, and visiting every principal city from the Danube to the Atlantic. In the autumn of this year (October) the infection had passed from Hamburg to Sunderland in England, breaking out nearly at the same time in London. In four months it had reached Edinburgh in Scotland, and but a few weeks later it appeared in Dublin, Ireland. From England the epidemic seemed to pass into France and Spain, and thence to Quebec and New York, where it made its appearance in June, 1832.   In Great Britain and Ireland 30,000 fell victims to the scourge; in Paris alone, 18,000.

These are the main streams through which this virus of death, in its first circuit, rolled over the whole earth.   Were I to return, I might show how these several rivers of death sent out their lateral branches, till, in their fatal course, they scarce left a nation untouched, by some reverted stream.   By some reflex current, Spain, Portugal and France, Piedmont, Genoa and Florence were reached from England; Egypt and Arabia from Persia; and Constantinople from the great Western stream.   At Mecca 20,000 died in four days, and in Cairo the mortality became so great that the sick went without care and the dead without burial.

It will be seen by this brief outline, that it is not true that this scourge only travels westward.   In its eastern route through Arracan and Malacca, we find it traversing the islands of the Indian Archipelago, extending its ravages into China, and passing the Great Wall and pervading many parts of Mongolia.

It has been remarked by a writer in the London *Times*, who has been at some pains to trace the ravages of this destroyer, that it was twenty years from its first outbreak in Bengal before it had completed the circuit of the globe.   Two years it took to over-run India; two, to pass through Persia to the Caspian Sea; and two, to spread through Europe to Great Britain.   During two years it paused in its career on the boundaries of Hindostan; and during six years it halted on the verge of Europe.   And the last reflex current, which invaded the southern peninsulas of Europe, did not reach its destination till 1836–7.   Gibraltar was not attacked till 1834—Piedmont, Genoa, and Florence in 1835—Naples in 1836—and Rome in 1837; or twenty years from the first outbreak in Bengal.

I need only remark that the pestilence which more recently passed over our land, pursued, with very little deviation, the track of its predecessors, traveling however more rapidly and committing fiercer ravages.   "Many cities," observes the same writer, "as for instance, St. Petersburg and Berlin, were attacked at the same season, and even in the same month, as in 1830.   The same streets, nay, the same houses, that suffered most severely before, have suffered the most severely now"—and towns which escaped then, were passed by in the late visitation.

There is much, I think, in the history of this form of pestilence, to indicate that it was one of those Divine judgments which should precede the coming of the Son of man—when he shall come to be avenged on his enemies and to be glorified in his saints.   It is governed by no laws which we can discover—is confined to no class of men—and is peculiar to no circumstances in life.   But, in what to us seems its arbitrary character and its fitful independence, we discover unmistakable marks that it is a special agent of God by which to inflict his last judgments on the earth.

Thousands of families in our land were, in a moment the most unexpected, clothed in sackcloth—tens of thousands of our citizens, of all ages and conditions of life, were, in awful suddenness, snatched away; all their fond relationships in time broken up; their friends left in bitterness to mourn, and they hurried away to the judgment-seat.   In some instances whole families were cut off in the course of a few days: in one instance a family of eleven persons.   In the small city of St. Louis, the mortality rose to one hundred a day—and in Cincinnati its ravages were scarcely less. In New York, 1400 were borne to the grave in a single week. Who was not shocked at the appalling facts which reached us from Sandusky City?   One writing from that infected place and amidst the victims of the devouring scourge, says:

"The condition of this city, at the present time, is most fearful and heart-rending, from the effects of the cholera.   For some days past, the epidemic has been making rapid strides, and it has now reached a crisis which threatens to involve the most awful consequences. Of a population of 3000, there are not more than 700 remaining. The deaths for the last two days amount to about 100, and are still on the increase.

"Most of the inhabitants who have escaped the dreadful malady have left the city in dismay. Business of every description is entirely suspended, and the various hotels, together with the post-office and the public stores, are all closed. Many of our physicians have fallen victims to the disease, and those who have escaped its ravages, have precipitately fled from the region of death. The sick are suffering in a dreadful manner for the want of medical aid and assistance.

"The living are not only unable to attend to the wants of the sick, but cannot bury their dead. There are none to be found to dig graves or make coffins. The markets are entirely deserted, and the few inhabitants remaining are under the necessity of sending to Cleveland, and other ports on the Lake, for provisions and medical assistance."

Like the plague or pestilence described in the Bible, the cholera broke in upon the people suddenly—made its dreadful invasion at "midnight"—gave signs of being inflicted by God for the sins of the people—and everywhere strangely extinguished the common sympathies of humanity. Friends, absent, dead, dying, or watching over those who are dying, are compelled to leave their dead to persons hired to clear them away as a nuisance to the living. This desolating, *hardening* effect of the cholera, quite identifies it with the prophetic descriptions of the Pestilence that should precede the coming of the great and terrible day of the Lord.

2. I said political revolutions—convulsions among the kingdoms of the earth, are to be looked for as precursors of the Millennium. Is there any thing in the present political state of the

world that verifies this sign? The fifth angel *poured out his vial on the seat of the Beast; and his kingdom was full of darkness; and they gnawed their tongues for pain.*

This we have interpreted of the papal nations—especially of the "ten kingdoms," which "give their power to the Beast"—which sustain the spiritual Babylon by their civil authority. Before Christ shall set up his kingdom, we have seen, these nations shall be thrown into hopeless confusion; and, inasmuch as their civil despotism is so identified with the spiritual despotism of Rome, that the two must perish together.

Do we at the present time discover in the condition of European nations any thing like the confusion, perplexity and darkness represented by the pouring out of the fifth vial? Do we find kings dethroned, dynasties dissolved, governments thrown into disorder, and a general distrust and uncertainty pervading all the affairs of those nations? We are all too well acquainted with the revolutions and civil convulsions of 1848, to need any details here, as a matter of history. But there were certain features in these revolutions which go very far to identify them as the events which are foretold shall immediately precede the reign of a thousand years.

The fifth vial was poured out upon the *seat,* or the *throne* of *the Beast;* and the effect should be, that *his kingdom should be filled with darkness:* i. e. the judgments should fall on the *ruling powers,* and as a consequence, they should be thrown into a strange confusion and perplexity, and that both rulers and people should act like men blindfolded, or like persons groping their way in the dark. Nothing could more accurately describe the present condition of Europe. If we were to describe the condition of Europe as the result of her late revolutions, in a single word, we should say it was one grand *disappointment.* I do not know a single result that proved in the end to be what was expected.

The most profound skill and the most undoubted bravery came as near accomplishing the objects aimed at as men blindfolded would accomplish their objects. France, with some noble spirits to lead in her affairs, annihilated the monarchy of Louis Phillippe and established a republic. And yet there was in the form of government adopted less of republicanism than there was either of monarchy, despotism, or anarchy. France realized nothing she sought and fought for; neither did any other nation of Europe. But what is more remarkable, they rather realized the very opposite of what they sought. I may here quote a paragraph from a writer of the time, containing some exceedingly just remarks, which will put this topic in a more correct light than I should be able to do otherwise:

"The new government, in place of securing to the people the liberty which they anticipated, is in many respects more tyrannical than the monarchy they overthrew. Instead of yielding occupation and abundance to the laborers of Paris, the French Revolution deprived them of employment and reduced them to beggary and starvation. Many of the men who were chiefly instrumental in establishing the republic, instead of obtaining the political station and enjoying the influence which they expected, have sunk into neglect or been driven into exile. The new administration, instead of favoring the liberty of other nations, has overthrown the Republic of Rome, and attempted to reinvest the Pope with the worst species of despotic power. The King of Belgium, who was ready to abdicate had his people desired it, holds his sceptre with a surer grasp than any other monarch in Germany. The Austrian Government, which appeared less likely to feel the shock of revolution, has been in greater danger than any other of subversion. Prince Metternich, who was thought to be more thoroughly master of the art of despotic rule, and more likely than any other minister to maintain his position, was the most easily baffled, and the most thoroughly divested of power. The Pope, who from his pretensions to the vicegerency of God and infallibility, it might have been expected, would be the most reluctant to quit his station, and if overwhelmed, fall with a degree of stateliness, was more easily induced than any prince to abandon his throne, and in a form the most undignified and abject. The population of Rome, which seemed less capable than any other of self-government, and less likely to offer a brave and effective resistance to a foreign foe, has conducted itself in a more orderly manner, displayed a nobler patriotism, and made a bolder and a more strenuous struggle for the defense of its liberties, than the people of any other capital that has been the scene of revolution. The Austrian monarchy, which has ever been fearful and jealous of Russia, has, by inviting the Czar to assist in the conquest of Hungary, assumed the relation of a dependent on him, and probably placed it in the power of the Czar to pursue what course he pleases, without respect to the wishes of Austria."

In a word (as I have before said), scarcely an event took place in the course of all those strange revolutionary struggles which was not the opposite of what was expected and desired. Both rulers and people missed their aim in all that they attempted, and all the calculations of human sagacity and forecast quite failed. It was a great political game played in the *dark*. The "*kingdom of the Beast was full of darkness.*" No symbol could more exactly express the condition of Southern Europe during that eventful period. The actors in the great drama were without concert or understanding of each other's movements, as men groping their way in the dark. Confusion, perplexity, doubt, and especially *disappointment*, were the most prominent characteristics of the recent European movements. Little has yet been realized but defeat and disappointment. What but disaster and despair have crowned the noble struggles for liberty, of the people of Paris—of Berlin—of Vienna—of Rome, Genoa, Milan, Florence and Naples? How completely thwarted all their endeavors for liberty! And how disastrous the revolt of the Sicilians; and how humiliating the defeat of the outbreak for liberty in Ireland! And poor Hungary—noble Hungary—whose heart did not throb a welcome to her among the sons of the free (who more worthy?)—and whose heart has not been pained at her melancholy fall!

But the other part of the prophecy seems to be meeting a no less exact fulfilment in the present condition of Europe: " *And they gnawed their tongues for pain, and blasphemed the God of heaven because of their pains and their sores, and repented not of their deeds.*" All these political convulsions, instead of conducting those nations to moral reformations, seem driving them on to infidelity and atheism; and their defeat and disasters seem not to be working a feeling of humility and dependence on the Divine arm, but is rather torturing, tormenting and maddening them on to a struggle of which, what has been, is but the beginning of sorrows. All Europe is trembling over a volcano. Its internal fires are boiling, and ere long we shall hear the explosion—and *such* an explosion the world does not often hear!

The present hostile attitude of the great European powers is awfully grand and dreadfully ominous of coming change. Stupendous armies are rallying to the combat. The most formidable preparations are making to shake the whole continent of Europe, and to drench the nations in blood. We wait in awful suspense the result. If it be not the final great battle (which we do not apprehend), it is doubtless a mighty conflict which shall, in dreadful certainty, hasten on the final battle. The contending parties in the late Italian war seemed not arranged for finality. The great confederated enemy, which shall finally range himself in deadly hostility against the nations that acknowledge and fear

God and contain the true Church, may first be allowed to fight against himself—one portion of this confederacy be made to prey upon, to weaken, if not to destroy another portion, before the final adjustment of parties for the great and last conflict.

If the confederation which we anticipate, viz., a confederacy of Russia as the representative and embodied strength of the Eastern Hierarchy, and of the Roman Catholic powers of Europe as the representative and embodiment of the Papal Hierarchy, were *now* to join hands in the conflict against the Protestant powers of Europe, the odds would be fearfully against the latter. It would be the alliance of the Bear and the Wolf against the Lamb. But the great King who rules among the nations knows full well how to set the Bear and the Wolf first in deadly conflict with each other; and not till they shall have expended their strength and wasted their resources in mutual combat, will he allow them to combine against his anointed.

Such we apprehend to be the character of the late war in Europe. *Before* the final adjustment of parties for the Great Battle, we shall probably witness a great slaughter among the aliens. They shall pounce upon and devour one another. Sanguinary battle-fields, accompanied perhaps by the Divine judgments, shall greatly weaken those powers; and yet more remarkable changes may, in the mean time, come over the face of European affairs, and especially over the embattled hosts of Rome and of the great Eastern apostasy, through a repetition of the revolutions of 1848. Europe, as I have said, is rocked on a volcano. There are working beneath her surface elements of tremendous power. Fearful are those internal, hidden struggles for liberty, and ere long they must find vent; and dreadful will be the explosion. The noble spirits of Forty-Eight are not dead. A decade of years has added strength to their arms, and new resolution and courage to their hearts. Kossuth and Mazzini yet live—or if *their* arms should be palsied, their mantles shall fall on others who shall rise in the strength of the God of Elijah, and in the sacred name of Liberty, marshal a countless host who have " not defiled their garments" with the wrongs of despotism or the corruptions of Rome.

The late war was very much a conflict of Rome with Rome. The progress of future hostilities will no doubt reveal new elements of contention, and new arrangements of parties. Unexpected revolutions may disclose new issues to be sought, until the great and final issue between truth and error, between great Babylon and the servants of the living God, shall be reached. We must therefore wait and pray, hope and trust till the end come.

Indeed, there seems much in the present political condition of the world which we are warranted in taking as preliminary to the no distant coming of the Millennium. A moment's reflection increases the conviction that the great crisis hastens on apace, heralded by the thunderings and lightnings and earthquakes of political convulsions—the turning the earth upside down—the destruction of all that stands not on the sure basis of truth and righteousness, and the speedy establishment of that better, that glorious kingdom which shall have no end.

3. Another indication that the time is at hand when the wicked shall meet a signal and awful overthrow, and the empire of righteousness be set up, is, I said, *the present extraordinary increase of religious knowledge, and the universal spread of the gospel.*

A distinguishing sign of such a period is that *many shall go to and fro, and knowledge shall increase.* The gospel must first be preached to all nations—the Bible translated into all tongues— the earth traversed in its length and breadth till a knowledge of the gospel become universal. The Press must send out the savor of life far and wide—the Bible must be read and understood—Christians be better instructed in the mysteries of re-

5

demption, and there be a general and rapid advance in Divine knowledge.

And is this not rapidly becoming true of the present age? It is very generally conceded that this sign is abundantly verified. Since the world began knowledge was never so widely diffused—science never so advanced—learning of all kinds so nearly universal. And the gospel was never known to so large a portion of the population of the earth. Indeed, there is scarcely at the present day a nation or a tribe in which the gospel is not already preached, at least to a portion of its inhabitants. Already has the Bible been translated into every principal language on the face of the earth. Already are the embassadors of the cross traversing every nation. Such are the facilities of communication that nations, which but a little time since were unknown to each other, are brought into neighborhood. By means of the press, of travelers, commercial agents and missionaries, they are brought within *speaking distance.* There is an advanced state of knowledge throughout the whole world. It is a day of unparalleled light, and light is increasing in a more rapid ratio than ever before. Already has the gospel become a *witness* to nearly the whole of the earth's population.

Zion shall arise and shine, her *light being come* and the glory of the Lord being risen upon her. But this *increase of light* shall, more surely than any thing else, rouse the slumbering foe and hasten on the conflict.

4. "That day shall not come, except there come *a falling away first,* and that *man of sin* be revealed, the son of perdition." We may expect, I said, first a very general *declension* and *apathy* in religion and sad apostasies, followed by the revelation of the "Man of Sin," a subtle, insidious, dangerous *infidelity* and *lawlessness* or insubordination, which, under the pretext of moral reform and religious advancement, shall trample on all order and

right, and become the most seductive, dangerous and deadly foe Christianity has ever had. Do we not see at the present day a falling away, both from the holding fast of the sound words of Christian doctrine, and more especially in reference to Christian practice ? Have not past years—the year 1858 excepted—been years of general *declension*—a period when there was a most woful withholding of the Spirit? And not only this, but there is a sad *apostatizing*. In one large portion of the Reformed Church, there is a strange retrograde movement back again into the bosom of Rome. And in other portions of the Christian Church there are departures from the simplicity of the gospel, and the purity of the faith once delivered to the saints.

And not only this, but there is, every year, a more and more manifest revelation of the " *Man of Sin, the son of perdition.*"

The discussion of our general subject would be left quite incomplete if I did not say more on this particular feature of the times and events that are to precede the Millennium, than can be said in the present chapter. The " revelation," development, growth, maturity and the destruction of this Man of Sin, and son of perdition, is all to take take place *before* the coming of Christ and the setting up of his earthly kingdom. He is to be destroyed *by the brightness of his coming.*

Reserving to some future chapter, to show that this man of sin is fast being revealed, I shall at present only add that I do not believe the Roman Hierarchy, the Papish apostasy, to be this " Man of Sin." This colossal system and mystery of iniquity is doubtless *a* man of sin—answering in many of its general features to that power described by Paul (2 Thess. ii). But it is evidently not specifically *the* Man of Sin there described. I think the attentive reader of that chapter will rather discover the description of a great infidel and atheistic power yet to rise, than the distinctive features of Popery, which have already existed. And if we were to translate the word "wicked," in the expression "Then shall that wicked be revealed," by the word *lawless* or *impious*, as with all propriety might be done, and substitute the word "lawlessness" in the place of "iniquity," in the phrase "Mystery of iniquity," we should much sooner recognize here the popular Infidelity of our times, than the Religion of Rome and of the Pope. It is to be that thing acted over again on a large scale which appeared in miniature, in France, in her reign of atheism and of terror—with this difference, that that was Infidelity with the grossness and comparative ignorance of the time; this shall be infidelity with the light and knowledge, the refinement and religion of the present times. It is to be a state of things in which human wisdom—human reason, shall be exalted above all that is divine—in which men shall be wise above what is written—when they shall be "heady and high-minded"—shall practically acknowledge no power higher than themselves. Indeed, I suppose, the apostle is here describing that same great power of unholiness of which he and Peter and Jude speak of as being about to prevail in the "last days." *

I suppose we have here a summary description of that last great and terrible scheme of the wicked one, which shall exist at the revelation of our Lord. Unlike the Papists, who are theoretically orthodox, the men of that day shall be *scoffers, walking after their own lusts*, brooking no restraint—lawless—self-willed—supercilious—*denying the Lord that bought them—despising dominion*, and *speaking evil of dignities.* That such shall be the next great and final form of sin in our world, and that sin is fast assuming this form—that the moral corruption of wicked men is now developing itself in such a form as we have here indicated, I think, will in the course of the discussion be made to appear.

*Paul, in 2 Tim. iii. 1—5; 2 Peter, iii. 3, 4; Jude, 4—8, 14—19.

In closing, I may just remark that the three points which have occupied our minds in the present chapter, give rise to three distinct reflections:

1. When the Judgments of God are abroad in the earth, we should *learn righteousness.*

2. When God is overturning the earth, and breaking up every false structure, and bringing to naught all things that do not please him, how ought we to *examine our foundation?*

3. As knowledge is increased—the gospel more widely preached —the light made clearer—duty made plainer, and new modes of usefulness opened to us, how are *our responsibilities increased— how our guilt?*

CHAPTER VI.

Characteristics of our Age—Modern Infidelity as the Man of Sin.

"And that Man of Sin be revealed, the son of perdition."—2 *Thess.* ii. 3.

In reply to the inquiry, "Are there indications at the present time of the near approach of the Millennium?" I have already spoken of *judgments*, of *civil convulsions*, and of an increase of knowledge and the extensive diffusion of the gospel, as indications that the day of Zion's emancipation is near. In alluding to the *falling away*, or the apostasies that shall precede that day, and to the consequent revelation of the *Man of Sin*, that shall be revealed, the son of perdition. I then hinted that I did not think this man of sin the Pope of Rome, or the Roman Hierarchy, but rather an infidel, atheistic power that should arise—a condition of unparalleled *lawlessness* and *impiety*. A great antichristian power—the last great exhibition of sin—the climax and consummation of the works of the Devil, the god of this world, before he shall be obliged to yield up his dominion on the earth and make an end of sin. As we expect that the coming and last dispensation of grace on this earth shall be the most glorious, the most morally magnificent of any preceding one, so we may expect the last dispensation of sin shall be correspondingly luxuriant in the wiles and the deep-laid schemes of the Pit. As one shall be the nearest approach to heaven of any thing ever yet known on earth, the other shall be the nearest approach to hell. In subtlety—in the power to deceive, if possible, the very elect—in the deep Philosophy of high-fallen intellect, all clad in a garb of an angel of light, we may expect the last great scheme of Satan to be his mightiest and his worst —more potent to deceive, more sure to destroy.

In what may in general terms be called *Modern Infidelity*, I believe we have, in germ at least, just such a system as I have alluded to. The religion of Rome, of Mecca, and the religion of the Pagans are little else than different illustrations of Infidelity. The last scheme shall be like them all—and yet unlike them all—shall have the same spirit, and the same end to accomplish, yet the *form* and the means of accomplishing that end shall differ. Perhaps we cannot better indicate it than to call it a *union* of Romanism, Paganism and Infidelity, clad in the garb of an angel of light.

The judicious and pious commentator, Dr. Scott, on this point, remarks: "Papal persecutors were often concealed infidels; and infidels concealed under any other mask, and opposing vital Christianity, may perhaps equally answer the prediction: for the peculiar opinions of this antichristian power are not specified. The prevalence of Infidelity in various forms, and the zeal with which principles of that tendency are everywhere propagated, when contrasted with the declining state of the Popish superstition, renders it not wholly improbable that the 'Beast' may change his ground and method of attack before he thus prevails against the 'Witnesses.'"

The probable change of ground, and method of attack and form, is, that the Beast will depute his authority to some subtle, delusive Infidelity clad in a Christian costume, which shall prosecute the warfare against the Witnesses more effectually, because more clandestinely, and shall overcome them and kill them.   Therefore,

5. I shall now direct attention, as the next characteristic of our times, to such a view, as I may be able to give, of MODERN INFIDELITY.   My object is, that there may be seen in it, first, the Man of Sin—sin matured into manhood—sin in its last great strength and malignity.   And, secondly, that there may be discovered in its peculiar development, the approaching, ominous close of the present dispensation, and the no distant approach of the Millennial period—the coming of the Son of man to set up his kingdom on the earth.

There is much in the present aspect of Infidelity which betokens a fearful conflict with the Truth at no distant day.   And we are scarcely in danger of overrating its importance as a sign of the times.

Infidelity, which in our day is extensively diffused, has changed its mode of attack.   In the days of Voltaire and the French Revolution it was bold, argumentative and overbearing.   It hoped to put down Christianity by logic and philosophy.   Argument was the weapon of its warfare.   Reason was exalted as the last court of appeal.   And *Paine*, in his too well-known work, " The Age of *Reason*," essayed to prostrate the fair fabric of Religion, and to remove its very foundations from the face of the earth, and fain to blot out its remembrance from the annals of the world. But he failed.   Reason, so far as she was capable of making a verdict on the sublime mysteries of Christianity, pronounced in her favor.   And never has Christianity prospered more—never spread her wings so widely and diffused such healing in her beams—never before overshadowed so much of the earth and scattered over its desert surface so much of her celestial fruits, as since Voltaire and Paine, and that unholy conspiracy against the truth, ceased to pour out the vials of their wrath. The Church has lived and prospered; and not the less so because of their hard reasonings and bold invectives.

It was then infidelity unmasked—infidelity fighting under her own banners.

But a change has come over the scene. The eruptions of the volcano, which then disgorged their fiery floods over all Europe, and rolled their resistless waves across the Atlantic to the land of the Pilgrims, have, at length, given place to the latent heavings and burnings of internal fires, deepening and widening, and preparing to burst forth again with redoubled fury. Infidelity has become subtle and covert, preparing rather to appear as an angel of light —to wear the form of Religion, in which she may the more effectually stab her to the heart. There is open infidelity yet, bold, obtrusive, threatening, from which the Church has something to fear. She may still be assailed and galled by its *violence.* Yet her danger lies, not in Pagan or atheistic, but in baptized infidelity—infidelity in and close about the nominal Church. There is the infidelity of Popery, covering the greater portion of the states of Europe and much of the New World; and the scarcely less extended infidelity in the Greek Church. There is the infidelity of portions of *Protestantism,* wearing the form of piety, and assenting to its doctrines, but denying its power. There is, again, the infidelity of *Socinianism* and all its kindred tribes, and of *Universalism* and all its pitiful fraternity, endeavoring to *reason* men out of their souls, or laugh them out of their inheritance in the skies. And there is yet the more daring and fearful infidelity of *German Neology,* which has usurped the seat of learning and raised its unhallowed form high on the eminence of *Christian*

Theology, striking a deadly blow at the vitality of our holy religion.

Modern infidelity is not so much besieging the walls of our Zion from without—erecting its scaling-ladders, or plying her well-formed bulwarks with its huge battering-ram, but it has insinuated itself within her very walls. It is lurking about her altar, and finds a lodgement in her strongholds.

This is what the page of prophecy has taught us to expect before that great and notable day of the Lord, and is what shall bring about that day. It is the "mystery of iniquity" working in the children of disobedience—the "spirit of devils, working wonders"—not in words denying God, but in works casting off his authority, and exalting itself above all that is called God or that is worshiped. It is an unclean spirit under a religious disguise—a threefold emanation from the Dragon, the Beast and False Prophet, described as *three unclean spirits like frogs*—amphibious—able to accommodate themselves to all circumstances—noisome and vexatious.

The danger of such an infidelity is immense. The longer it works the more formidable it becomes. It is the enemy *within* the citadel. While allowed unmolested possession, it is not tumultuous. But attempt to dislodge the foe and cast him out, he stamps the earth in his rage, he shakes the forest with his roaring.

But we must ponder this topic a little more leisurely—must iuquire more in detail what there is in the present developments of infidelity which betokens its speedy collision with the truth.

I shall dwell on this topic the longer as I believe we may here discover the lineaments at least—the incipient developments—of that great antichristian system, the last and most formidable antagonist of the Christian Church.

Where, then, shall we look for these fast-maturing germs of the last great antichrist? I hesitate not to say I think I see them vegetating and rapidly maturing in the *Owenism*, the *Non-Resistance*, the *Fourierism, Transcendentalism*, and Come-outism of our country—in the *Socialism* and *Chartism* of England—in the *Communism* and *Fourierism* of France—in the *Radicalism* and *Free Societies* of Switzerland—and in the *Pantheism*, the "*Friends of Light*," and the *Hengelianism* of Germany.

These are but different names by which, in different portions of the world, the same thing is called. The animating spirit is the same; it is a lurking, subtle, masked infidelity *suited to the times*. At one time it mounts the car of Reform, raised to a dizzy height above the common herd, speeding its way ahead, leaving consequences at a fearful remove behind; again, you find it the judge and censor and fierce advocate of an elevated piety, ready at a blow to demolish all of piety there is in the world for the sake of erecting on its ruins the stately, transcendental fabric of its own imagining; or you meet it, with the besom of destruction in its right hand, prostrating all law and authority and human government—or presumptuously entering the sanctuary, stripping the man at the altar of his sacerdotal power, casting the Bible into the labyrinths of distrust and perplexity, disbanding the Church, if possible, and filching from her the sanctity of her Sabbaths, and all this, forsooth, for some *better thing*, which is to be introduced when the ground shall be cleared of all present incumbrances.

Its pious design, under the pretext of a grand system of Reform, in government, society and religion, is to prostrate all existing institutions, whether civil, social or religious, and to build anew, not after the fashion shown to Moses in the mount, but after the fashion dictated by the god they worship, the "spirit of the age."

A brief examination of some of these systems of skepticism, which, of late, have sprung up almost simultaneously in different and widely distant parts of Christendom, yet one in spirit, will verify what I have said. No one yet delineates the full-grown Beast. Some portray one feature more prominently, some another, yet the spirit and tendency of all is essentially the same.

Take for an example the Socialism and Chartism of England, which differ scarcely but in name from the *Non-resistance* and "Come-outism" of America, and we shall see on what *moral* basis the whole system is founded.

While true Christianity promotes the civilization and refinement of the world, strengthens the bonds of the social compact, and improves and elevates the social character of man, Socialism, the doctrine of Robert Owen as illustrated in his settlement at New Harmony, and enforced in his public and private teachings in this country and in Europe, would break up the very fountains of the social principle. It is a lawless, restive, licentious spirit which spurns the bonds of civil restraints. It would have no law, no government, no restraints. It is but the *concentration* and maturity of views, feelings, and doctrines which had their origin, not in this pernicious system, but in the human heart.

Though diametrically opposed to Christianity, Owen, true to the genius of modern infidelity, did not avow this till his followers could bear it. But "now," says a writer in a late English newspaper, "Owen and his followers have completely thrown off the mask, and are at present employed throughout England in the most undisguised and wicked attempts to set aside the scheme of Divine revelation, and to subvert Christian morality. Owenism aims at sweeping away all the existing forms of religious belief." Prayer and all other forms of worship are the objects of ridicule and contempt—the Being of a Great First Cause doubted —native depravity and personal responsibility boldly denied. The Bible is virulently opposed and spoken of as written by ignorant men. Salvation through Christ is abused and rejected. It aims, in a word, at the complete subversion of the present order of religion and of society.

" Marriage is denounced as a state of deceit and immorality; and, to the reproach of human nature, *female apostles travel through England, unblushingly declaiming against marriage* as the cause of the crimes and miseries which afflict the sons and daughters of men, and offer plausible pleas for the indulgence of unrestrained licentiousness."   And strange as it may seem in the nineteenth century, this system is not so opposed to the public taste, not so odious or startling (though directly tending to license the most shameless immorality) that it does not find there numerous advocates.   Yet it is to be feared that such sentiments are as rife, though not so ripe in America as in England.

If such a leaven be at work, so extensively and in such a place, is it not a precursor of a convulsion?   This looks more like an attempt to " slay the Witnesses"—to suppress the truth and trample under foot the Church of God, than any thing we have yet seen.

Or, go to Germany and you will meet the same thing: the name and the costume is changed, but the body and soul is the same.   There this rising conspiracy against the truth call themselves the " Friends of Light."   The Friends of Light have undertaken to carry out, practically, what the Rationalists had proposed, theoretically.   The appeal of the one was to Reason, exalting it above all they call God or worship; that of the other to the passions, stirring up popular feeling, and exciting popular prejudices.

An intelligent writer of the present day (G. de Felice) thus speaks of the Friends of Light, as to the manner in which they treat the Bible.   " They do not receive the Bible as supreme authority in religious matters.   They say that there are in this book errors and contradictions, and that what was written eighteen hundred years ago, *does not suit our enlightened age."*   These

Friends of Light concede that the Bible contains *words of God*, or fundamental truths, which *they* can distinguish from the dross by the *spirit of the Lord* which is in them. But when you come to inquire what this spirit, dignified as the spirit of the Lord, is, they do not hesitate to say it is *the spirit of the age*. And as every man will interpret public opinion to his own liking, it follows that this judge and discriminator of God's word is no more nor less than a man's *individual reason*. By this convenient method they can conduct a controversy, and sustain themselves in any thing they wish to believe, and reject what they will. They have only to declare a passage which stands in their way to be *not a word of God*, or if it ever were a truth, *now obsolete truth*. In this way they seem, to superficial observers, to support a subtle, sinuous system of infidelity from the Bible, while at the same time they are effectually undermining all belief in the inspiration and authority of the Scriptures.

How nearly akin such views are to those embraced and exemplified by men of like passions in this country, I leave to the judgment of those best acquainted with both their theory and practice. The Friends of Light in this country may not congratulate themselves on much originality in their new-modeled errors. The transcendentalists for subtlety of logic, and the various castes of ultraists for misguided zeal, have their prototype and counterpart in the old world, and that too, as a fruit of German Neology, or Modern Infidelity.

My design is only to point out some of these simultaneous and similar developments in different parts of Christendom, of this rising system of false, subtle, yet Christianized Infidelity, which I have supposed is to be the last formidable antagonist of the Church.

It matters little which of the affianced *isms* I have named, we select in order to discover their disorganizing and ruinous tendency, and their ultimate plunge into real if not undisguised Infidelity.

Take, if you please, for our next example, *Fourierism.* This is no doubt regarded by many as only a harmless piece of foolery—harmless except to them who foolishly embark their all into the hands of a gang of land-sharks, never to come out from thence till they have lost the last farthing. But this is but the beginning of the miseries of Fourierism. It is based on principles destructive of all law and order, of all morality and religion. It is pregnant with the popular infidelity of the day.

This charge finds ample support in its own professions; and yet its professions are evidently but a partial index of its spirit and real character. It is based on new doctrines both of philosophy and religion—doctrines, when carried out, utterly subversive of the old-fashioned doctrines of Divine revelation. They proclaim their intention " to reorganize society," that is, to destroy all its existing relations, and shape it to suit themselves ; *to abolish the marriage* relation, and substitute in its stead universal concubinage. Their design is to unsettle and destroy in society all that has hitherto been settled; and morality and religion they treat as unceremoniously. Contrary to all experience, to conscience and the Bible, they teach that the *passions* are *not* to be restrained and governed, but to be allowed " free course and development."

They make sin to be " merely a weakness incident to the infancy of our race, instead of an evil in each individual soul." The worship of God is stigmatized as a " servile and superstitious adoration," and indeed the whole scheme of revealed Religion is thoroughly and contemptuously discarded. Its forms are treated with levity and ridicule, and its spirit denounced as tyrannical.

I will quote a paragraph from Mr. Ripley, one of their leading writers, and we shall find their position, as to infidelity, defined in their own words. He is replying to the charge of Infidelity preferred against them. He says:

"*We* ARE *infidels in respect to the prevailing religion preached in our Churches. I say we* REPUDIATE *the Christianity of our prevailing Churches, because we believe these Churches reject Christianity. We reject the religion of the Churches,* because we do not see in them that spirit of *devotion to man* which the gospel breathes ; we see in them no attempt to realize the promises of Christ, that men shall be clothed with more beauty than the flowers of the field, and that all *earthly things* shall be given in abundance unto them. We *do* aim at the destruction of the present order of society. We do look for a new heaven and a new earth, and in this respect we are content to bear the charge of infidelity."

Who does not discover here the sentiments and almost precisely the language of another class of errorists and fanatics in our own country? They reject the religion of the Church *because* the Church is not more *devoted,* not to God, but to *man,* and does not realize the promises of all *earthly* things. They would fain have it understood that they, without either the pretension or attempted practice of piety themselves, cannot tolerate the Church because she is so corrupt. Pious souls, they ; they cannot breathe in so tainted an atmosphere as the Christian Church, and therefore they will regale their pure spirits in the dismal regions of doubt and skepticism.

Did time allow and need require, it would be easy to point out the characteristics of other kindred germs of this modern Infidelity, and, stripping off the Christian guise which for the present they assume, to show the latent, active infidelity which is rampant within. There are the *Radicals* of France, the *Humanitists* of Germany, and the *Propagandists* of Switzerland, whose object is described to be the subversion of all existing morals—the "destruction of the social, political and religious organizations of Germany. The *Propagandist clubs*, which have become fearfully numerous in Europe, especially in Switzerland, have taken an advanced step, thrown off their disguise, and speak of " God and the immortality of the soul as old and threadbare trash." " Religion," say they, " is dung." Again: " Religion is all a battle of smoke;" and " vengeance is a natural act of justice; and we should desire to see the outbreak of great vices and outrageous crimes rather than *that virtue which annoys* and that worn-out morality with which they *fatigue the people*." Any thing but that old morality of the Church—that *threadbare virtue which annoys* —the wicked.

Yet, notwithstanding the bitter hostility of these Propagandists against all evangelical religion—their downright *atheism*—they ape a character for piety. Says Standon, one of their leaders, writing to a fellow-champion : " As I spend much of my time at the house of the curé, and frequently dine there, I pass for the most pious and orthodox person in the world. You may imagine how droll I look in this character." " I assure you I have a terrible penance to go through in playing this pious part I have assumed " —" attending regularly at church and joining in religious meetings every day, I every day become more irreligious."

It is easy to see that a kindred spirit pervades all these systems. They all bear the mark of the Beast, some more, some less distinctly. They are agreed in leveling all existing institutions with the dust, whether of government, society, the family, or religion, and all agree in doing this for the sake of introducing a purer and higher form of Christianity.

They agree in their bitter invectives against the Christian Church —in their unmeasured abuse of her ministry—in their strange tamperings and irreverence with the word of God—in their vandal tramplings under foot of the " powers that be," and in the novel doctrines concerning the holy Sabbath.

None of these systems, or rather parts of the great System, has yet fully developed itself. I only attempt to point out the forming lineaments of the Beast that is to make war against and destroy and kill the witnesses for the truth. We see that Beast, as yet, scarcely out of the shell; yet we may judge of his enormous dimensions and his great power to hurt and to kill, by these faint outlines.

Already he speaks as the Beast, although he appears in the garb of a lamb. The war-cry against the Church and clergy, the Bible and the Sabbath, which commenced in Europe, has found a distinct echo on this side of the Atlantic. And here more especially has it been achieved under the cover of a pretended piety, and with the pretext of introducing a purer Church and a higher order of piety. Here it has mounted the rostrum of Reform, and assumed the tone of benevolence and philanthropy, and from these heights of popular feeling, has more effectually struck the fatal blow.

No language has been too abusive and too base to suit the purpose of these pretended Reformers in their attacks on the Church and her ministry. The clergy have been denounced as a " brotherhood of thieves, and the Church the habitation of devils"— " below the savages "—" destitute of common humanity "—" more savage than the cannibals of the South Sea Islands "—" their religion had burnt out their humanity."—" The grog-shops nearer the kingdom of heaven than our Churches."—" The clergy the most guilty and corrupting body of men in the land "—" unworthy and dangerous spiritual guides." (Gerrit Smith.) They must, they say, " rip up the Church and grind them to powder." They would do great things, glorious things—make earth a Paradise for us, could they but annihilate the Church and her very troublesome ministry, and remodel the Bible to suit the *spirit of the age,* and suitably dispose of that old Jewish day called the Sabbath, and a few more things which have become antiquated by a too long use.

Yet these men, while with one hand they raise the axe of extermination and strike the very foundations of our religion, with the other they extend a " bland and patronizing condescension " towards what they please to call Christianity—but not the Christianity *of the Churches;* that they' repudiate and hate, but the Christianity which they fancy will emerge from the ruins of the moral deluge they hope to produce. But first we must submit without a murmur, or demur, to a complete prostration of all existing moorings and landmarks; and when we have surrendered all and left the ground, they will build—what, we must wait and see.

Surely, did the Devil ever act more wily, to turn Reformer—to burn with zeal for the purity of the Church—to outstrip Howard and Wilberforce in his philanthropy—to separate himself from the Church because she is so corrupt—to mourn over the defection of her ministers, and all this that he may carry out, in a manner suited to the times, the great scheme of deceiving the nations of the earth! " Truly," says one, " the work of Satan grows and expands itself side by side with that of the Lord, and this word of Revelation is proved to be true : the Devil is come down among you having great wrath, because he knoweth that he hath but a short time."

Did names and human authorities prevail, many might be adduced to show that I have not, in what I have said, widely deviated in the opinions here advanced, from the sentiments of many wiser and better, and, in intellectual and moral worth, more exalted on Zion's walls, and able more distinctly to read the signs of the times. Says one:

"Infidelity is among us in its most subtle guise. A false and superficial philosophy is the order of the day. The most disorganizing principles are openly broached in education, politics and philosophy—all under the guise of an extraordinary philanthropy, and a pretendedly higher faith than is to be derived from the teachings of the Church and the authority of Revelation." "The danger, we contend, is real and imminent. The remedy can only be found in a stern resolution on the part of those who have an unwavering faith in the Bible, to guard, by every means in their power, all who are under their influence, from the insidious attacks of this subtle enemy."

No one need go into any very lengthened examination of either of the *Isms* I have named, to discover, with Prof. Norton of Cambridge, "*the latest form of Infidelity.*"

But I will dwell on this topic no longer: nor should I so long, but for its practical importance at this time. When the Enemy changes his mode of attack, then is the time to be on the alert, ready for his next assault. No matter if he be an angel, if he preach any other gospel than Paul preached and Paul's Master dictated—if he invade the fold, and assail the Shepherd, and scatter the sheep—if he set up other standards, or demolish those Christ has erected, he is an enemy; receive him not; and go not after him. For many false prophets have gone out into the world who will so nearly imitate the true, that, if it were possible, they will deceive the very elect.

I cannot forbear, however, further to confirm what I have said, to quote a brief paragraph or two from the pen of Dr. J. W. Alexander. In a discourse on "Modern Infidelity," he says:

"The beginning of the infidelity of the present age, unlike the vulgar infidelity of the preceding one, was with *a show of great learning and science.* The new sciences of astronomy, geology, ethnography, and ethnology, have been invoked to prove the

Bible false; and metaphysical reasoners, with a show of erudition and acumen never surpassed, have endeavored to crush the doctrines of the Gospel.

"The infidelity of our age *affects to be religious.* Finding that man, despoiled of all the religious emotions, became a Marat or a Paine, a tiger or a swine, the arch-enemy found he must remodel his devices, and bring in a religion better than that of the Bible; thus becoming most dangerous, when transforming himself into an angel of light. This new form of error employs almost every term of theology and experience in a false and deceptive sense, often applying the most sacred words of gracious truth to matters of literature, scenery, the fine arts, love, and alas, even to sinful indulgence. Some of the foremost poets of our day are chargeable with these insidious tactics; so that a father has need to look well to the books which lie upon his daughter's table, as splendid presentation-copies.

"Under the present phase of infidelity *much is said of God.* If frequent repetition of the sacred name could sanctify a cause, theirs would be hallowed indeed. But their God is not our God; not the God and Father of our Lord Jesus Christ; not the God of the saints; not even a personal God. The more they talk of God, the less they believe in him. In their disguised atheism the term implies the sum of all things, or the everlastingly unfolding process of causes; or the universal reason, as existing in all minds. Sometimes, in their glorification of humanity, they utter the scriptural phrase, 'God is man;' but their inward meaning is, that man is God. Man is the object of their adoration. The highest manifestation of God, say they, is the human mind. This they dishonestly name at times, the incarnation. Never before has the world seen so large a body of infidels, really denying every thing like a proper revelation, yet full of great swelling words about the Spirit, the God of history, the union of virtue and beauty, and the excellence of religion.

"The infidelity of our age *connects itself with freedom and social progress.* The cry is, that Christianity is a failure; that the Church has not made men happy; that whatever good the Bible has accomplished, its work is done, and we must have something better. It is a part of this scheme to glory in humanity as such; to assert the independence and self-sufficiency of man; to deify the creature, and pushing the rights of man to a Jacobinical and impracticable extreme, to install lawless freedom in the pulpit. Thus, strange as it may seem, philanthropy, unsanctified, may lead unsound minds to unbelief; and there are no more reckless or bitter opponents of Christianity than a number of writers, lecturers, and editors, whom we once knew or heard of as ministers of Jesus Christ."

In conclusion, the inquiry forces itself upon us, what lesson of instruction ought we to gather from such a subject? If the enemy has taken the field under a new guise, we should be ready to meet him. In professions, in zeal, in subtlety, he may outstrip us. We must be prepared to meet him on the arena of personal piety, and turn against him the battery of God's everlasting truth. We must be " strong in the Lord and in the power of his might." We must put on the whole armor of God, that we may be able to stand against the wiles of the Devil. For we wrestle not against flesh and blood, but against principalities, against powers, against the rulers of the darkness of this world, against spiritual wickedness in high places. Wherefore take unto you the whole armor of God, that ye may be able to stand in the evil day, and having done all, to stand. Stand, therefore, having your loins girt about with truth, and having on the breastplate of righteousness, and your feet shod with the preparation of the gospel of peace; above all, taking the shield of faith, wherewith ye shall be able to quench all the fiery darts of the wicked; and take the helmet of salvation, and the sword of the Spirit, which is the word of God: praying always with all prayer and supplication in the Spirit, and watching thereunto with all perseverance and supplication for all saints; and for *me*, that "utterance may be given unto me, that I may open my mouth boldly and make known the mysteries of the gospel."

CHAPTER VII.

More Signs—Paganism—Popery—The Hierarchy of England and of Scotland—Increase of religious knowledge—Stupidity and listlessness of the
wicked—Extensive revivals of Religion.

" Can ye not discern the signs of the times?"—Matt. **xvi. 3.**

MEN are usually wise in their secular affairs. They look about
them—detect adverse influences—arrest their progress, and adapt
means to the accomplishment of ends so as to secure their own
interests. We are often not a little astonished at the discernment
with which men, who in other matters are deficient, manage their
own affairs. They are not generally lacking where they need
wisdom for their own secular benefit. They can discern the face
of human affairs and judge pretty correctly what will come to pass.
They, too, can judge of the face of the sky. They are worldly-
wise, as well as weather-wise. Yet they do *not discern the signs
of the times* in the *moral* world. Sad, indeed, is the stupidity of
man in this respect. Christ here upbraids the wise ones of his
time and nation, because they could see nothing in the unusual
movements of HIS day—in his teachings and miracles, in his character and labors of love, which betokened a great moral revolution
—the establishment of a new order of things in the religious world.

We may be living in a similar disregard of the signs of our times.

It is often said we live in a remarkable age. So we do—though not exactly in the sense implied. It is remarkable as a *preparatory season* FOR *a remarkable age.* It was for this reason I instituted the proposition in a former chapter, viz.:

That the characteristics of the present age indicate the speedy approach of the final and universal triumph of the kingdom of Christ; and by consequence, of the great conflict between truth and error.

I have spoken of some of the characteristics of our age, or signs of our times. I shall now speak of others.

7. *Paganism gives portentous signs of dissolution;* yet its dissolution may not be expected without a terrific dying struggle. Look at Paganism as it now is. It is a waning system. Into whatever quarter of its dark domains you cast the eye, you find it shorn of its strength. It is old, worn out, decrepid and ready to decay. In all its multifarious developments and excrescences, it was formed for a different condition of society and of the world, from what the world now presents. Satan originated it for a gross state of ignorance and barbarism. But the world has advanced, and undisguised idolatry is too gross a religion for this advanced order of things. Its days are numbered, not only on the page of inspiration, but numbered in the necessity of the case. The atmosphere in which Paganism once so freely breathed—the soil on which it once took so deep root and thrived so prosperously, has been changed, and now its poisonous leaves wither and its wide-spread branches are falling off. No system of idolatry on the whole face of the earth is in its full force and youthful vigor. Every system of *European* idolatry has long since sunk into the shades. Scarcely vestiges enough remain to tell what it was. The idolatry of Western Asia, of Persia and Arabia, has fled before the rising sun of Christianity; and the grosser systems of superstition and image worship of the Pacific Ocean have been

completely overwhelmed by the irresistible tide of gospel truth. The principal remaining systems are those of Brahminism of India, and Boodhism of India and China, and these are but the mere shadows of what they once were. Their power over the minds of the people is rather nominal than real—at least, rather a matter of habit than of principle. European power, intelligence, and religion have come in upon them like a flood, and they cannot withstand the invasion. As soon might you expect midnight darkness to tarry before the rising sun. Everywhere do they show marks of decay, and give premonitions of a no remote downfall. Hundreds of villages have within a few years renounced the long established, but now antiquated religion of their fathers, and embraced the Religion of the Cross.

As proof of this assertion, I will present two or three testimonies as specimens of the delightful intelligence which is reaching us from month to month.

"The feeling," says Mr. Bariero, "is becoming general that some extraordinary change is near at hand, which is to be effected by the diffusion of Christianity. Well may the people look for such an event when they see so many signs of it in the neglect of rites and ceremonies essential to Hindooism. Recently, two men came from a place not twelve miles distant to inform us that nearly one thousand persons—in consequence of reading some of our tracts—were desirous of putting themselves under our protection. The same company mention half a dozen villages where a similar change has been produced simply by the reading of Christian books."

An Episcopal missionary writing from Southern India (Mr. Pope), says: "Since my appointment here, nine devil temples in this division of the district have been either destroyed or converted into Christian prayer-houses; and of the twenty-two villages in connection with the Episcopal mission, the whole of the most respectable and influential inhabitants are under instruction.

A few days ago a large temple was made over to me within a furlong's distance from my bungalow. The whole utensils of the temple have been brought to me, and the property transferred to the church in the village." The idol has been demolished—and the temple converted into a church.

And, what is much in point, the Brahmins (Hindoo priests) and the principal men of the nation are engaged in fierce and fearless controversies touching the merits and demerits of their national religion. Not a few native newspapers are freely and boldly assailing the mighty colossus of Hindooism in every vulnerable point, undermining its foundations and breaking down its superstructure. And what has been reared, and for centuries stood in darkness and ignorance and cruelty and despotism, must necessarily fall before the light of truth and a religion of purity, freedom, light and love.

The late withdrawal by the British Government of their support of idolatry in India, has taken away the last substantial prop of Brahminism and Boodhism throughout the vast territories of England in the East. Those systems which have so long held in thraldom dire one-half the population of the globe, need now only to be left to be pervaded by the light of truth which is already profusely shining on them, and to the many and powerful providential agencies* which are operating there, to fall by the weight of their own ignorance and corruption.

The late act of toleration of Christianity in China, by the emperor, and the removing, by the British Government in India, of the unrighteous and cruel disabilities of Hindoo converts, especially as touching the *right of inheritance* (a change of religion

---

* Such as commerce, intercourse with Christian nations—subjection to a Christian government—light, intelligence, European education and science—and a thousand invasions on their usages of caste and religion.

heretofore forfeited all right of inheritance), further weakens the hold of Paganism on the common mind by removing obstacles to the free action of the gospel.

Since writing the above, India, China and Japan—all those vast and populous regions over which these two great systems of religion have so long retained an iron sway—have undergone revolutions which presage the no distant downfall of idolatry. The late insurrection in India, the war with China, and the recent treaty with Japan, are such revolutions. But we cannot review those events in this connection. They deserve a separate consideration, which we shall give them by and by.

These are signs of the times, betokening the approaching overthrow of this mighty system of idolatry. And we speak advisedly when we infer that the teeming millions of its deluded votaries (as many have already done) will soon abandon a system of priestcraft and cruelty under which they have so long groaned.

But we have no reason to expect from what we have seen in like cases, such a mighty revolution can take place without a conflict. Satan will not yield his seat and his great power without a struggle.

8. *The present condition of the Romish Church furnishes another of the characteristics of our age which betoken a great moral revolution.*

The Church must remain in the wilderness—exist in a state of abandonment by the world, during the conjoint spiritual despotism of Mohammedanism and Popery. The former spread its dire ravages over the eastern portion of the Christian Church, and was the scourge of what is known as the Greek Church; and the other breathed its withering influence over the western portion.

We have reason to believe, both from prophecy and from present appearances of the Papal power, that *its* days are as nearly numbered as those of Mohammedanism. Its existence is limited to twelve hundred and sixty years—and these we believe are nearly expired. And, in accordance with such a belief, we find the Papal Beast shorn of much of his power; yet maddening and raving, and strengthening himself in the things that remain. The court of the Inquisition has for the most part been disbanded and its dismal prisons broken down; the block, the stake and fagots, and the multifarious and skilfully invented instruments of torture and death, are scarcely known only as matters of history. That ghostly despotism which once knew no bounds to its rapaciousness and despotism, rioting on the ignorance and stupidity of its countless millions, now has found a limit and meets a merited rebuke in the gathering ranks of a fearless Protestantism. Though the Pope still lords it over the consciences of a great multitude of the human family, where his ecclesiastical domination is still undisputed, yet his political dominion has nearly ceased, and is yearly diminishing. He can no longer make and unmake kings, and give empires to whom he will. His secular arm is palsied. He entreats rather than threatens—negotiates where he once coerced. So feeble, it is said, and really powerless has the Pope already been for some years past, that but for the presence in Italy of a large Austrian army, he would not have been safe even in Rome. Hence the inference, and with no slight probability, that his Holiness feels all the anxiety he manifests, for the *extension and prosperity of the Romish Church in America.* He may need America for an asylum when he can no longer riot on European soil.

There can be no doubt that Popery is on the wane in the Eastern continent. One of the most magnificent and extensive empires that ever existed was the Portuguese empire in Asia. That empire was but a province of the Romish Church. Nowhere perhaps has Rome ruled with more cruel tyranny, over hundreds of millions of our race. The history of the Inquisition of Goa is written in human blood. But that empire now lives only in the annals of its despotism, intolerance, cruelty and blood-shed. The vast domains, from the Red to the Chinese seas, over which it stretched, have been given into the hands of Protestants. Indeed, while Rome is gaining a few poor proselytes from Oxford and the ranks of High Churchism, both in England and America, or from the ranks of ignorance and infidelity, she is elsewhere losing kingdoms. *Spain*, though far enough from the outer limits of an evangelical religion, is weary of the merciless domination of Rome, and is seeking to free herself from her spiritual yoke. Debased Portugal, debased by the " Mystery of iniquity" which worketh in her, threatens to throw off the Pontifical authority. Yet Popery is in still greater danger from the puissant arm of the Czar of the Russias. Nicholas not long since raised the fearful hand of persecution against the Romanists of his empire—though Nicholas be not justified, yet Rome is humbled: * " They that take the sword shall perish by the sword." As they have measured to others, so shall it be measured to them.

Yet, perhaps, the most portentous sign of Babylon's approaching fall is to be seen in the progress of Protestantism and evangelical religion in certain Catholic countries in Europe. Whole communes in France have recently renounced their allegiance to the Pope and embraced the religion of the Bible. The gospel is preached by faithful and self-denying evangelists, and the doctrines of a pure Christianity are inculcated by the books and untiring labors of colporteurs throughout the length and breadth of this great Catholic country, and with the most cheering success. But what is the most distinctive sign of the times is the conversion

---

* The supposition that the autocrat of Russia shall humble Rome, does not necessarily militate against our theory, that Russia and Rome shall finally join hands in the last great day of conflict. Herod and Pilate shall in that day be made friends.

from Romanism of so *many Romish priests.* While Rome, from a sense of her own weakness, no doubt, and her inability much longer to hold control over the minds of her deluded millions by any thing like fair and open means, has called again to her aid her Janizaries, the Jesuits, and found it necessary to return to some of her grossest and most shameful superstitions, such as the exhibition of a pretended garment of Christ, and other marvels quite as sensible. On the other hand, her more intelligent priests leave her communion in disgust. Scores of Romish priests have renounced Rome within the last ten years, and it is believed that numbers more wait but for a favorable opportunity. In a single " department (Saintonge), no less than forty parishes are open to the labors of evangelists." In another department, says a French paper, *thirty-nine* parishes have rejected the mass, and are longing for the Bible and a Christian ministry." "More than one hundred places in France are calling for evangelical ministers—and the number is increasing rapidly."

Such are but specimens of the evangelical work now going on in France—all tending to undermine Rome in her stronghold.

" Never," says Mr. Roussel, a celebrated French pastor, " have the Roman Catholic people been more disgusted with the superstitions of their Church and the avarice of their priests, than at present ; and never has there been a more favorable opportunity of declaring the gospel to them." And it is a presage of much good that this opportunity is altogether lost. Says a late report of the Foreign and Evangelical Society: " There are few villages in France, if any, where the word of God has not been offered and in which some copies have not been left. And though the priests may burn the Book of Life, and utter a thousand lies against it, the people begin to perceive that the Romish religion and the Bible cannot exist together." Two hundred thousand copies of the Bible have been distributed in France the past year, and almost wholly among Roman Catholics. But Rome and the Bible cannot live together!!

More than six hundred persons, the entire inhabitants of commune (Villefavart), were last year converted to Protestantism by the simple reading of the Scriptures—and this in the face of the most violent opposition of the Romish priests.

But more remarkable and significant yet are the present religious movements in France and Ireland. In those countries, so long and so decidedly given over to Rome, the Spirit is poured out from on high. Whole counties are pervaded by the blessed influences, and revivals, characterized by all the general features which distinguish the late revivals in our own land, are this day in progress there. Sinners are awakened, convicted and converted, and great numbers are added to the Church. We have met nothing before which looks so much like the predicted end of the Man of Sin. The Lord shall consume him with the *Spirit of his mouth,* and destroy him with *the brightness of his coming.* The Papacy can withstand any thing but such a revelation of God's Spirit, and of his word. The demonstration of the Spirit in the preaching of the word is wonderfully fulfilling the prophecy in these countries.

And the Papacy has been scarcely less seriously galled by the arrows of God's Truth, in *Belgium* and *Switzerland,* and more recently in Tuscany. In Belgium more than 250,000 copies of the Bible, and a larger quantity of Christian tracts and books, have been distributed within the last fifteen years. In Tuscany the word is having free course, and we may be sure it will be glorified.

Ominous signs of coming change have from time to time appeared in the Romish communion. Ever and anon oppressed humanity, pressed beyond the point of endurance, boldly resists. Such an outburst of resistance transpired a few years since in

Germany, under the leadership of Rongé and Czarski; and may be repeated in this country, under the leadership of Father Chiniquy, of Illinois.

A few years since (Oct. 1844), John Rongé, Catholic priest in Germany, roused to indignation by the audacious conduct of Bishop Arnoldi, of Treves, in exhibiting for pay to great multitudes of people (500,000) an *old coat*, which he impiously called *the coat of Christ*, issued a most spirited letter to the Bishop and the people of his charge, in which he speaks in merited and unmeasured terms of rebuke of the shameless imposition and traffic, and calls on his clerical brethren to arouse and throw off the despotism of Rome, and emulate the noble spirits of Huss, Hutten and Luther.

The consequence of this bold, Luther-like movement was to rouse the Catholic mind in Germany in a degree unknown since the Reformation in the sixteenth century. Rongé raised a giant's voice and wielded a giant's power. Immense crowds surrounded him where he went, and though priests and political power, and prejudice and superstition and ignorance most bitterly opposed him, and the Papal Beast was ready to stamp him under foot, yet his cause lived and prospered. It gathered strength daily, and carried terror to the very heart of Rome.

A new Church was formed, called the German Catholic Church, protesting against the errors, corruptions, superstitions and fooleries of Rome, and incorporating much of Protestant and Bible truth. It embraced a large number of clergy and people of Germany.

Though this movement did not mature into the full realization hoped for, and by many confidently expected, yet it was a movement in the right direction, but not altogether of the right spirit. It was lacking in the evangelical element. There was something of Luther's soul in it, without Luther's holy fire. The movement was not sufficiently pervaded with the gospel, and evangelical piety. Yet it was not a vain effort. As a bold protest, as an uncompromising *resistance* against error and corruption, it fulfilled a mission; it struck a blow at the colossus of Rome which she will not cease to feel. Germany has felt it. It was a blow for freedom.

Nor was the wonderful movement by any means confined to Germany. "Not only," says a late account, "it seems to be diffusing itself into all parts of that country, but it is spreading even into Barvaria and Austria, which are the most Roman Catholic countries in all Germany." It found its way into Poland, into the Polish part of Prussia, and gave no doubtful symptoms of a speedy eruption in France. Nor did poor Italy lie prostrate beneath the vandal foot of the Beast without giving some signs of struggling life. The late movements there in favor of political liberty, instigated by the galling of the yoke of ecclesiastical bondage, are but the sympathetic struggles which Papal Europe is making to be free.

I referred to the movement at St. Anne's, Illinois, under the leadership of Father Chiniquy. It may be premature yet to express an opinion as to what shall come of this movement. It is a bold and noble protest and resistance against the unwarrantable oppressions of Rome. It will do a work—probably will accomplish something important in the right direction; "and though Father Chiniquy may not be *the Luther* for whom we look, yet he may be a Wickliffe, or a Knox, gathering materials, securing resources, and preparing the way for the great and final work. God takes time—seldom begins and finishes a work by the same agent, or in the same generation. One sows and another reaps. He employs a succession of agents, as from step to step the work goes forward, till it draws near to its consummation; then he raises up some controlling spirit who finishes the work Moses, Luther, Washington, were selected for their respective missions, and brought on the great theatre of action, just in time to give completion to their work.

In due time our Luther will come. The great and final blow will be struck, and great Babylon will fall.

The late war in Italy has largely contributed to the same long-looked for result. Ostensibly, it has done much in breaking down barriers, removing obstacles, and preparing the way for the introduction of the Bible and a preached gospel in Sardinia, and the nations of northern Italy. Yet, really, it has done more, in destroying the prestige of an old order of things in religion and in politics, which, incubus-like, had settled down on those nationalities, like the curse of the apostasy. The leaven is at work. The effervescence may be terrible. The result will be sure.

Switzerland, too, is a volcano, heaving from its very centre. One hundred and fifty ministers in the canton of *Vaud*, no longer able to endure the exactions and control of the Neological Church authorities, have formally separated themselves from their connection, and, like the Free Church of Scotland, become independent. They have given up their sanctuaries, parsonages and salaries, that they may have liberty of conscience.

Again Rome shows another sign. She madly presumes, in some quarters, to raise the hand of *persecution*, and again to play the tyrant and oppressor. I refer to the infamous transactions of the agents of Rome at the *Society* and *Sandwich Islands*, and the scarcely less alarming indications in France herself. The unoffending inhabitants of these Islands were compelled, at the cannon's mouth, to receive and protect the very emissaries of the Beast, and to give place, on a soil already consecrated to a holy Religion, to the temples of the mystery of iniquity, and in addition to this, to give countenance to a traffic in intoxicating drinks, which once spread desolation over those fair Isles.

Such is the spirit of Romanism at this very day. Shorn of

its temporal power, it cannot depose kings and trample down empires as it did, yet it will still trample on the weak with the same cruel oppression, and drink the blood of saints with the same zest, wherever it can.

But why speak of the remote Islands? The same things, marked if possible by more violence and hatred of the truth, have transpired in Madeira, Madagascar, and in semiprotestant France. The late relentless persecutions of Dr. Achilli, and the Madiai, are illustrations of the spirit of modern Rome.

There is evidently a *movement* of the Beast, which presages a convulsion, indicating weakness at the centre, and a struggle to renew life at the extremities. Dreadful as the great conflict shall be, we may hope it shall be the last.

It may be that Rome feels her seven hills trembling beneath the ponderous excrescence of papal tyranny and corruption. It may be that she feels that Rome—that Europe is not the place for the Mystery of Iniquity longer to work, it having worked there so long already. Or it may be that His Holiness feels himself, in Italy, too much shut out from the great centre of the world, commercial, civil, literary or religious, and too much removed from the further sympathies of European Governments much longer to be sustained; and for any or all of these reasons, he would fain try his fortune in the New World.

As a forlorn hope, he may be looking across the Atlantic for a retreat. Nor is it althogether unlikely that such a plan may be carried into execution, and that the American Church may yet feel the power of that scourge which has been so severely felt by the Church in the Old World. May God avert such a calamity. But should it come, it is no more than our ingratitude and short-coming in duty deserves, and no more than the present state of the Romish Church seems to demand. The very struggle Rome finds it necessary to make for the preservation of her waning power, is the best evidence of her weakness. She is now rousing her wasting energies for one more desperate effort before she meet her doom, which hastens on apace. Such renewed efforts have been made in India, China, and Japan; and recently it was reported that a French general had gone to Rome to announce to the Pope that the Emperor of Burmah will not only tolerate, but encourage and aid Catholic missions throughout his empire. The emperor has built at his own cost spacious schools, and will provide funds for the support of the European professors who will be attached to them. He is about to erect a hospital to be administered by French Sisters of Charity, and means to build churches where the converts are sufficiently numerous.

9. Another indication of a great moral revolution, is *the recent shaking of the Hierarchy of England and Scotland.*

The religious establishment of England, especially, has grown to an enormous stature. We have no occasion to discuss the expediency of a National Religion. It is enough for our present purpose to allude to some of its excrescences. It doubtless incorporates much in its system which must be done away before the coming of the latter day of glory. And He who ariseth to shake terribly the earth, is now shaking this establishment to its centre. It has long been conceded by the evangelical part of the Church that there is imperative need of Church Reform. But recent developments have shown that the evils complained of are not so superficial as was supposed. There are causes already there at work, which go a great way to confirm the idea advanced under a former head, that before the much desired downfall of Papal Rome, the Man of Sin will increase in power, ancient error will be revived under new and specious forms, and truth and righteousness experience such a conflict with sin as has never yet been known. Both in England and America there are many such indications. But what I more particularly allude to here is, *the recent Theological movement at the University of Oxford, England.*

This ancient, rich and learned Institution, over whose enchanting grounds, and within whose venerated walls, and through whose extensive and costly libraries the writer once had the pleasure to roam, has long been the rallying point, as well as the radiating point of Church of Englandism. But as you now catch the sound from those high battlements of Zion's walls, surely you hear not the voice of "Protest" against the "Mystery of iniquity" that worketh in the spiritual Babylon; but it is the well-known voice of the Beast.

Some years ago, Dr. Pusey, Regius Professor of Hebrew and Canon of Christ Church in that University, began to publish certain new and startling doctrines in what were called "Tracts for the times." In these he apologized for the errors of Popery —called the Romish Church the elder sister of Episcopacy, whose *faults* are to be treated with much tenderness; and advanced sentiments diametrically opposed to the Reformation. He indeed speaks of Protestantism as a thing much to be lamented, and the Reformation as a misjudged act.

Such sentiments, too, have met the sympathy and support of other principal Professors of the University.

At first these innovations—or rather this attempt to revive old popish and ancient errors—attracted little attention, and did not excite much alarm; but within the last few years, they have spread with astonishing rapidity into almost every part of the English Church. Many of the high dignitaries of that Church have avowed these principles; and some of the most popular and widely circulated periodicals of England give them currency.

In these Tracts the great and distinguishing Protestant doctrine of *Justification* by *faith* is denied, and branded as the offspring of fanaticism; while the old Romish doctrine of *Bap-*

tismal Regeneration is openly avowed. Prayers for the dead, the worship of saints and angels, belief in Purgatory, crossings, holy water, festivals and fasts, and perhaps the whole routine of Romish rites and observances are gradually being introduced. Indeed, the design seems to be to resuscitate as fast as the people will bear it the rites and tenets against which Luther and the Reformers of Germany and England so strenuously contended, and to oppose which rivers of Protestant blood have flown.

And what is a more sad and alarming sign of the times, the religious state of England is such that a no inconsiderable portion of the Established Church is prepared to embrace a system so delusive and destructive.

These things are portentous of what may shortly be. Amidst the general convulsion, the fabric of Episcopacy is receiving a fearful shock. It may be rent in twain—or, more, it may be demolished, and the tottering Church of Rome be pillared on its ruins.

And fain would I add that America is not infected with this poison. Already have its pestiferous streams found their way across the Atlantic. The leaven is at work here. Admirers of Oxford, who do not fear to commend the Popery of *Protestant* Oxford, are not few on our side of the water. Nor did this new flood from the mouth of the dragon find the Church in question so well rooted and grounded in the truth and so fortified by habits of unadorned piety as not to be overcome. Not a small portion of the laity, and a large portion of her clergy have embraced the fascinating dogmas of Oxford. A test question (relating to the ordination of a young man who had one foot in Rome and was willing to put the other there) arose a few years ago, which leaves no room to doubt that a decided majority of the largest, richest and most influential Episcopal Convention in this country are the friends of Pusey and Oxford. And what is found true there, would probably not be found untrue elsewhere if the test were applied.

Romanism gives ominous signs that she is rallying for the great struggle.

No one can have been a careful observer of European history, for the last half century, without observing the strange advances of the Papal power in countries professedly Protestant. Although as a political system it has lost its hold, as an ecclesiastical power it seems endowed with a strange vitality. Three centuries since, the clouds of superstition seemed to have almost entirely receded from Central and Western Europe. But the dark shadow seems returning again. Puseyism counts its beads and mutters its mummeries in the very sanctuaries that once listened to the truths of a primitive gospel. Mysticism and infidelity dispute the sway of the German mind, with a State religion, Papal in every thing but in name. The very cities where Luther preached, and Melancthon wrote, now boast their priests and their Romish conventicles. All over Western Europe, the emissaries of the Papal hierarchy seem to be fast regaining the soil from which the Reformation so lately expelled them. "How," says an able writer, "is this phenomenon to be explained? In what manner may we account for the startling fact, that amid the blaze of science, the spread of education, the wide diffusion of intelligence, the awakened spirit of inquiry and of progress; in lands blessed with an open Bible, a free gospel, and all the appliances of religious instruction, an old tottering hierarchy, foul with pollution, laden with abhorred memories, and reeking with the blood of murdered saints, should come forth from the gloom of the dark past, and flaunting its tattered traditions in the eyes of the nineteenth century, be welcomed and embraced?"

The solution of the difficulty doubtless lies in the fact that the Beast is allowed to rally his already decayed energies for the final encounter. The great apostasy has always, when it could, been a persecuting power. Its terrific mission has been to make war with the saints and to kill them. And before it shall be finally overcome, he shall rise in great wrath, because he knows his time is short.

Another kind of process has been going on in the *Kirk of Scotland*. Already has the work of the divorce of Church and State begun, and going forward with rapid and irresistible strides; and probably the ball of revolution, started on the heights of the Grampian Hills, will never be stopped, till, gathering magnitude and strength as it advances, it shall prostrate before it every proud tower of hierarchal domination.

The Kirk of Scotland, though Presbyterian, has, since the union of the two kingdoms, been like the Church of England and Ireland, a *National Church;* and as such, no particular parish could choose their own minister, or transact their own ecclesiastical affairs unmolested by Government. The Patron or lord of the Manor—the owner in a sense of the peasants or working people and of the lands they occupied, has the ecclesiastical right of choosing and imposing on a parish such a one as he will; and the only alternative the Church and Society have, is either to retain and support a man who is offensive to them, or reject him at the hazard of a legal prosecution, yet still support him—and in addition to this, support the man of their choice.

To many parishes these burdens became intolerable. A manly —a *Scottish* resistance was made, which has resulted in a large secession and the organization of a new Church, on independent and evangelical grounds. And it is predicted that a Reform is there began, which shall not stop till every Church in the British Isles shall be disenthralled from the trammels of the State and be made free with the liberty of the sons of God.

10. We must not overlook another characteristic of our times

of an opposite character: I mean *the stupidity and listlessness of the wicked at a period like the present.*

The period preceding the great conflict is thus described by Daniel: "Many shall be purified and made white and tried, but the wicked shall do wickedly; and none of the wicked shall understand, but the wise shall understand." Even in the midst of such superabundance of light, the wicked shall walk in darkness—in the midst of extraordinary privileges they shall remain unmoved, uninstructed, unprofited. While the truth is proclaimed about them and enforced upon them they remain stupid and unconcerned as the marble. It is not open infidelity, but a listlessness, which admits the necessity of religion and assents to the truth, yet indulges in its stupidity. No effort seems to reach them. Preaching is powerless—exhortation unavailing—judgments ineffectual, mercies unheeded—death does not move a muscle. This is but too true of a large class of the ungodly: *none of the wicked shall understand.* They will harden their hearts and blind their eyes that they may perish.

The extensive religious revivals of modern days present another evidence which identifies our age with the age that should precede the final triumph of the Church. Great numbers shall be gathered in, and many shall be zealous for God before that great and notable day of the Lord shall come. But this is a topic which has already assumed an importance as a sign of the times, and an efficient agency in the great moral revolutions which are coming on the earth, that has placed it among the great and leading movements of the day. We shall therefore assign to it a separate place of consideration.

CHAPTER VIII.

"I will show wonders in heaven above, and signs in the earth beneath; blood, and fire, and vapor of smoke: the sun shall be turned into darkness, and the moon into blood, before that great and notable day of the Lord come."—*Acts* ii. 19, 20.

"THE day of the Lord" is a day when God shall vindicate his cause and magnify his name—the day of the manifestation of his power and the execution of his judgments. And the "great and notable day of the Lord" is a period when he shall do this in an extraordinary degree. Every deliverance of his people—every instance of his executing vengeance on his enemies, may be termed the day of the Lord. But when he does this in a signal manner, it is *the great and notable day of the Lord*. The deliverance of the children of Israel out of Egypt, and the corresponding infliction of wrath on his enemies was a day of the Lord. So was the destruction of Jerusalem, and the preservation of the people of God, in that awful event.

This is particularly what is meant here. But as in general it means any period when God signally manifests himself—and, more emphatically than any other, the judgment-day, I shall not be deviating from the spirit of the passage if I apply it to that great conflict of sin against righteousness, and the consequent vindication of his cause on the part of God, which shall take place previous to the complete establishment of Messiah's kingdom on earth.

"I will show wonders in heaven above, and signs in the earth beneath"—great changes and wonderful events both in the Church and out of it—"Blood, and fire, and vapor of smoke"—wars, calamities, conflagration of towns. "The sun shall be turned into darkness, and the moon into blood"—such calamitous events as shall then transpire shall cast a gloom over the moral and political world, such as resembles that dismal appearance of the atmosphere when the sun is eclipsed, or the moon is shorn of her silver brightness by a thick haze or a dense vapor. Such shall be the gloomy aspect of the world before the eventful period, called the "great and notable day of the Lord." But soon after there shall be a period of a very different character. A change comes over the scene. The darkness is dissipated—the vapor is cleared away—the blood dried up—the fire is quenched. Peace smiles again. Prosperity shines. Righteousness reigns. The period is described in these words: "the kingdoms of this world are become the kingdoms of our Lord and his Christ."

There is a general expectation that such a period is at hand; and the expectation seems but a simple response of ancient prophecy. It is becoming then that we should read these signs, understand their import, and be prepared for the coming of the "great and notable day of the Lord." The aspect of the world is peculiar, and such as to indicate a mighty convulsion as not distant. What this shall be, we should, if not aided by the light of prophecy, be quite unable to form a conjecture. But with this Divine guidance, we more than conjecture it shall be the last great conflict of sin against holiness which shall precede the Millennium.

I shall name other "signs of the times" which indicate the approach and prepare the way of the coming of the great event. And the next that claims our attention, as verified in our present age, is—

11. *The present condition of the Mohammedan Empire.* Constantinople, the present centre and head of Mohammedan power, is the keystone of dominion in the great world of religion and politics. Any movements, therefore, in that quarter are especially ominous of coming change. What we assert is, that present appearances indicate the no remote downfall of the Turkish Empire and the Mohammedan religion, and the consequent pleasing, dreadful, humiliating, glorious results of that great event.

Satan has always been careful to keep organized against the true Church of God some mighty confederacies and counterfeits. The spirit of this hostility has been essentially the same in all ages of the world, though it has worn a form suited to the times, places, and the condition of the Church. Before the rise of the Sun of righteousness—or the introduction of the Christian dispensation, Paganism presented a sufficient barrier against a holy religion. The Church then was less aggressive, less powerful and diffusive, and presented less to the eyes of the world which could excite alarms or engender fears. With the exception of a few insignificant spots, Satan sat entrenched in the strongholds of idolatry over the whole face of the earth. Gross, absurd and corrupt as Paganism was, it was not too much so to be allowed to stand in an equally corrupt world. The world's morality was then such as could tolerate it. But Christianity threw a new light over the world. There was now a grand moral advance. The Church was enlarged and enlightened. It was more holy and powerful. It now became *aggressive*. During the life of its Divine author, it began to overstep its former prescribed boundaries; and at his death, astonishment must have seized the foes of the true Church to hear him issue the command, clothed in the power and baptized with the affection of a dying request, that his followers should never cease their aggressions till they should subjugate the entire earth to the dominion of Immanuel.

This was alarming, but it did not immediately give the alarm. Earthly dominion was then in the hands of Paganism, and in a few years it became more so by the subjugation of the Jewish nation to the Romans. The great author of Christianity was dead—he had died an ignominious death. The spell that held the disciples together seemed broken—their number was so small, their condition so humble—the reputation in which they were held so low, that the most timid in the ranks of the foe felt no alarm. But to the utter confusion of the world, Christianity lived and prospered. After a little while it was heard of in Arabia, in Mesopotamia, in Asia Minor, in Athens, Corinth, and in Rome. And behold it has appeared in the very household of *Cæsar*.

This, however, gave no very general alarm. The apathy which the empire of sin had acquired by its centuries of undisturbed dominion was not yet broken. At length it is proclaimed that the hated religion of the Nazarene has appeared in the forum—in the council-chamber, and in the hall of legislation—in the public arena of the bustling world, and in the walks of private life—in the halls of science and among the humblest cottages of the hamlet, yea, that scribes and Pharisees, high priests and rulers, kings and emperors, were numbered among its disciples; and the enemy began to be alarmed. The besiegers were brought to the very gates of his stronghold.

At length the great Constantine is born. He is converted to Christianity—espouses the cause of Christ; Christianity is known in the palace, and anon it is the religion of the Roman Empire.

Hitherto the Enemy had looked on with astonishment, wondering whereunto this thing would grow, yet believing that the bloody mouth of Persecution, which stood ready to glut his insatiable maw with the blood of the saints, could not fail to exterminate the rising sect. Paganism, which had for ages stood an impregnable bulwark against all former encroachments on the dark domains of sin, was no longer suited to its purpose. Its *spirit* would do, but its form—its garb was too uncouth, too offensive to the taste and sentiment of the age—savored too much of barbarism and ignorance, to allow it any longer to be a fit instrument by which to oppose the then formidable growth of the Christian Religion. A new Power must now be formed suited to the new state of the world as modified by the introduction and progress of Christianity. It must be a grand delusion—and be so constructed as to meet the threefold demand of the Pagan, the Jew, and the Christian—and withal contain nothing that should disturb the quietude of the carnal heart.

Mohammed arose. He commenced his public mission in 609, only three years later than the generally received date of the rise of the Papal Beast. Mohammedanism was a religion for the times. It was a new edition of the same old error. It was Paganism and Infidelity and Licentiousness dressed in a costume suited to the new order of things under the gospel dispensation. It incorporated in itself so much of each of the prevailing religions as should satisfy their respective votaries. Mohammed chose out a common ground. The Jew, the nominal Chistian, and the more enlightened heathen would acknowledge the existence and unity of God, and the duty of rendering to Him some service; while to the carnal mind a sensual Paradise would be altogether congenial.

The Church had become corrupt, and Mohammedanism became the scourge of the eastern portion, as Romanism did of the western.   Mohammed was a reformer among the Pagans, though a corrupter of the truth, and a False Prophet to Christianity.   His system was a most cunningly devised fable—a fit instrument by which to ensnare the unwary souls of men.   It was Paganism modified and modernized and fitted to a more enlightened state of the world.   It was Satan's second grand scheme to subjugate Asia and Africa to himself.

The corrupters of Christianity, who prepared the way for the rise and progress of Mohammedanism, are represented, in the ninth chapter of Revelations, as a " *Star fallen from heaven unto the earth*"—to whom was given the "*key of the bottomless Pit.*" "*And he opened the bottomless Pit.*"   The propagation of his false doctrines let loose the powers of hell, and encouraged wicked men in sin.   "*And there arose a smoke out of the pit as the smoke of a great furnace, and the sun and the air were darkened by reason of the smoke of the pit.*"   Here was Mohammedanism.   It was a grand *delusion* which either blinded the eyes of men, or so bedimmed and perverted their vision that they could only see as through a glass darkly—as men see when the sun and the air are darkened by a dense smoke.

There could not be a more exact description of Mohammedanism as a *religious* power.   But Mohammed was not merely a False Prophet—a corrupter and destroyer of religion; he was a *scourge among the nations*.   He had a political as well as a religious dominion.   Follow on in the description: "*And there came out of the smoke locusts on the earth; and unto them was given power as the scorpions of the earth have power.*"   That is, great armies of Arabians or Saracens were raised up by the policy and craft of the Mohammedan imposture, which spread desolation among the nations of the earth.   They were numerous as locusts; and arose from the same quarter from which the greatest swarms of locusts originate.   Yet in their power to hurt, they are as *scorpions.*

And the shapes of the locusts were like unto horses prepared unto battle; and on their heads were as it were crowns like gold, and their faces were as the faces of men.   And they had hair as the hair of women, and their teeth were as the teeth of lions.   And they had breastplates, as it were breastplates of iron; and the sound of their wings was as the sound of chariots of many horses running to battle.   And they had a king over them, which is the angel of the bottomless Pit.

What more accurate description of an Arabian army?   Numerous as swarms of locusts from the southern desert—vindictive and deadly as the scorpion—consisting principally of horsemen—with turbans on their heads resembling crowns—with their long hair, as the Arabians are accustomed to wear it—and although, like women, they may wear some marks of timidity and gentleness, yet they have teeth like a lion.   They ravage and devour without mercy.   They have *faces* of men—appear *like men,* yet they are unchained tigers.

They were a well organized army—had a king over them—were actuated by one spirit, as one commissioned from the bottomless Pit.   They harmonized in their object, the prostration of the Church—were protected by a strong civil power—had *breastplates of iron.*   They produced a great tumult in the world—flew from one country to another like an army with chariots and many horsemen.   At first they favored and flattered; but there was a sting in their tail.   They at length stung like a scorpion.

They had power to do hurt for *five* months—one hundred and fifty days—or, according to prophetic language, one hundred and fifty years.

Mohammed began publicly to declare his mission in the year
8

612, and the power of his violent agressions was suspended on the building of Bagdat, in 762—one hundred and fifty years after. The *smoke* continued—the power of religious delusion did not cease, but the flying, furious, stinging, scorpion-like locusts ceased their ravages. The fierce military character was abated, yet their civil and religious power and dominion over the fairest portions of the world was continued, and is to continue till it shall have accomplished in all twelve hundred and sixty years. The period of its existence (which was cotemporaneous in its beginning) is the same as that of the Papal Beast.

What I have described is the "first woe" of Mohammedanism, or the fierce and cruel ravages of Moslemism during its first one hundred and fifty years. During this period it spread its gloomy desolations over the whole Eastern Roman Empire. Arabia was already in the hands of the Prophet before his death. Syria, Persia and Egypt are soon made the vassals of his proud successors. The banners of the Moslems wave over thirty-six thousand cities, towns and castles, subjugated to the new conquerors within the first twelve years; four thousand Christian temples destroyed, and fourteen hundred Mosques dedicated to the Prophet.

Africa was subdued—the Moors are converted to the new Religion, and in their turn descend into Spain and establish a magnificent empire there. "The victorious standard of the Crescent was raised on the cold mountains of Tartary, and on the burning sands of Ethiopia." "On Mount Lebanon and by the waters of Babylon; under the pyramids of Egypt, and to the Mozambique and Madagascar, the standard sheet of Mohammed was unfurled."

The "*second* woe," or the second grand aggressive, blood-thirsty stride of Mohammedanism may be looked for in the rise of the TURKISH POWER. The Turks, recently so formidable and constituting so important a portion of the Mohammedan Empire, were not an original part of this dominion. They were a tribe of *Tartars* from beyond the River Euphrates—often called Othmans or Otomans, from Othman their chief, who assumed the title of Sultan. Suffice it to say these Tartar hordes, after various and extraordinary success, in which they subjugated Persia and Western Asia, and formed four governments on the east side of the Euphrates, had hitherto been held in check. But in the year 1281 these " four angels which were bound in the River Euphrates, were loosed." The Turks burst forth on the Saracens—carried their conquests from the Euphrates to the Danube—overrun the whole Mohammedan Empire—took *Constantinople*, the capital of the Roman Empire, in 1453—took possession of Syria, Greece, Egypt, and conquered most of Europe.

These wars and conquests reached up to the year 1672, being three hundred and ninety-one years from their incursions west of the Euphrates. This answers precisely to the length of time predicted for the continuance of the " second woe," or the woe of the Turkish invasion. " *The four angels which were loosed, were prepared for an hour and a day and a month and a year.*" That is, for three hundred and ninety-one years, the very time occupied in the above conquests.

Since that time the Turkish Empire has stood the grand centre of Mohammedan power, and the formidable barrier between Christianity and Paganism. It has occupied the central portion of the earth, and been the keystone in the arch of empire. It is the balancing power among nations. But for this fact it would have been demolished long since. Consequently, when it does fall, it must produce a crash among the kingdoms of the earth.

The same remark might be made in reference to the Turkish power on *the religious world,* but that would be to anticipate another part of our subject.

Russia has always looked with an eagle-eye on Turkey. She

now waits to seize on her prey. France waits to realize her long indulged dreams of making Egypt (an important part of this dominion) her tributary. England fears for her wide domains in the East if Turkey shall be dismembered; while France, England, Austria and Prussia have a common interest in opposing the encroachments and the consequent aggrandizement of the autocrat of the North, the grand Czar of Russia.

Thus it is that Turkey is the pivot of power. The great desideratum among the nations is, how to preserve the *balance* when this pivot shall be destroyed—for destroyed it soon must be. Mohammedanism is rotten at the core. It has always nourished within its bosom the seeds of its own dissolution. Its vigor was long since departed. Infirmity, disease and age have long since betokened its downfall. The keen-eyed statesman has long since seen it. The courts of the great Powers of Europe are perplexed, not as to the probability of the speedy overthrow of this power, but as to the manner that it shall be disposed of so as to preserve the balance of power among the nations. The moment the banners of the Crescent shall be furled on the towers of Constantinople, there will be a tumult among the nations—some to preserve what they have, others to gain what they have not.

If such be the relative position of the Turkish Empire, it is easy to see why, politically as well as religiously, so much importance is attached to the downfall of this power.

What, now, are the facts in regard to it? They are these: The arm of this empire is broken—the sceptre is departing—her glory is eclipsed—her strength is weakness. Long ago would she have fallen but for the interested interposition of those who were not yet prepared to divide the spoil. But now her days, to all human appearance, are numbered. She cannot be pillared up much longer. She must fall—and that speedily—perhaps within a few years.   But this event shall be followed by a mighty revolution.

Am I not right, then, in pointing to the present political aspect of the world as indicative of a general convulsion?   Precisely what that will be we may not determine.   Yet we are not left without some landmarks by which we may be guided in our inquiries here.   Let us turn to them for a moment:

The overthrow of Mohammedanism is, I think, foretold in the following passage from the sixteenth chapter of Revelations: *"And the sixth angel poured out his vial on the great river Euphrates, and the water thereof was dried up, that the way of the kings of the East might be prepared."*

The Euphrates, it is well known, is the very centre of Mohammedanism.   To the north, at the head of this river, lies Turkey, the very fountain of Islamism; at the east, Persia; at the west, Arabia, Syria and Egypt.   The land of the Euphrates is the very land of the Mohammedan delusion.   Here it has held undisputed sway over the fairest portions of the world.   Thence it has sent out pestiferous waters to poison the souls of men.   It is therefore well symbolized by the *river Euphrates*—and its downfall by the *drying up of the waters* of this river.   The power of that great empire shall wane and waste away until it shall cease to be.   So it has been for many years past, losing its vigor and diminishing till only the shadow of its former greatness remains—and to all human probability it must soon cease to be. But what shall be the consequence?   The account proceeds: *" And I saw three unclean spirits like frogs come out of the mouth of the dragon, and out of the beast, and out of the mouth of the false prophet.   For they are the spirits of devils working miracles, which go forth unto the kings of the earth, and of the world, to gather them to the battle of the great day of God Almighty."*

First the body shall die, and the eagles shall gather together to divide the carcase. The kings of the earth shall come to seize the spoil. But the spirit shall live. It shall be a spirit of a three-fold power: 1st. The spirit of the Dragon or the Devil—the spirit of Idolatry or of Infidelity; 2d. The spirit of the Beast or Popery; and 3d. The spirit of the false Prophet—the same old spirit of Mohammedanism.

These foul spirits of the Pit now issue forth on the annihilation of the great antichristian power—the great scourge of a pure religion. They practice all manner of deception, even pretending to work miracles. Their grand design is to stir up the kings of the earth to the last great conflict—to the *battle* of *the great day of God Almighty.*

This great battle, the battle of Armageddon, is the result of that last and fearful confederacy of the powers of darkness against the Church of Christ.

The signs of the times are portentous. The world is in commotion; the political world seems to move from its very centre. The fountains of the great deep seem about to be broken up. It labors and heaves from beneath and betokens another deluge. Not a deluge like that which broke up the material surface of the earth and cast the mountains into the sea, and turned the sea into dry land—that remodeled the entire surface of our globe, but a *moral* and *political deluge.* A convulsion that shall cast down the high mountains of despotism and break to pieces the strongholds of ecclesiastical domination, and throw into fearful commotion the stagnant ocean of common minds. We seem to be in a transition state—passing the threshold of some mighty change. The world is about to be shaken to its centre. Those things that may be shaken shall be removed; and those things that cannot be shaken shall remain. Every nation's as well as every man's works are about to be tried, that it may be seen of what they are. The hay, wood and stubble shall be burnt; the

gold, silver and precious stones shall come out seven times purified.

Already does the earth give signs of such a convulsion. The
world is becoming too much enlightened much longer to bear the
galling yoke of despotism. The genius of Liberty is too rife in
the world much longer to be trampled under foot by a bull of the
Pope, or to crouch to the thraldom of Pagan or Mohammedan
priestcraft. These mountains, however, cannot be cast into the
sea without a convulsion that shall shake the whole earth. Already, to all human appearance, it is beginning to work.

But there is another and a less despondent phase of affairs in
Turkey. In the midst of the wanings of the Crescent and the
drying up of the waters of the Euphrates, new fountains of moral
and political life have sprung up and are beginning to cheer the
desolations of that land of despotism. Christianity, in its primitive life and purity, has entered Turkey. And Christian civilization has there entered on its benign mission. The gradually
vanishing away of old systems and polities does but make place
for the ingress of the reforming institutions of a better religion
and a better civil polity.

But remarkable and ominous of change and promising of a
radical reform as the decay of the old regimé is, these are not
the features in the present history of the Turks and of the Moslem religion, which the most obviously betoken a revolution that
shall put out of the way one of the most formidable obstacles
with which Christianity has now to contend. We refer rather
to the civil and religious resuscitations which are there transpiring at the present day. The past few years have wrought marvellous changes in Turkey. The destruction of the Janizaries,
and the death-blow thereby struck to the despotic power of the
Ottoman empire; the abrogation of the death penalty on account
of a change of religion, and the free toleration of all religions;

the extensive introduction of the Press and the publication of a great variety of newspapers and periodicals; the translation of the Bible into the principal languages of Turkey and its free and extensive circulation among all classes of people, and the recent increased attention paid to education, especially to *female* education, are signs of the times of no doubtful import. Recent movements of the Sultan in reorganizing the schools of his empire, and especially in putting upon a more prosperous footing than ever before, schools for girls, indicate the determination of the Sublime Porte to carry out the schemes of reform already so auspiciously begun.

And what is yet more to our purpose, European civilization has been very extensively introduced, and Christian missions have made known, in every principal place in the empire, the religion of the New Testament. These are the things which are inaugurating a new era in the land of the Moslems, and which indicate coming changes of a most delightful character. Agencies are undoubtedly at work there which shall not fail to work out a glorious emancipation.

Whether, therefore, we watch the receding wave of the old and decaying order of things as it returns again to the dark chaos whence it rose, or whether the eye fix on the inflowing and gradually strengthening tide of the new order, we are instinctively impressed with the idea that great changes are at hand. Turkey can scarcely fail to be soon revolutionized. And we think we are not mistaken in the intimation already made, that a revolution in Turkey will be the signal of revolution in most of the nations of the earth.

What shall be the immediate results of such revolutions we cannot predict; but sure we are that the mighty hand of God will be in them, and an immense revenue of glory shall accrue to his name. He will break to pieces, as with a rod of iron, the power of reigning despotism; he will rebuke the pride of man; he will strengthen the hands of the nations that serve him, and weaken the power of those who will not have him to reign over them. He will, in all things, open the door among the nations for the free and universal diffusion of the gospel.

It will be seen that we do not anticipate a violent death for this great system of religious delusion. In this respect its end shall signally differ from its great contemporary, the Romish Apostasy.

These views might be abundantly confirmed by intelligent witnesses, at present residents in those countries; men who have, for more than a quarter of a century, been identified with these reforms and who know whereof they affirm. The Rev. Dr. Goodell, who has done good service in Turkey for the last thirty years, speaks thus hopefully of the prospects of the work. He says: "A wide and effectual door is opened before us to labor for the evangelizing of this Mohammedan and corrupt Christian land. Behold what things God hath wrought! War has come and brought many evils in its train, but it has also brought the Bible, ministers of the gospel and many praying hearts here. It has given liberty to distribute thousands of copies of Bibles and Testaments to those who are denied this blessed book in their own land. It has broken the wall of bigotry and prejudice that can never be built up again between Mohammedans and Christians, and opened the Mussulman mind largely to Bible and Gospel influences. It has officially pledged religious liberty to all classes, even native-born Mussulmans in the Turkish Empire, and that, too, with the sanction of all the great powers of Europe. Having thus accomplished the great designs of God, the late war ceased, and peace was proclaimed amidst universal rejoicings. And the way is now opened for evangelical Christians to enter in and take possession of this land for our Lord and his Christ. The signs of the times call upon us to gird ourselves with one heart and one mind for the work.   There will doubtless be a great conflict in the overthrow of Moslemism in the opposing of the flood of infidelity and licentiousness that will follow, and in the establishment of a pure and evangelical Christianity, but the result is sure as the Word of God."

In commenting on the late Hatti Sheriff, which he regards as the turning-point in the history of the East, the Rev. Dr. Schaffler says: "The entire war seemed made for the Hatti Sheriff, the late firman of the Sultan, granting liberty of conscience to all the subjects of the Porte.   Before this was proclaimed, the allied powers tried to make peace, but it was impossible.   God's purpose in the war was not yet accomplished.   But when religious liberty had been pledged from Constantinople throughout the Turkish Empire, then the conferences met at Paris, and peace was at once concluded.   A good Arminian brother said, 'This war was not made for the queen, the emperor, or the sultan, but for the Lord Jesus Christ, to pave the way and to open every door for the spread of the Bible and the preaching of the gospel in this land.'   A great leaf was soon to be turned in the history of the East; it was now trembling in the hand of Providence, and we believe there is written on it glorious things for the triumph of the gospel of Christ.   Hatti Sheriff, being interpreted, signifies *sacred writing.*   This was to prepare the way for God's sacred writing—his Hatti Sheriff—to go forth in all the languages and lands of the Mohammedan empire."   Almost the only substantial fruit of the Crimean war was the decree securing religious liberty.

"Nor did the renunciation of the claim to inflict the death penalty," says the Rev. Dr. Riggs, "appear alone.   The same edict proclaimed the entire equality of the subjects of the empire, of whatever faith; and besides, it comprised twenty points of reform, all proposed by the English embassador, and seconded by the embassadors of the other allied powers, who were thus led, in the wonder-working providence of God, to demand in Turkey a more complete toleration than they grant in their own empires."

Indeed, the united testimony of the whole missionary corps in that benighted land, comes to us in accents the most cheering, proclaiming " the morning cometh." " There was never a time," say they, " like the present in this country. The word of God has free course. Christians, Jews and Mohammedans, in the great cities of the country, in the interior, in the mountainous regions—Kurds and Kuzzlebashes—accept the Word. The dwellers in the rocks and in the plains, shout to each other, and every prosperous year is outdone by the year following. Our experience is that the time for the evangelization of the East has come."

Such are the signs of the times in that land which stands as the key-empire of the world. Change and commotion there betoken change and commotion among the nations. On the one hand, we have seen the Turkish Empire toppling to its fall, and is only propped up by the strong arm, and preserved in its integrity by the complicated interests of foreign powers. The no doubtful premonitions of the overthrow of the Moslems are ominous of mighty changes ; and at the same time preparatory to the things which must shortly come to pass. Soon we may expect to witness a crash among the nations. The dying struggle of Islamism shall be the signal of a wide-spread commotion. On the other hand, we have witnessed at work there, under auspices the most promising of success, a series of reforming elements and agencies, which are working out results as sure as they are ameliorating and benevolent. Yet we do not expect the Sun of Righteousness will arise on those lands so long darkened with the devouring locusts of the false Prophet, except he shall arise out of the thick darkness and the tempest. Yet we expect he shall soon arise.

When the great drama shall end, when the most colossal system of imposture which the world ever witnessed shall dissolve away and be no more, then shall he who overturns and overturns, come and set up his kingdom on the earth. The duration of this imposture, we remember, is nearly coeval with that of the Romish Apostasy. We therefore expect, in the waning of the Crescent, to witness the downfall of great Babylon.

In all these commotions and overturnings the Christian hears the stately steppings of his Prince. The pestilence and the sword may go before him, but righteousness and peace shall follow in his footsteps.

But what shall the sinner and the ungodly then do? The earth is tottering beneath him—it shall reel to and fro like a drunken man—and if he have not laid up for himself a good foundation for time to come, he is indeed in want of all things. When the day of the "Lord's vengeance" shall come, then may we know that the "year of the redeemed is come."

CHAPTER IX.

Movements in the camp of Israel, indicating the approach of the latter-day glory—The present condition of the Jews, a (12th) sign of the times.

In designating what should be the signs of the coming of the Son of man, I said the "restoration to the land of their fathers, and their conversion to Christianity, of THE JEWS," should hold a prominent place. We have purposely reserved what we would say on this topic for a separate but brief chapter. It is the design now to show that *the present condition of this extraordinary people is such as to indicate the no distant approach of the glorious era foretold.*

But what has the world now to do with the descendants of Abraham—with these despised and everywhere spoken-against Jews? Are they not cut off and cast out, repudiated and cursed of God? Why should those ancient rebels be now called up to honor the King when he shall come in his glory? What have we to do with them? Much every way; and chiefly because God will honor them more prominently than he ever has done as an instrumentality by which to carry forward the glorious work of Redemption. Salvation is of the Jews.

(125)

We here do well to go back and inquire at the mouth of the living oracles, what is the mind of God in respect to Israel? Has he done with that extraordinary people? Are his purposes all fulfilled, his promises through them all performed? Will he use his ancient covenant people no more as prominent instruments by which to carry on the great work of human salvation?

As preliminary therefore to the main design of the present chapter, and as a means of confirming our faith in the permanency of God's covenant with Abraham to the end of time, it will not be amiss to refer to a few particulars respecting this singular people which can scarcely fail to inspire in us fresh hopes that God will yet make the seed of Abraham bear a very signal part in bringing in the latter-day glory; and make us feel the more confident, as we see any movements among the Jews betokening their return to the land of their ancient inheritance, and their acknowledgment of the Messiah, that such a day is at hand. But why does any movement in the camp of Israel, or a movement in reference to this people have such a strange significancy, and why is it taken as an index of corresponding movements in the Church of God, and among the nations of the earth? It is because of *the peculiar relation* in which this people stand to the purposes and covenant promises of God.

Such has been the past history of the Jews—such God's covenant and its promises—such the whole course of his dealings with them—their singular dispersion and more singular preservation—and the no less remarkable predictions concerning their future—as well as the prominence in human affairs which in all ages has been allowed to individuals of that nation, while at the same time the great mass of them were still crushed under great oppression—all these things indicate that this people hold a position in relation to the Church universal and to the world, which can scarcely fail to invest every thing which belongs to them with a peculiar interest.

When Christ said "Salvation is of the Jews," he announced a fact which runs parallel with the whole history of this wonderful people—and more significant, probably, in relation to its future than its past. The destiny of the world is strangely bound up in the destiny of Israel.

But let us inquire a little more particularly what there has been so singular in the relative position of the Jewish Church and nation in the past history of the world—and what there is in God's promises, and his obvious purposes towards them in the future, to indicate that they are to have any special agency and influence in the conversion of the world and the bringing in of the latter-day glory? what that should make us feel that any movement among that people, or in respect to them, is especially auspicious and encouraging? There are some things in connection with the *original grant* made to Abraham—something in the form of the promises and blessings appended, which more than suggest that a glorious future yet awaits that people. Israel should become *a great nation.* This has been but partially fulfilled. In the palmiest days of the Hebrew Commonwealth this grant was only in part appropriated. And as the land was given as an *everlasting possession*, it yet remains for a future occupancy.

Another feature in the covenant with Abraham, was that *his name* should *be great.* He should be denominated, not the Father of his country only, but the *Father of the faithful.* No other name is so universally honored by the whole family of man. "Jews, Gentiles—Mohammedans and Christians, vie, one with another, in their reverence to the memory of this great man," and glory in their real or supposed descent from him. Never was a name so immortalized on earth—so interwoven with the saint's hope of eternal life—appended, as it were, to every grant of pardon at the court of heaven.

And not only so, but he should be a remarkable channel of *transmitting* blessings and honors to others, without limit. *Thou shalt be a blessing*—a fountain whose streams shall bless a world. Do we value the Bible? do we esteem above rubies the institutions of Religion—the Sabbath and the Sanctuary?—Is Christ precious, the chicfest among ten thousand? These are boons through faithful Abraham.

And we observe another thing here. God singularly identifies his interest and aims in the affairs of this world with Abraham and his descendants: "I will bless them that bless thee, and curse him that curseth thee." To raise a hand against Israel, is to fight against God. No people, no nation has ever opposed, persecuted, and harmed Israel and prospered. This, all history has abundantly verified; not in respect to the spiritual seed of Abraham alone, but scarcely less remarkably, in respect to his natural seed.

Another significant fact in relation to this race, is *its singular preservation*. They have remained a distinct people 4,000 years—and, impliedly and prophetically, since the promise of a Saviour to Adam. There is not another such instance in the annals of the world. The Assyrian, the Babylonian, the Greek and the Roman—where are they? The tide of empire rolls on, rising and falling—flourishing and decaying, till the revolution of empires is scarcely less looked for than revolution in any other mutable thing. *Not one of the nations which oppressed Israel is now to be found.* How different the fate of the Jews! The earth has been overturned and overturned—the foundations of empire broken up—kingdoms on kingdoms wrecked, and nations dissolved into their elements, yet the nation which the King is pleased to honor, has stood like a tower amidst embattling hosts. Amidst a spiritually barren world, she remained from century to century as a garden in the desert, the only spot on which the eye of moral beauty could fix with delight. Founded on a Rock, Israel stood and prospered, while the beggarly elements of the world were dissolving about him.

And though now scattered to the four winds and cast among people of every language and latitude, they lose none of their identity. They stand separate and alone amidst the endlessly changing population of the globe. But why has this people been so remarkably preserved a separate and distinct people, if God has no further special use for them? If his future purposes concerning them are simply that they shall acknowledge the Messiah like any other nation of unbelievers, why all this special care of them?

In other respects, too, this singular people hold a most extraordinary position in relation to all the other nations. They were the chosen depositories of God's grace for a perishing world—Zion, his earthly dwelling, the place of his peculiar presence—of his promises, of the covenants, of the living oracles of the truth—of the advent of the Messiah. They were the *dispensers* of salvation to a dying world; the *channel* of *transmission* of the waters of life. And they were, too, the *key-stone to empire*. Ancient monarchies rose, prospered, and faded away according to the good pleasure of God as touching Israel. They were the grand radiating point of light—the fountain of moral influences for a lapsed world.

And, what is more remarkable, the first agents, the most efficient and successful, in the early diffusion of Christianity, were of this same stock of Abraham. Under the auspices of this Jewish, apostolic agency, the gospel, in spite of all governmental power arrayed against them, and in spite of all the opposing power of the world, the flesh and the devil, was, in about thirty years, made known to every nation under heaven. And not till a Gentile agency was substituted in the place of a Jewish, did the missionary spirit of the primitive Church subside and the Church herself become corrupt. Most emphatically was this great *salvation of the Jews*, both in its introduction and its diffusion among the nations.

And more remarkably yet, shall this same feature characterize the final conversion of the world and the establishment of Messiah's kingdom on the earth. The prophets are full of the most glowing expressions as to the leading influential part which the seed of Abraham shall take in the final evangelization of the world.

There are here two classes of predictions : the one relating to the profound and overwhelming *conviction*, which the restoration to God's favor, and the fulfilment of so many prophecies, and the verification of so many promises shall produce on the mind of the whole Gentile world ; and the other relates to the direct *instrumentality* which the Jews, when converted and restored to the land of their fathers, shall have in bringing about the desired event. The conversion, after so long a time, of such a people— the manner of their return—the forbearance, faithfulness, goodness, mercy and judgment of God displayed in it—the great practical attestation it will furnish to the truth of prophecy, will produce a *moral impression* on the mind of the nations, more powerful than we may readily conceive. When the " light" shall have come to Israel, and the " glory of the Lord shall be risen" on the restored house of Jacob, " the Gentiles shall come to her light and kings to the brightness of her rising." When God shall " arise and have mercy on Zion, the heathen shall fear the name of the Lord, and all the kings of the earth thy glory." " They shall be in the midst of many people, as a dew from the Lord, as the showers upon the grass." " When the Lord shall build up Zion

—restore his ancient covenant people—he shall appear in his glory."

The restoration of the Jews—after the fulness of the Gentiles shall be brought in—is everywhere held up as the spiritual resurrection of the whole Gentile world. The great apostle to the Gentiles has left us no room to doubt of the meaning of the many prophetic visions to which I have scarcely more than alluded. "Now," says he, "if the fall of them be," as by all conceded, "the riches of the world"—the means or occasion of bringing the gospel to all the nations of the earth; and the "diminishing of them the riches of the Gentiles, *how much more their fulness?*" Or "if the casting away of them be the reconciling of the world, what shall the receiving of them be, *but life from the dead?*" The resuscitation of the dry bones of the house of Israel shall be the regeneration of the world.

Precisely *how* converted Israel shall become the regenerator of the whole Gentile world—be *as life from the dead* to the vast realms of spiritual death, we may not be able fully to explain.

Yet we can see how the *conversion itself* of such a people shall so reassure the people of God in his faithfulness to fulfil his promises and execute his purposes, shall so verify a long and interesting series of prophecies, shall send home conviction to the mind of skepticism and infidelity, and so solemnly enforce on the mind of the entire world the truth of Divine Revelation and the certainty that not a jot or tittle of all that God hath spoken shall go unfulfilled, as to be an overwhelming means of the conversion of the whole world.

But vastly more than this is doubtless true. The Jews once converted shall have a most successful *agency in* the conversion of the world. They shall be again, as they once were, the most energetic and effective missionaries. Scattered as they are among all nations and acquainted with every language on the face of the earth; inured to every climate; familiar with the religion, philosophy, literature, the manners and customs of every people; possessed of immense learning and greater wealth, and endowed with uncommon energy and perseverance, they will be prepared, if once energized with the omnnipotent Spirit, to go forth, such missionaries as the Church has not had since the days of the Apostles.   Rather, they would become missionaries—every man in the land of his own home; and thus a thousand lights would be kindled in the heart of every nation and kingdom on the earth.

Thus possessed of the gift of tongues, and aided by a thousand modern facilities in the way of improved modes of travel; of translations of the Bible into almost every language ; of the Press in its, at present, astonishingly increased power; of the present condition of education and of free principles, they may be expected to evangelize the world with an apostolic rapidity.   They would bring to bear on the world a moral power which no other people can.   This power, at present almost dormant, if once quickened into life, will tell delightfully on the world's regeneration.   And then shall it be acknowledged in a depth of meaning not now comprehended, that SALVATION IS OF THE JEWS.

If such be the relative position which this extraordinary people occupy in the coming conversion of the world to God, and such the part they are to act in that illustrious event, we may feel no difficulty in accepting any movement among this people as a signal of a great and universal movement among the nations of the earth.   Their conversion shall *precede* the general conversion of the world ; and as we see signs of a resuscitation of the house of Israel, we may confidently expect that the consummation of all things is at hand.

But do we see such a movement among that people ?   Does

the cloud which has so long settled down upon them seem to be rising, and are the tribes again on the march? I think they are; and a cursory glance at their present condition will abundantly justify such an opinion.

I shall not indulge much in details here in reference to the present condition of the Jews. What I would say to illustrate my proposition, has been said in another place.* Such is at present the civil condition of the Jews—such the feeling and sympathy for them on the part of the Christian Church—such the intellectual and religious movements among themselves—and such their favorable disposition to receive the gospel, and its present success among them, as to hold out no doubtful indications that the time to " favor Zion" draws near. And then shall the " Gentiles come to her light and kings to the brightness of her rising."

But a few years since the Jews, among almost all nations, were compelled to live under the most oppressive *civil disabilities*. They were outlaws—had no rights. It was no sin in the eyes of the world, and scarcely of the Church, to abuse and persecute a *Jew*. But how changed his civil condition now! Those oppressive acts have been repealed by almost every nation. This movement among the nations—this abatement of prejudice, is a prognostic of coming good—an index that the long night of their abandonment approaches its close, and the day of their redemption is at hand.

And more than this: there is a movement in the camp of Israel itself—a shaking among the " dry bones." Jewish mind is roused —their prejudices abated—their bigotry less rigid. Many gladly receive the New Testament, and the teachings of the missionary; and yet more entertain a growing distrust of the Talmud and the teachings of the Rabbies. Weary of their vain waitings for the

* Chapter nineteenth, vol. i. of " God in History."

Messiah, some acknowledge, and others entertain a half-formed conviction, that He has come already.

Such a state of mind, when taken in connection with the growing interest and sympathy in their behalf on the part of the Christian Church, is a star of hope for benighted Israel. Neglect and contempt had soured and alienated their minds against all Christendom. They looked on Christians as *enemies*, in whose hearts there was no flesh to feel for a Jew. They are now beginning to learn that Christianity has *a heart* to pity, and an arm to embrace the long forgotten children of Judah.

And there is another sign in the Jewish horizon. It is a movement in the Jewish mind towards their beloved Jerusalem. And there are movements in Palestine and in reference to the Holy Land which seem to be inaugurating a state of things * that shall at no distant day invite the return of the scattered tribes to the land of their long-cherished hopes and desires. Says an intelligent Prussian, "there is a general movement of inquiry, and a longing expectation abroad, that something will take place to restore them to the land of their fathers." "For better or for worse," says another, "they are on the move. Old chains are being severed. Old opinions, associations and observances are being broken up."

And here I cannot forbear quoting the very valuable testimony of Rev. Mr. Bellson, a converted Jew and Missionary in Posen, and late candidate for the Bishopric of Jerusalem: "I am more than ever impressed that the Jews are hastening to a great crisis. It must be evident to any common observer, there is a great move-

---

* Dr. Magowan, resident at Jerusalem, says: "An extraordinary change has come over Jerusalem. It is no longer a city which 'no man seeketh after.' It is now the resort of the wealthy and the great ones of the earth. Large purchases of houses and lands are made by agents of European governments, and establishments on a large and magnificent scale will be shortly made in the neighborhood." Lady Polack, a wealthy Jewess, has purchased the Mount of Olives—a Railway is about to be constructed from the Mediterranean to Jerusalem.

ment among them. This wonderful people, who for 1800 years remained unaltered, have undergone a marvellous change within the last forty years, especially the last twenty years. They are in a transition state. Thousands, convicted of the hollowness and rottenness of Rabbinism, and therefore thrown it off, feel a vacuum in their souls, which Christian truth alone can fill. The Talmud is sinking fast, and its giving up the ghost cannot be far off."

Such are facts connected with the present condition of the Jews. And do they not afford increasing and decisive evidence that the time draws near when the Father of Jacob shall again smile on his wayward, wandering children, and bring them back to their native hills, and accept their services in their beloved Zion. God has not cast off his people. They are dear to him as the apple of his eye. "The Lord shall arise and have mercy upon Zion, for the time to favor her is come."

But we must not forget that the destiny of the nations is suspended on providential movements connected with the Jews. Any divine purpose fulfilled to Israel, or any movement in their camp, *involves in it a series* of purposes and movements towards the Gentile world. We are then again conducted to the conclusion that the Church of Christ is approaching a crisis which will soon bring her into sore collision with the enemies of the truth— a crisis in human affairs of intense interest to the whole race. Truth is rapidly approaching its fiery trial and final consummation. The two belligerent parties are arraying themselves for the conflict. There will be no neutral ground—if not for God and the truth, we are against him. But God will conquer—the truth will prevail.

How important, then, that we be found on the Lord's side. Never has there been a time when the people of God were more loudly called upon to put on the whole armor, and having done all, to stand. "For we wrestle not against flesh and blood, but against principalities, against powers, against the rulers of the darkness of this world, against spiritual wickedness in high places." We have need of all the courage, all the decision, all the piety, all the holy energies of prophets, apostles, reformers or martyrs. While the great Head of the Church is, in such quick succession, accomplishing his great purposes; while he is hastening on all things to their last and great consummation, shall we not stand in our lot? Shall we not cheerfully yield to him our poor services, and give him our unworthy instrumentality? Now is the exigency in God's cause on earth, and if we will not step in *now* and come to the help of the Lord when the mighty oppose, are we worthy of our high calling? Can we expect to be called in to share in the victory if we are not ready to bear the burden and danger of the warfare? Loudly, indeed, do the signs of the times call on all who profess the name of Jesus, to be up and doing.

CHAPTER X.

IN previous chapters I have pointed out several appearances
which go to sustain the proposition "that the Christian Church,
the 'witnesses' for the truth, approaches her last and great conflict with the Beast:" and not with the Papal Beast merely, but
the Beast under his modern guise, and in his new mode of attack
—a great, conjoint Antichristian Power, made up of the Infidelity of Paganism, Mohammedanism and the Papacy, modernized
and nominally Christianized to suit the *spirit of the age*, its ruling
deity; and yet incorporated and nominally lost in the fogs of
modern Infidelity; which we represented as a subtle, covert Infidelity, disguised under the garb of a pretendedly purer Christianity, laboring by every plausible means to undermine and kill
what it calls the "Christianity of the Churches" by many a well-
directed, yet covert blow at the Christian Church, her ministry,
her Bible and her Sabbaths. It was shown, too, that this peculiar species of Infidelity, this last great resource of the Devil, to
prop up his waning empire and to oppose the Church—this most

effective, and most-to-be feared form of Infidelity, has sprung up of late almost simultaneously in different countries of Europe and of America, organized under different names, but one in spirit and in aim.

I shall now name one or two indications more of the approaching conflict.

14. *The present striking want of reverence—loyalty—respect for authority, indicates some great revolutionary struggle.*

Our age is characterized by a fearful spirit of *lawlessness*. The yoke of restraint is galling. Men talk of *their rights* as if they alone of all the world had rights. The impulse of the age is to resist as oppressive, all laws and restraints which do not favor their own wishes or interests. Hence outbreaks of violence in the shape of mobs and riots. Hence the difficulty of enforcing laws for the suppression of sin, as Sabbath-breaking, intemperance, gambling. Men are determined *to do as they please,* despite the will or pleasure, the peace or interest of others. This is the spirit of the age. It is unrestrained selfishness. Covetousness is the sin of the world—and would to God it were not the sin of the Church. It is a selfish age.

Now whoever will be at the trouble to examine, will find *this* to be the characteristic of the times which *should* precede the last great conflict. Says St. Paul (2 Tim. iii. 1—5): " This know also, that in the last days perilous times shall come. For men shall be lovers of themselves; covetous, boasters, proud, blasphemous, disobedient to parents, unthankful, unholy, without natural affection, truce-breakers, false accusers, incontinent, fierce, despisers of them that are good, traitors, heady, high-minded, lovers of pleasure more than lovers of God ; having the form of godliness, but denying the power."

Here is portrayed a spirit of general insubordination, and of recklessness of obligations throughout all the varied relations of life.

From the violator of national treaties, or "truce-breakers," down through all the social, religious, domestic and individual relations, to the pert and disobedient child, the prophetic eye of Paul foresaw there would be an all-pervading spirit of *lawlessness.*

How far this description applies to *our* times facts must determine. Is the present or is it not, a day of peculiar *selfishness,* pride, self-conceit, insubordination and blasphemy? Is our day inglorious for *covenant-breaking,* in the Church and out of it?—in the nation and among societies and individuals? Is not the present an age of unblushing licentiousness, of impatience of restraint, developed in a thousand forms, whether of pride, or the love of power, or pleasure, or sensual gratification? Men scorn that law, human or divine—that public sentiment—that the fear of man or God, should interpose between them and the gratification of their desires.

Was there ever a time when men were so "high-minded" and "heady"—so wise in their own conceits—so "fierce" in the support of their own dogmas?

Again, the apostle Peter says: "*In the last days, there shall come scoffers, walking after their own lusts*"—determined to live as they please in spite of social or religious restraint, or of law, human or divine. And Daniel says in reference to the same period: "*The wicked shall do wickedly*"—shall abound in wickedness. It is *hatred* of *authority*—*rebellion* in the broad sense of the term. Who is God that we should serve him?—who is man that we should regard him? We will not have this man to reign over us. Let us break their bonds asunder and cast away their cords from us.

If you will allow the mind to recur for a moment to some of the developments of our age, you will not hesitate to identify them as fulfilments of the predictions of the apostle. There is, in the first place, a want of respect for *established institutions.* Yea, more, there is a hatred of them. In religion, in morals, in politics, in social and domestic relations, large classes of men tread with vandal step on the long-tried institutions of their fathers, and trample down the long ago venerated structures of wisdom and experience. I have already pointed to numerous and extensive organizations, both in this country and in Europe, whose end and aim is to prostrate at their feet all law and authority—to break up the foundations of all social order, to put far away religious restraints, to sever marriage ties and scatter family relations to the four winds. They would leave men to act as dictated by passion. Under the magic spell of "Men's rights" and "Women's rights," they subvert *all* right, all order, all decency.

There is, in a word, a fearful tendency to throw off the bonds of restraint. The fire of loyalty in the old world, burns with less strength than it was wont to burn. Among the nations of Europe there is the appearance of a mighty convulsion at hand. Men are growing restive under the yoke of despotism. The principles of liberty, political and religious, have taken deep root, and are now beginning to bear fruit. Men no longer feel themselves to be the *property* of a sovereign or a master, but assert their unalienable rights as *men*. Nations, societies, churches, individuals, are evidently now passing through a *transition state*. Commotion and overturning is the order of the day, indicative of the breaking up of an old order of things and the introduction of a new. Much that is wrong will be broken up, much that is right. Such are fearful times because there are so many fearful energies at work.

The most careful and honest observers of the signs of the times see, or think they see, portentous sights. They tell us "perilous times" are at hand, and warn us to be prepared. And, inasmuch as the aspect of our times corresponds with the *predicted forerun-*

ners of that great convulsion which shall shake heaven and earth—the Church and the world—the warning is not a needless one.

15. *The Church gives signs that the "great and notable day of the Lord" is at hand.*   God has begun to humble his people, to make them feel their dependence on sovereign power and free grace.   But is the Church humbling *herself* and feeling her dependence?   It is one thing to *be humbled*, another to be *humble*.   God may, for our sins, bring us low, yet in our pride and self-righteousness we may exalt ourselves and still provoke the divine indignation.   There ure but too many indications, at the present time, that God is about to allow his Church again to be prostrated in the dust, and the enemy for a short space to triumph over her.   All over Christendom are ominous signs.   The apostasies from the faith and the apathy of the Church at such a day as this, betokens a day of trial.   There is something, too, in connection with the very *revivals of religion*, and the *benevolent enterprises* of the Church, not without alarm.

There is not a more marked dispensation of mercy towards Zion than is to be read in the revivals of religion of late years. The windows of heaven have been opened, and showers of grace, rich and copious beyond any former precedent, have fertilized our parched and mourning Zion.   Many hearts have been made glad, and thousands begun the song of redeeming love on earth, to be consummated in higher and holier strains on Mount Zion above.

But has not this richest boon of heaven's love been abused? Has not strange fire been laid on the altar?   Has not the ingratitude and presumption of man cast a cloud over the brightest radiance of heaven towards our benighted world?   In our self-dependence and complacency we were beginning to feel, *we* could *make revivals*—we could convert souls, I had almost said—we could open and no man shut.   We were vain in our imaginations, and God brought a blight over our fairest prospects.   We humbly and confidently hope the late wonderful work of grace is mixed with more faith and dependence and humility than any previous work which has blessed the Church, and that its results will be altogether happy and lasting.   But should not all our high-raised hopes be realized, we need not marvel as if some strange thing had happened.   The heavenly is still mixed up with the earthly.   Too often does the gold become dim, and the most fine gold changed.

The same may be said in respect to other measures of the Church.   She contributes funds for the evangelization of the world; sends out men; engages many agencies in her behalf, and presses on with a zeal worthy so good a cause.   The Lord of the harvest prepares the way and prospers their going forth.   So many are ready to give—so many more to *talk* and wish a good cause well, and so many have been willing to go abroad, that we are in danger of feeling that the conversion of the world rests on *our* shoulders; and as the work advances, to look upon it as if *our* hands had wrought out salvation for a perishing world.

In proportion as such becomes the state of the Church, we may look for a rebuke.   Spiritual pride goeth before destruction, and a self-righteous spirit before a fall.   God will not give his glory to another.   He is a jealous God.   If his people get proud of their works or their graces He will rebuke them.   Persecutions will arise; unexpected forms of error assail; conflicts betide, and they seem shut up, so that no power on earth can relieve them.   The great Head suffers them to be brought into straits that they may learn where their strength lies.

Is not such the condition of the American Church, if not of the Church universally, at the present time?   God has in a remarkble manner opened our way to the Gentile world, and provided unprecedented facilities to enable us speedily to fulfil the command: "Go ye into all the world."   Yet what is the present condition of the missionary work?   It stands hovering between hope and fear. Hope beckons onward. Fear suggests that the wide and effectual door now open, may, through the apathy of the Church to enter, be in a measure closed, and the dark cloud, which seemed rising and scattering, soon again settle down on the broad plains of Idolatry. Every enterprise is, for the want of funds and missionaries, retarded, or again in danger of being suspended. Has not the Lord a controversy with his people that he will not accept this service at their hands, and allow them the honor of final success? And may we not expect that before Zion shall spread her wings over the whole earth and shadow the nations, before her Lord shall clothe her in the strength and beauty of heaven, for her final and glorious triumph, he will bring her into the very dust of debasement, divesting her of all self-reliance.

These things intimate that the Church, like every thing beneath the skies, is not perfect—that there is much in the Church which does not please God. He will, therefore, sift her—humble her— deliver her for a time into the hands of the *Philistines* for her chastisement; yet God will not cast off his people. Though he chasten them, they are dear to him as the apple of his eye.

16. In connection with the apathy and defection of the Church, I name as the last sign of the coming conflict which I shall mention, *the abounding wickedness of the wicked.*

If, as you cast your eye over the face of society, you discover vice to be bold and aggressive; sinners hardened in sin; infidelity covert and disguised, sapping the very foundations of our Religion under the delusive pretext of introducing a more excellent way; if an all-pervading selfishness characterize the intercourse of man with man; if rectitude and honesty be rare, and our age so corrupt that man is scarcely expected to act except as prompted by selfish interest—if there is found to be, as has been intimated, any thing like the forming of a grand *confederacy* of the different systems of iniquity and infidelity, a rising up of a new form of the Beast, animated by the same spirit of hostility to the truth, yet in the stolen robes of the truth; and if, on on the other hand, when iniquity comes in like a flood there be but few to set up a standard against it, apathy having come over large portions of the Church, you have but too much reason to regard the signs of the times as ominous—just what are foretold as precursors of the great conflict—fulfilments of such scriptures as I have quoted: "The wicked shall do exceeding wickedly"—"Iniquity shall abound"—"The love of many wax cold"—Sin shall become reckless and unrestrained. "Iniquity shall come in like a flood," and few shall be found to raise a standard against it.

This, in connection with the *predicted apostasies* and the rising up of *false prophets* which should immediately precede the "perilous times" of the latter days, confirms the view of the subject I have taken. St. Paul says expressly that "*that* day shall not come except there come *a falling away first*, and that Man of Sin be revealed, the Son of perdition." The *abounding of sin* is to be accompanied by a great apostasy or *falling away* in the Church. Both these are found sadly true of our times.

A few years past have been remarkably signalized for apostasies both in the Church and among her clergy. Recall what I have said of apostasies in the Church of England, and recall what, in many a sad case, has transpired elsewhere, and ours will be marked as a day of *falling away*.

And equally, I apprehend, shall we find the present a day of *false prophets*—and of *just such kind* of false prophets too as should characterize the period in question. They should be subtle, plausible teachers, ostensibly, of the truth—so complete a counterfeit of the true as with difficulty to be distinguished—"inasmuch, if it were possible, to deceive the very elect."

Facts must determine whether such prophets, teachers, guides or leaders have risen up all over Christendom, zealous in some particulars, denunciatory in all, loose in moral principle, and utterly defective in the the groundwork of truth and righteousness.

" When the Son of man cometh shall he find faith on the earth?" an interogrtory implying that when Christ shall come to set up his kingdom nearly the last ray of Christian piety shall have expired. The Church shall have been brought into a state of debasement the most helpless and hopeless, from which nothing short of the omnipotent arm of her Immanuel can deliver her. The witnesses are now slain. They lay dead in the streets; and the enemy send gifts one to another, and rejoice over them. The Church never saw a darker day. But this is the hour of the gracious interposition of her Lord. The faith of the Church needs now to be, in some remarkable manner, reassured. The enemy have been allowed so strangely to triumph over her—she is so completely overwhelmed—the gates of hell seem so to have prevailed against her, that she begins to waver in her faith, to half doubt the promises of her Lord. Since the fathers fell asleep they despair of his coming.

Such a state of the Church seems aptly represented by one of the closing scenes in the life of John the Baptist. He had understood himself to be the forerunner of Christ. He had pointed out the man of Nazareth to the multitude and declared him to be the Lamb of God, the Messiah, that taketh away the sin of the world. He had heard his words and witnessed his wonderful works; and had unreservedly recognized him to be the expected Messiah: and he fully believed in the *increase* of his kingdom and its universal extension over the whole earth. Yet when he had been cast into prison, and the enemy allowed to triumph over him, and darkness and doubt allowed to come over his soul, his faith staggered. Had he not been mistaken? If he *were* the

10

Christ, and himself, as he had supposed, were his forerunner and his personal friend, why had these things befallen him?

Under such feelings of painful suspense and failing faith he sent messengers to Christ to ask if he were indeed the Christ, or should we look for another? Under his darkness and doubt and extreme depression by the enemy, he needed a reassurance of the divinity and faithfulness of his Saviour.

So the Church at the time of which we speak. In her extreme depression and apparent overthrow, she now needs a renewal of her faith—a reconfirmation of her hopes. And "the coming of Christ with clouds" with his mighty angels, and flaming fire, will be precisely the kind of confirmation which the depressed and down-trodden saints will then require. Yet we do not suppose the coming, at this time, will be *personal.* He shall be revealed in great power—shall "come with clouds," judgments, mighty providential displays. These may be the " mighty angels "—"the flaming fire," by which he shall discomfit his foes: and these the manifestations by which he shall reassure his people; or, as the apostle says, shall " be glorified in his saints and be admired in them that believe."

But I need not pursue this branch of the subject. The signs of the times indicate a mighty conflict at hand. The fountains of the great deep are breaking up. You may see it in the present state of the Church—in the commotions on the great political arena of the world; you may see it in the genius of revolution abroad on the dark and turbid waters of Paganism, and amidst the restless billows of Infidelity. And especially you may see it in that general *restiveness* of control which has so strangely seized on the minds of men in all the relations of life. Ours is an age of rebellion, not yet fully developed, but smothered for a more fearful explosion. It is a warfare between Rulers and ruled—*abused authority* on the one hand; *abused liberty* on the other. We watch with intense interest the awful progress of the car of war, as at the present hour it rolls over Europe. Its carnage is dreadful; its commotions fearful. It is the awful power of God to break down and destroy—to remove out of the way those great and formidable civil despotisms and hierarchies which hinder the progress of his kingdom. But we confidently expect, when the smoke of the battle-field shall have passed away and the " confused noise " of the warrior and " garments rolled in blood " shall be forgotten, sweet Peace shall return to the earth, and the angel preaching the everlasting gospel shall ploclaim that the kingdoms of this world have become the kingdoms of our Lord and of his Christ.

It will again be seen that the position attempted to be established in these chapters leads once more to the conclusion that the " Witnesses," by which I understand a succession of godly men, essentially embodied in the visible Church, *are yet to be slain*— that *their slaying* means the great conflict which truth and the true Church is yet to encounter from the combined enemies of the truth—that the Beast, the personification of this combined hostility, shall change the mode of his attack—put on a Christian garb, and, under the pretext of carrying out the *spirit of the age*, shall essay to break down and trample under foot our old landmarks, prostrate the walls of our fold, and for a little space, sorely gall the flock. This rousing up and rage of the Beast shall be a consequence of the increased light and real progress of the truth, producing the conviction that the Church will triumph and eventually make all men feel the strength of her cords and the tightness of her bonds. Seeing this—that *his time is short*, Satan will enter the field with redoubled rage—marshal his forces under new colors—colors stolen from the armory of heaven—and snatching from their hands the very weapons of the sacramental host, Apollyon mounts the car and is ready for the last great encounter.   He now comes up to battle, not as heretofore by *divisions*, but with all the powers of darkness confederated, and now animated by one spirit, hatred of the Church and the truth.

That the affairs of the Church and of the world are verging to such a crisis I have little doubt.   And that it will terminate in the complete overthrow of the wicked, and, after a temporary (a three and a half years') prostration of the Witnesses, they shall then arise in their strength and glory—Zion shall put on her beautiful garments—her light shall shine, "fair as the moon, clear as the sun, and terrible as an army with banners."   The wicked shall triumph, yet their triumphing shall be short, and their overthrow signal and final.

I have before me an opinion on this subject, which, from the circumstances of the case, I regard as peculiarly valuable.   It is a joint letter from the American Mission at Constantinople, signed by Messrs. Goodell and Dwight, than whom no two men are more advantageously situated, or better qualified to form a correct opinion on such a subject.

"We notice," say they, "the wide-spread alarm and the stern hostility which the slightest success in turning men from darkness to light awakens; and we can scarcely be mistaken as to the influence of future and more decided progress.   A mighty revolution must take place, and in the course of its accomplishment, the ecclesiastical and moral world will be shaken to their very centre. We cannot hide from our eyes the approaching struggle, the gathering storm.   We wish not to hasten it prematurely, but we dare not try to avert it.   It will come, must come, and ought to come.   No one of our plans can be accomplished without it, no one of our prayers heard, no one of our hopes realized.   We pray that God may pour out his spirit on this people, but that cannot be without producing instant commotion.   We long for the conversion of sinners; but this soonest of all things will turn upside down this ecclesiastical world. There is no possible way to avoid this but by concealing the light of the truth."

Ever and anon we descry some new premonition of the coming conflict. A voice from the same Mission, after the lapse of years, utters again similar notes of alarm. The commotions in India (connected with the Sepoy mutiny) come as an earthquake, shaking the whole Mohammedan world. They have strangely roused the sleeping animosities of the Moslems against Christianity. And it is easy to see how the inflammable spirit of Mecca should take fire at the first intelligence of the insurrection; and how easy it would be, when the King of nations shall permit, to light up the torch of war among all the nations of the earth. A confederacy of Pagan and Mohammedan nations against evangelical Christian nations, in which nations that represent a corrupt Christianity might very naturally be drawn in, would of itself at once bring on the great Battle. In a late letter the Rev. Dr. Hamlin, of Constantinople, says: "The rebellion in India has communicated a singularly excited spirit to the Turks. The fanatical party make great and effective use of it. Tens of thousands believe that it originated in efforts of the English to make Mussulmans Christians by force; and that all the English have done here for freedom of conscience is only to prepare the way for the same violent conversion of Mussulmans in Turkey.

"This storm will probably soon pass over; but it is an indication of what we must anticipate in the future. The excitement against missionaries, personally and as a body, is just now very strong. Fearful indeed is the trail that is laid, and, when the signal shall be given, the least spark will set the whole on fire." And who has not been shocked at the horrid details of the late Syrian Massacre! This is but another explosion of the same internal fires, which are boiling, and surging, and gathering strength for a final and dreadful eruption. The Moslem's hatred to Christianity is as virulent as death. Though smothered for a time, it has lost none of its power: and his "wrath" shall be all the greater when he shall "know that he hath but a short time."

The Evangelists, Matthew and Luke, have left on record a vivid and thrilling description of these times: "*The sun shall be darkened and the moon shall not give her light, and the stars shall fall from heaven, and the powers of the heavens shall be shaken.*" Or as Luke has it: "*There shall be signs in the sun and in the moon and in the stars, and upon the earth distress of nations, with perplexity, the sea and the waves roaring.*" Which, in plain language, means, there shall be a most alarming *prostration* of *authority*. *The sun shall be darkened*—authority shall be subverted—restraint resisted. *The moon shall cease to give her light* —the light of the Church shall be dimmed, her authority rejected and disdained. *The stars shall fall from heaven*—ministers of the gospel shall fall, some by apostasy and sin, more by being driven from their charges, and bereft of their influence, and the authority of their instructions lost because of the commotion of the times, and the disorganizing spirit of unreasonable and wicked men. Many in the Church and more out of her will think they can do God no greater service than when sapping the foundations of confidence in his ministers, or thrusting them from their sacerdotal orbits. *The powers of the heavens shall be shaken* —unheard of commotions in the ecclesiastical world. *Upon the earth distress of nations, with perplexity, the sea and the waves roaring*—political eruptions, commercial distresses, the outbreakings of violence among the common people in the form of riots, and mobs, and revolutions. *The sea and the waves roaring*—men of loose principles and infidel sentiments, "rising in ungovernable rage, throwing off all restraints, and spreading consternation and panic" among men.

If there be something in *our* times which looks like this, then, "lift up your heads," ye saints, for "your redemption," after a short and severe rebuff, hastens on apace.   And "mourn," ye sinners, as ye see "the Son of man coming in the clouds of heaven, with great power and glory:" for he comes, "revealed in flaming fire," to take vengeance on them that obey not the gospel.

We venture to add to this chapter a few paragraphs which recently appeared in the *Puritan Recorder*.   They are so much in harmony with our views, and withal so pertinent to the *times*, that they seem to claim a place in this connection:

" Christ foretold, that preparatory to his coming, there should be, ' *upon the earth, distress of nations, with perplexity.*'   He has not clearly defined what coming of his is to be thus preceded.   Nor is it needful for us to have such a definition; for it seems that the introduction of every new era of light to his kingdom, has its period of conflict and painful trial to precede it.   The whole creation groaneth and travaileth together in pain, to be delivered from the bondage of corruption.   There are doubtless to be many of these bitter throes and pains, before the full consummation of the glory of Christ.   But if ' distress of nations ' is one of the precursors of a brighter day, we have now the means of quickening our hopes for its advancement.

" The pressure of God's hand upon many of the nations of the world is now heavy.   Our own nation is having a remarkable experience.   In the midst of an abundance of all the products of the field, an actual famine of bread is staring us in the face. Immense multitudes of the people have been thrown out of employment, and thus out of the necessary means of subsistence.   And the financial crisis which here began, is now extending itself over the nations of Europe; so that the commerce of the world is to feel the stroke of the palsy in every limb.

" But this financial crisis is only one item in the present distress of nations. Our mother country, having had scarcely time to breathe freely after the exhausting war with Russia, has found herself suddenly involved in another war, and that with the whole of Eastern Asia. Over her vast domains in India the curse of civil war is sweeping; and the hundred millions in China seem to be at war, not only with the most powerful of foreign nations, but also among themselves. How much of the distress of nations is involved in such a wide-sweeping extent of warfare, it is not easy for us at this distance to conceive. Here, then, we have, 'upon the earth, distress of nations, with perplexity; the sea and the waves roaring, and men's hearts failing them for fear, and for looking after those things which are coming upon the earth.'

"In such clouds as these, the Redeemer is wont to come when he extends his spiritual reign upon the earth. In the figure of the poet, these clouds are the dust that waits upon his sultry march when he visits earth in mercy. These judgments which are abroad, awake more of expectation and of hope, from their coming at a time when so many evangelizing agencies are abroad in the world, accompanied by so much of the quickening breath of the Holy Ghost. Never since the primitive days of the Christian Church, was so much done, and with so much success, to extend the gospel to those who have it not. It is well for us to look upon these remarkable providences, as intended enforcements of God's word of grace now sent forth to the nations. God, in saying to his Son, 'Thou shalt break them with the rod of iron; thou shalt dash them in pieces as a potter's vessel,' says in the same connection—'Be wise now, therefore, O ye kings, be instructed, ye judges of the earth; serve the Lord with fear, and rejoice with trembling; kiss the Son, lest he be angry, and ye perish from the way when his wrath is kindled but a little.'

"But we commenced these few remarks with a special reference to the spiritual impression upon our own nation, to be received from our present distress. It is obvious, at a glance, that our calamities are in their nature adapted to rebuke our most prevalent sins, and lead to that spiritual impression which is needed by us as a people. If God were about to pour out his Spirit on the churches, and on the masses of our people, these providences might operate as an admirable means of the conviction of sin, and of turning men to God. And who shall say, that this is not the great purpose of these remarkable visitations? In this view, these are times which invite and encourage special earnestness in our supplications for the outpouring of the Spirit. When God's judgments are abroad in the earth, it is a time for the inhabitants thereof to learn righteousness. Then, especially, is a time to hope and pray for the putting forth of his saving power."

The closing remarks of this writer seem prophetic. God has " poured out his Spirit on the churches, and on the masses of the people;" and " these providences " *have* operated " as an admirable means of turning men to God." And we may now believe that this *is* the " great purpose of these remarkable visitations."

It only remains to add here, that if there is discovered a seeming discrepancy between the *unfavorable* features pointed out in the foregoing chapter, and the favorable features of our age as they at present appear in connection with the extensive and delightful religious revivals of the present day, I have only to say, there is no discrepancy. This is only what was spoken of by the prophet Daniel: " Many shall be purified, and made white and tried; but *the wicked shall do wickedly.*" As light increases, as divine influences are more active, and their effects more ostensible, and as the ranks of the adversary are seen to be thinning, and his cause waning, he is wont to come to the rescue. The only wonder is that he has thus far, during this extraordinary religious interest, kept so quiet. Men of all ranks and conditions in life, in great numbers, deserted his ranks, and we may be sure he will not quietly submit to his disasters. He will ere long rise in his great wrath, knowing that his time is short. He will stir up wicked men to *do more wickedly.* " *The wise shall understand,*" but *the incorrigibly wicked shall not understand,* but be allowed to go on to their own eternal undoing. We shall see if the great enemy of all good will allow his vassals to succumb, without a struggle, to the new order of things which the Lord, by the late wonderful effusion of his Spirit, is now inaugurating in our land. In what form the reaction will come we know not, but we believe it will come.

CHAPTER XI.

The Great Battle—The slaying of the Witnesses—Their restoration and ascension to Heaven.

"And when they shall have finished their testimony, the Beast that ascendeth out of the bottomless Pit shall make war against them, and shall overcome them, and kill them."—*Rev.* xi. 7.

WE have all along kept in view the idea of the great conflict which awaits the truth before its final triumph. It is time that we define more definitely what we mean by the Great Battle? what it shall be? when? and where? Its character is perhaps no where more accurately delineated than in the eleventh chapter of the Revelation, in the account of the "slaying of the two Witnesses." This, we believe, represents the great Battle of God Almighty, the Battle of Gog and Magog, or of Armageddon—the battle of the great day. It demands some special consideration.

Who are these witnesses? When did they begin their testimony, and when shall they end it? What is meant by the slaying of the witnesses, and when shall it be? What their restoration and ascension to heaven? These are queries all of which we may not satisfactorily answer; yet much that is satisfactory may be said.

Who are these Witnesses? Some say they were certain eminent *individuals*, as Moses and Aaron, Elijah and Elisha, or Moses and Elias. Christ sent out the twelve, and also the seventy, two and two. I do not suppose these were *the* Witnesses. They were witnesses for the truth, but do not meet the conditions in the case. Nothing less, I apprehend, is here meant than a *succession* of holy men and fearless prophets and teachers, who, during the period in question, bear testimony to the truth, and sustain the true Church. Such a succession of men there has always been in the world. These are the two candlesticks, with each its seven branches and lamps, emblematical of the Church universal, as the light-giving body to illuminate the surrounding darkness. These two candlesticks are accompanied by two "olive trees, which, by means of conductors, convey their oil continually to the lamps." Hence the lamps of the candlesticks could never go out.

Such is the true Church, or the *succession of witnesses* for the truth. Fed by an unction from on high, they are a bright and shining light, that shineth brighter and brighter till the perfect day. In whatever age or nation, they are the light of the world. They have power to prophesy a thousand two hundred and three score days, or twelve hundred and sixty years.

A *second* question arises as to the *commencement* and termination of this period of time. The whole period of their prophecy is co-eval with the existence of "the Beast that ascendeth out of the bottomless Pit," and also with that of the false Prophet—two events which had their commencement and are to have their termination, nearly or quite at the same time; and I may here add —though this is not the time to furnish the proof—that the restoration and conversion of the Jews, and the gathering in of the Gentiles or Pagan nations, are two *other* exceedingly important events, which, it seems, are to take place at the same time with the two above-mentioned.

The Papal Beast is generally said to have arisen in the year 606. This was when the Pope became universal Bishop. A hot contest had for some years previous, been carried on between the Bishops of the Eastern and Western Church; the one, the Bishop of *Rome*, and the other, of *Constantinople*. *Boniface*, then Bishop of Rome, in the year 606, prevailed on the then reigning Emperor, *Phocas*, to declare the Bishop of Rome universal Bishop or Pope. Here separated forever the eastern and western Churches; the former was afterwards known as the Greek Church, and the latter as the Latin, the Roman or the Roman Catholic Church.

Here we have the full-grown Papal Beast—but as yet *without his horns.* For it was not till the year 756 that the Pope became fully established as a *temporal prince.*

Here lies the difficulty of determining the precise time when the twelve hundred and sixty years begun. If we fix their date in the year 606, they will terminate in the year 1866. This at first seems too short a period into which to crowd so many and such mighty events as must transpire before or at the termination of that period. But when we reflect on the wonderful changes of the last few years, how many and how mighty changes both moral and physical have taken place, and what are now the signs of the times in reference to a mighty onward progress, it need not greatly stagger our faith to believe that within this short space the gospel may be so universally diffused over the earth, and take such deep hold on the hearts and consciences of men—change laws and customs, that the wicked, no longer able to brook the restraints of piety, shall burst "the bonds and break the cords" of the godly, and come out and make war on the saints of the Most High; that they shall, to all human appearance, overcome them and kill them; that God shall then in some remarkable manner avenge the cause of his elect—completely overwhelm the powers of antichrist—the confederated hosts of Popery, Mohammedanism and Infidelity, or rather of a new power made up of all that "opposeth and exalteth himself above all that is called God or that is worshipped; that the Jews shall be restored to the long-lost favor of God, and to their long-forsaken and desolate land—and that their restoration shall be a glorious signal, and, in a great measure, the means of quickening into spiritual life the whole dead body of the heathen world. And then shall commence that glorious era of a thousand years when peace shall reign and righteousness shall prosper and be ascendant throughout the whole earth.

It is no more difficult to conceive that all I have supposed will take place in the brief term of six years, than it was as many years that what has transpired, should have taken place. Who, but a few years ago, could have conceived that the whole world should so soon be thrown open to receive the gospel—the Bible be translated, published, and read in one hundred and sixty different Pagan languages—the Christian Press, free as the air we breathe, be scattering, as on the wings of the wind, millions and millions of the leaves of the tree of life, until there is scarcely a nation, or a tongue, or a people that may not already read the wonderful things of God in the tongue in which they were born?—And that funds to such an amount, and men in such numbers should be engaged, and so much land should be possessed? Nor are the moral, civil and political changes which have taken place less remarkable.

There seems, therefore, no reason for rejecting the idea that the notable twelve hundred and sixty years commenced in 606, on the ground that the small space which remains of it now, is not sufficient for the accomplishment of all its events. There is time enough, and all this too without a miracle. Indeed, should the Great Dagon at Rome fall prostrate before the ark of the Lord in half six years, and Mohammedanism explode with the Turkish Empire, and Pagan nations meet their hastening doom, we need not be surprised. All things are fast hastening to such results. Six months, indeed, might suffice to set all the nations on earth on fire—to dash the nations one against another: and another six months suffice to overthrow the armies of the aliens—to clear away the smoke of the battle-field, and to plant on the ruins of the nations that would not serve the King Jehovah, the foundations of the everlasting kingdom. A thousand years with the Lord is as one day, and one day as a thousand years.

But if we fix on the other date, as its commencement, viz., 756, then we add to the unexpired period of the reign of the Beast and the prophesying of the witnesses in sackcloth one hundred and fifty years, making the unexpired time one hundred and fifty-six years instead of six. The true date is doubtless not sooner than the first, nor later than the second, but purposely left in this obscurity, because it is not given unto us to know the "times and the seasons."

Another thing that demands a passing remark concerning the witnesses, is *the condition in which they appear.* They are clothed in "sackcloth," indicative of their humble condition, the contempt cast on them by the world, and their own affliction and grief on account of the wretched condition of the world, and the estate of the Church.

· "Clothed in sackcloth" well represents the general condition of genuine piety in our world. In another place the Church is represented as a "woman" so tormented and persecuted by a "great red dragon," which had "seven heads and ten horns," that she was compelled to flee away and hide herself in the "wilderness"—a most apt illustration of what has been the real condition of the true Church, or genuine Christian godliness, ever since the corruption of the Church and the origin of the persecuting powers of Rome. Rivers of blood have flown. Perhaps the ingenuity of man was never more taxed than in inventing modes of torture and of death for those whose only crime was to worship God agreeable with the dictates of their own consciences. The *fashion* of the *world* has always been to cast a pure Religion out, and to compel her to seek the lodging-place of a wayfaring man in the wilderness. False or corrupt Religions have not unfrequently been called to sit in high places, but in no nation has holiness been *popular*. It has been tolerated, but not a passport to popular favor. The witnesses are clothed in sackcloth.

A *fourth* characteristic of these witnesses is, that they *are sustained by a supernatural power*. They stood before the God of the whole earth, and received power from him. And they are protected by the same omnipotent arm. " If any man hurt them, fire proceedeth out of their mouth and devoureth their enemies." God will avenge the cause of his elect. By the power of holiness they shall be a terror to evil-doers—one shall chase a thousand, and two put ten thousand to flight.

What is meant by the slaying of the witnesses, and *when* shall this event take place, and by whom? Their death is the violent and complete suppression of their testimony. If by the witnesses be meant the succession of those who profess and contend for the faith once delivered to the saints, then the suppression of their testimony must be their death. The people of God will then be prohibited from bearing witness to the truth. Ministers may not preach ; Churches may not be opened ; Christians may not assemble for worship ; Bibles may not be published, circulated or knowingly read ; all benevolent societies will be suppressed ; the Christian Press prohibited ; Christian schools abandoned ; and all religious instruction interdicted. Righteousness will be sent away into the waste, howling wilderness, to sit solitary and to mourn. Wickedness will sit in high places and triumph over downcast piety. Every remaining vestige of piety, or the pious, shall be treated with savage contempt.

This I understand to be meant by the slaying of the witnesses —which I gather from the account given of the transaction in the following passage: " And when they shall have finished (or shall be about to finish) their testimony, the Beast that ascendeth out of the bottomless pit, shall make war against them, and shall overcome them, and kill them. And their dead bodies shall lie in the street of the great city, which spiritually is called Sodom and Egypt, where also our Lord was crucified. And they of the people, and kindreds, and tongues, and nations, shall see their dead bodies three days and a half, and shall not suffer their dead bodies to be put in graves. And they that dwell on the face of the earth, shall rejoice over them, and make merry, and shall send gifts one to another, because these two prophets tormented them." The wicked had a long time been held in an unwilling bondage by the restraints of their piety, but now they had at length broken away, and rejoiced in the hope of henceforth living as they should list. Piety being, as they supposed, dead, they hoped they might revel unmolested in the way they should choose.

A query here naturally arises as to the *time* of this disaster. Is it already past, or is it yet to come? I have no doubt it is yet *to come*. Several past eras have been fixed on as the time when the witnesses were slain—as the period when the saints of the valley of Piedmont, the Vadois, the Waldenses, the Albigenses, etc., so severely suffered. These were days of cruel persecution. Few could then openly profess the Lord that bought them, without sealing their testimony with their blood. There have been times of *triumph of the persecutions* of the Church in France, Germany, Bohemia and Italy. But there was in none of these instances that *general* suppression of the testimony of the people of God, nor that complete and vociferous and public triumph of

11

all the enemies of godliness, which is here described. But what is more in point, none of the mighty conflicts of iniquity against the Church of the living God, occurred at *the right time* to make them coincide with the event spoken of in our text.

This dread overthrow is to take place as the *result* of the dying struggle of the Papal Beast. He is then to arise in his last wrath, and to rage and lay desolate more than ever, *because* " his time is short." This, of consequence, must fall at or near the close of the above-mentioned twelve hundred and sixty years—or at or soon after the year 1866, as its nearest point of termination.

And, further, the slaying of the witnesses shall be attended by an *open avowal and general rejection of Christianity*—and a jubilee of triumph over its supposed final suppression, as if the demons of the Pit had broken loose to keep jubilee on earth over the final overthrow of the hated cause. Such a time seems yet to come.

Another no less interesting inquiry here arises : *By whom shall the witnesses be slain ?* The text replies, *by the Beast that ascendeth out of the bottomless pit ;* by which has generally been understood, the Papacy or Romish Church. In all its essential features it no doubt is so. It is the " antichrist that should come "—the *antichristian, antireligious* power that should oppose itself to all godliness. This does not shut out the idea, but rather encourages it, that it is more of a *confederacy* of iniquity against every thing which bears the form of piety, than any particular form that religious persecution has yet assumed. It is not so much Paganism, Papacy, or Islamism, as it is a joint and inveterate and vengeful hatred of the truth, which shall then make one united, general and desperate onset against the Christian Church. It is the " man of sin," armed rather with the panoply of *infidelity,* than with any particular form of hostility to the truth that has as yet appeared in our world.

It is only analogous to what we know to be the subtlety of the Serpent, to believe that he may, and that he often does change his *mode of attack.* He has heretofore come up to the encounter by *Divisions,* each bearing its own respective banner, such as Paganism, Infidelity, Popery and Mohammedanism. The spirit of the corps has always been the same—the spirit of Infidelity. The grand object of attack has always been the same—the kingdom of the Redeemer. But there has never yet been a general rallying of all the forces towards a single point.

Such a time, it seems to me, is yet to come. The grand line of demarcation shall at length be drawn. The powers of light and darkness shall then be arranged on their own respective sides. The neutral ground shall all be left as a common arena. The army of the aliens, led on by the arch-spirit of darkness, shall embody in it all that opposeth itself to the empire of holiness. This is *"the man of sin."* Its name is "Legion." It embraces all the antichristian powers of earth, whether found in the garb of Christianity, or on the altar of the Pagan, or under the banner of the Crescent. It is one grand infidel confederacy, roused from its native torpor. Long had it slumbered in the dark caverns of spiritual death. Light broke in. A ray penetrated through the black folds of night and came even to the seat of the Beast. He roused from his lair as if a star had fallen from heaven. Another follows and another, till the surrounding darkness becomes visible —sin is unmasked—abominations unveiled—the moral turpitude of ages exposed—sin shown in its own original and undisguised hatefulness—character exhibited *as it is*—virtue honored and vice despised—righteousness exalted and sin trodden down ; and how long, think you, before the monster will be roused and shake the earth with his roaring ? Sin cannot bear the light. Darkness is its native element. Light makes sin mad—the more light the more outrageous he is.

Hence as the gospel shall penetrate, as it is now fast doing, into Pagan, Mohammedan and Popish darkness, the mystery of iniquity shall be exposed; and when this shall be done up to a certain point, "the man of sin," the universal genius of iniquity, shall arise in the madness of his strength, rally the joint forces of wickedness, and, by one mighty, bloody onset seek to sweep Christianity from the earth. And so successful shall they be that they shall seem to have effectually done it. Their conquest appears to be complete. The witnesses are slain, and their dead bodies, in contempt and savage triumph, left unburied in the streets three days and a half.

In other words, the infidel power shall triumph, Christianity be prostrate—no one may safely raise his voice in her defense—the Bible shall be proscribed—the pulpit closed—the press muzzled—missionaries recalled—religious instruction prohibited—the fires of persecution lighted, and almost every vestige of Religion destroyed. Yet the good seed shall still remain.

If it be asked, then, if this shall be a conflict with carnal weapons—a conflict of flesh and blood? I can only answer that I see not why, in one of its aspects, it will not be. There is in the different descriptions we have of the great battle every appearance of it. There seems good reason to suppose it will be a mighty and bloody conflict between Christian and antichristian nations. But not solely nor principally this; it will be a mighty moral conflict. The united powers of darkness will be roused against the children of light, and shall "overcome and kill them." A Religious profession may yet cost as much as it ever did in the darkest, cruelest days of the Inquisition. And there may be those that now read this, who shall not taste of death till all these things shall be fulfilled. Therefore be ye ready.

Do you ask why I suppose the "Beast" here spoken of, who shall overcome and kill the witnesses, to be an infidel confederacy, made up of all the haters of godliness, rather than simply the Papal Beast? I reply, that this better agrees with the character given of this power by the Apostle Paul, in his second epistle to the Thessalonians, than the papacy does. Though the papists have to a shocking extent been concealed and real infidels, yet, in *theory* and *profession*, they are as orthodox as the Church of England, or the Presbyterian Church.

Is it asked again, why preach the gospel to the nations of the earth, if there is soon to be so complete an overthrow, and all seemingly to be cast to the four winds? I answer: The gospel is the very thing which shall bring about the mighty, and, to the enemies of God, the awful revolution of which I am speaking. It is the diffusion of the truth which shall rouse the latent energies of the opponents of all righteousness, and bring on the last great day of conflict. We might as well object to, or at least call in question, the utility of a preached gospel, or of any religious instruction, on the ground that it will rouse the slumbering energies of the foe and be followed by some disagreeable conflict.

What I mean may be illustrated as follows: Yonder is a province of Idolaters. The quiet of spiritual death reigns there. Sin riots and revels there, with none to molest or make afraid. Darkness covers that land, and a gross darkness the people. At length a messenger of truth arrives there. He plants and unfurls his banner for the first time on this unpropitious soil. A conflict now begins. It is the conflict of truth with error—of holiness with sin. Truth is the aggressor. Many seeing the righteousness and purity of its cause, range themselves under its banners. Its progress at first is slow and so gradual as to excite no alarm. The means seem so inadequate to its professed end that it excites rather ridicule than serious apprehension. But the Bible works its way—leveling all opposition—exalting valleys, and making low mountains. It changes manners, customs, and laws. It attacks and brings to the ground their strongholds. It prostrates principalities and powers. It erects a new empire; and all this by such apparently insignificant means as a preached gospel—education and the Press.

The alarm is now taken. Individual opposition at first appears. It becomes more and more consolidated and general, until a complete confederacy is organized, and there is a simultaneous rising up to crush the new Religion. So irritated have the opposing party now become—so sorely do they feel themselves restrained in their *rights,* that they are prepared to engage in a war of *extermination.* Nothing but the eradicating of the offensive party, root and branch, will now serve their purpose. They rise in their might and rage, and do the bloody deed. But they have forgotten that the blood of martyrs is the seed of the Church.

All now appears " dead," and they rejoice and send gifts and congratulations one to another. But the progress of the good cause, so far from its being finally arrested and all that has been done being *lost,* is scarcely impeded. A desolating tornado has passed over and laid all prostrate; but this is but the presage of a reanimation more stable and glorious than ever.

6. *The restoration, or resurrection of the witnesses.*

" And after three days and a half the Spirit of life from God entered into them and they stood upon their feet; and great fear fell upon them which saw them." After this short suspension (three and a half years, according to prophetic language) and this overthrow of the witnesses, God will avenge the cause of his elect —He will vindicate his own cause and exalt it far above all that it has ever yet known. It shall be as life from the dead. And in so extraordinary manner shall it be effected as to confound and to fill with consternation all those mighty, vaunting hosts that were so recently congratulating themselves and one the other over the final overthrow of a hated Religion. What a contrast ! one day they were indulging in excessive and open mirth over a prostrate foe; the next day they are in their turn laid low and overwhelmed beyond the hope of recovery, and those they hated are again alive—their strength renewed, and they shielded by the arm of Omnipotence. And more yet; for,

7. *They shall ascend into heaven.* "And they heard a great voice from heaven saying unto them, Come up hither. And they ascended up to heaven in a cloud; and their enemies beheld them." This, like most of the chapter, is figurative language. The slaying of the witnesses, as I have explained it, means the suppression of all efforts for the instruction and extension of the Church; their restoration the re-establishment of all such efforts under far more favorable auspices than ever. Their ascension to heaven must consequently mean that God now, in a special manner, approves and accepts them. Before, they had been clothed in sackcloth—dwelt in the wilderness—been forsaken, cast down, afflicted and tormented. They had eaten the bread of affliction and drunk the waters of affliction. But now had the Beloved appeared and lifted up their heads, and put a crown upon them, and set them in a high place, and made them kings and priests, and put their enemies under their feet, and put a new song in their mouths—even praise to Him that sitteth on the throne.

Such shall be the great *reaction* of that wonderful drama. The saints who so little time ago were dethroned, and cast down and dispossessed of the earth, are now suddenly invested in more than all their former dignities and exalted, as it were, to heaven in *the sight of their enemies.* "They ascended up to heaven in a cloud; and their enemies beheld them." "And the same hour was there a great earthquake, and the tenth part of the city fell, and in the earthquake were slain of men seven thousand [a definite for indefinite number]; and the remnant were affrighted, and gave glory to the God of heaven."

Now follows a great slaughter of the foes of the Church. Multitudes fall by the sword; multitudes are swallowed up by the judgments of heaven as by a mighty earthquake; and many beholding the arm of the Lord made bare over his enemies, are affrighted, turn away from their rebellion, are converted and give "glory to the God of heaven."

The saints of the Most High now have the kingdom. Antichrist is put down; and it is proclaimed, "The kingdoms of this world are become the kingdom of our Lord and of his Christ: and he shall reign forever and ever." This is the Millennial Morn —this the day when God shall lift up the heads of his people— when the New Jerusalem, come down from heaven as a bride prepared for the bridegroom, shall shine forth in her beautiful attire as the glory of this lower world.

The view we have taken of the Witnesses—who they are and what they signify—we believe to be abundantly confirmed in the prophetic descriptions of these events both in the Old and New Testaments. But we must defer the consideration of these for the present. In the mean time we may indulge in two reflections:

1. What a pleasing confidence the saint may indulge in his God.

2. What confusion and disappointment shall finally overwhelm the wicked. "Hand joined in hand" they thought to prosper. They made themselves strong in sin, they boasted of their iniquity, and "because sentence against an evil work was not executed speedily, their hearts were fully set in them to do evil." They thought themselves strong and began to afflict the saints of the Most High. Then he confounded and overthrew them, and none could deliver out of his hand. To the wicked God is a consuming fire.

What madness then to live at enmity with God! "Fear not

them that kill the body, and after that have no more that they can do. But I will forewarn you whom ye shall fear: fear him who, after he hath killed, hath power to cast into hell: yea, I say unto you, fear him."

May we all be faithful witnesses for the truth, that our unworthy names may be found written in the Lamb's book of life.

CHAPTER XII.

The year 1858—The financial crisis and the Great Awakening.

SINCE writing the preceding chapter God has done great things for his people. A previously mentioned sign of the coming of the Son of Man is signally verified. The year (1858) has been remarkably distinguished as the year of the right-hand of the Lord and the day of vengeance of our God. It has been signalized by one of the most powerful *revivals of religion* ever known in the Christian Church: in power another Pentecost; in extent and continuance, more than a Pentecost. And this delightful event was heralded by a convulsion which shook terribly the earth. The FINANCIAL CRISIS burst on the commercial world like a tornado, threatening for a time to demolish the strongholds of Mammon. In one short year both the heavens and the earth were shaken that "those things which cannot be shaken may remain."

The year has, in like manner, been signalized, in another part of the world, by one of those virulent outbursts of Idolatry and barbarism against civilization and Christianity which ever and anon convulse the nations. And again was the year signalized by an unwonted triumph of human skill and power in the successful laying of the Ocean Telegraph. Nor would we overlook the pleasant fact that the first intelligence conveyed through the submerged wires, was a message of *peace*, a proclamation of the next event of the year, announcing that the great Empire of China no longer stands aloof in proud isolation, from the nations of the earth, but has become as one of us; throwing open her wide domains to the religion of Calvary, and inviting its embassadors to unfurl there the banners of the cross.

The four events alluded to, together with the opening of Japan by commercial treaty, and Africa by late explorations, are especially characteristic of the last year. The year 1858 was the year of the right-hand of the Lord. Morally, physically, politically, it was a great year: and its events are no doubt in some special sense preliminary to, and the precursors of, that great day of the Lord whose speedy coming they herald. They are signs of the times, and it becomes us to note them as such. They proclaim the approach of the acceptable year of the Lord, *and* of the day of vengeance of our God.

A brief review of these events will abundantly confirm such an opinion.

I. The *financial crisis* and the GREAT AWAKENING. We join these together because we believe that in the mind of God there is such a connection. Such a concussion in the commercial world had perhaps never been known before. It was a thunderbolt. It was the earthquake, the fire and the storm, which made men stand aghast, and wonder amidst the wreck of their earthly hopes, and bade them give heed to the "still small voice" which was about to speak. Engrossedness in things seen and temporal had become our besetting sin. We had gone wild after Mammon, and needed to be taught the instability of all earthly good. And in a moment when least suspected the clouds gathered and the storm burst upon us. The whole commercial world was thrown into convulsions. Princely fortunes were in a moment scattered to the winds; business relations and prospects which had been regarded firm and hopeful, were ruthlessly invaded—stability in all earthly good became as the "baseless fabric of a dream." Never did Providence administer a more unexpected and scathing rebuke to all who were "hastening to be rich;" never were all classes of men, the employed as well as the employers, the poor as well as the rich, made to feel the uncertainty of all human affairs. And from the ruins of their earthly treasures and the wreck of their earthly hopes they seemed to hear that "still small voice" say, "Set not your affections on things on the earth." And men listened to this voice. Business men betook themselves to the place of prayer, and sought the durable riches. The work begun in our great emporium of trade where the financial convulsion was felt most severely; and thence has extended through the length and breadth of our land.

The great commercial revulsion of the closing months of 1857, doubtless had much to do in preparing men's minds for the gracious visitation of 1858; a year ever to be remembered as the "acceptable year of the Lord." Never before did the windows of heaven open so widely, and so rich a rain of righteousness descend.

For back of all these thunder-tones of rebuke, God had been preparing those quiet, invisible influences which were about to sway the mind, well nigh, of a nation, and perhaps set in motion a wave of influence which shall not lose its power till it shall have rolled over all the nations of Christendom.

II.   It is more especially the design of the present chapter to contemplate the Great Awakening of 1858 as one of those remarkable outpourings of the Spirit so often predicted by the ancient Seers, which shall precede that "great and notable day of the Lord"—when the Lord shall come to gather into his fold an innumerable multitude to commence his Millennial reign on the earth; and when he shall come in his signal judgments to take vengeance on them that obey not the gospel. The present extraordinary work of grace seems a realization of the many precious promises of a special divine influence on the Church in the "last times," and a delightful presage of the coming of the Son of man to reap the harvest of the earth and reign in righteousness among the children of men.

God has promised that he will in the last days pour out his Spirit in rich profusion—that he will fulfil his promises and consummate his purposes—that good times await the Church of the living God. This sin-smitten earth shall yet rejoice in the sunshine of the divine favor. That which was spoken by the prophet Joel, and had its first and partial fulfilment at that Pentecostal season when a few thousand were converted under the preaching of Peter, shall have a final, universal, a far more glorious fulfilment in the outpouring of the Spirit on the widely extended tribes of the present Israel, and in the great turning to the Lord which shall follow.

The Christian dispensation was to be a dispensation of the Spirit. Christ must go away that the the Spirit might come. He had finished the great work of expiation—the framework of salvation—the body had been made ready, and now it only remained that it should be quickened by the inbreathing of the Holy Ghost. If Christ went not away the Quickener might not come. The outgushing of the Spirit at Pentecost was his advent—the inauguration of the glorious part he was destined to act in the new order of things under Christ. The wonders then wrought were the earnest, the first fruits of the rich harvest which should distinguish the new kingdom of the Redeemer, but more especially should mark the closing period. The Pentecost was a specimen, not so much of what should immediately follow, as of the power and blessedness of Immanuel's reign in the last days, when the King shall gird himself and ride forth to the conquest of the world. When he shall come to make a short work on the earth, then shall the Spirit be revealed in his great power and glory. That which appeared as a glimpse at the Pentecost—an exception and glorious manifestation compared with any thing that had gone *before*, shall, in the appointed time, become the *rule* and order of the Spirit's operations. Only believe and you shall see yet greater things—greater wonders of mercy, greater miracles of grace, more extraordinary manifestations of the divine power in the conversion of sinners, more wonderful answers to prayer. The wonders of Pentecost shall be outdone—if not in the *power* of the Spirit's working, yet in the extent, and the longer continuance of his blessed influences, and the greater numbers brought under his converting and sanctifying power.

Peter, in the words of the prophet Joel, speaks of an order of things which should *begin* at that Pentecost, but should be consummated in the last days. For her encouragement the Christian Church was thus, at the very outset, allowed to witness at least a transient display of the mighty power which should thenceforth be engaged in her behalf. This was heaven's pledge, gloriously to be redeemed in the " last times."

Our faith in the coming of the latter-day glory is well founded. It has its pledge. All we need is the *repetition* and the *continuance* of the power of that day. And we seem to see that pledge about to be redeemed. The Lord is making bare his arm—the sacramental host is being endued with power for the work because the Holy Ghost is come upon them, and why should we not expect the scenes of a perpetual Pentecost? May we not regard the present great religious movement as the beginning of such a season ?

The Pentecost was an occasion of thanksgiving for the *first fruits* of the harvest—the partial ingathering and pledge of the full harvest. May we not in like manner regard what our eyes now see as the first fruits of a glorious spiritual ingathering, tokens of the full and final ingathering of souls into the garner of our God; when we shall go up from year to year to worship the King, the Lord of hosts, and to keep the feast of Tabernacles!

It is the *relation* which we believe the work in question *holds to the coming kingdom of the Redeemer* which clothes it with the profoundest interest. Let us, therefore, advert to some of the *characteristics, circumstances* and *results* of this work, as confirmatory of what I have intimated—identifying it with what we have been wont to look forward to as the fulfilment of prophecy and the precursor of the Millennium.

1. The work has been characterized *by extraordinary influences of the Spirit.* In this respect it has been truly a Pentecostal season. The word preached has been with power, because made efficacious by the Holy Ghost. The reading of the word, exhortation, religious conversation, the social prayer-meetings, the ordinances of the Church, and all the various means of grace, have all seemed to possess unwonted power. Thousands who have come to the religious meetings to scoff have gone away to pray. Strangely is the truth brought to bear on all classes of men and under all circumstances. A gentleman on his way to the noon prayer-meeting, passing through Washington Market, meets a young man who tells him the good work has reached that great and busy mart of trade. The young man, taking from his pocket a list of names, says, "There is a list whom we have been praying for in different praying circles. I have carried them to the meetings for prayer—we have prayed for them one by one, and now all on this list are converted." Presenting another list, he said, " Here I have another list of nine. We are now praying for these; and we pray for them one by one; and we follow them up, not only with our prayers, but with personal

conversation, entreating them to become reconciled to God."
"Learning," says the gentleman, "that I was going to the Fulton Street Prayer-Meeting, he begged me to ask you to remember these nine young men in your prayers, and ask for their immediate conversion."

The good work was as the coming of the Son of man, without observation. It was heralded by no prophetic tokens of coming good. It began, seemingly, "without human contrivances, and when no one seemed to be expecting it," and so effectually has a *lay* agency been in the work as quite to refute the evils of wicked and unreasonable men, who fain would attribute such a work to the cunning craftiness of priests.

From the market you may pass to the pier, to the busiest haunts of trade—to the counting-room or the hotel, and you are surprised that this same blessed agent, whose office it is to convince of sin and to quicken into a new spiritual life, has been there before you; and there remain the evident memorials of his blessed workings. And so you will find it if you repair to our watering-places and fashionable places of summer resort. It is not all fashion, not all worldly pleasure there now. The Bible, the Sabbath, the Daily Prayer-Meeting have been admitted, yea, welcomed, because the Spirit has been poured out from on high, and another spirit pervaded the hearts of many who the present season resorted thither for the healing of their mortal maladies, or the recruiting of their wasted energies. Now they drew waters from the wells of salvation to heal the moral maladies of the soul.

Or you might go to the fashionable restaurant, or even to the beer saloon, and you are not altogether beyond the limits of the Spirit's influences. A gentleman is dining in a restaurant. A conversation occurs with the waiter which leads the gentleman to inquire if he wished a copy of the Bible. He said he did.

"Do you ever attend the noonday prayer-meeting?" "No," said the waiter; "we are obliged to be here at our business all day and till ten o'clock at night. But we then have a prayer-meeting in the house among ourselves." Who would expect to meet, among the busy, bustling herd at a large eating-house, a company of young men who retire at that late hour to pour out their supplications and plead their wants at the throne of grace? Surely God is there and we knew it not. His gracious visitations seem, as never before, to be blessing every department of human life.

But there is related an incident yet more marvellous, and illustrating yet more impressively the all-pervading power of God's blessed spirit. A thoughtless young man goes into a beer saloon; such a one as the wretched young Gouldy left, and went directly home to make his father's house the scene of his shocking murders and his own suicide. The young man while partaking of his refreshments, heard a company in an adjoining apartment, separated only by a curtain, discussing the Gouldy tragedy, and alluding, in connection with it, to the Fulton Street Prayer-Meeting. Some at first laughed at the idea of a prayer-meeting having any claims on them. Others said it was not a thing to be laughed at; "There is something in it, and we will go and see." The young man who listened, responded, "There may be something in it, and I will go and see too." He was deeply impressed that he had immortal interests at stake. As you entered that saloon you thought it a godless place. But God was there. The invisible agent was at work, and you knew it not. May his blessed influences soon become so universal and all-pervading that the sinner shall say, "Whither shall I go from thy spirit? Whither shall I flee from thy presence?"

Meetings for prayer have been singularly marked by evidences of the Spirit's presence. "One cannot be in one of these prayer-meetings more than a few minutes, without feeling it is holy

12

ground, because the Holy Spirit is present in his silent but amazing power." And we are made conscious of the blessed influence as we listen to the different requests for prayer. We feel, as never before, that there is a deep and tender solicitude felt for the undying spirit of man.

2. Another delightful characteristic of the work in question which seems to identify it with the predicted reign of righteousness, is the *unwonted spirit of prayer* which pervades the Christian Church. It was the prevalence of the spirit of prayer that preceded the wonderful season of Pentecost—rather, it was this which brought down the blessings of that day. The disciples were commanded to wait in Jerusalem for the " promise of the Father," which was the baptism of the Holy Ghost. But did they wait idly? No; " all these continued with one accord in prayer and supplication, with the women." With united heart and voice they called mightily on God for the promised blessing, the outpouring of the Spirit. And the blessing came in overwhelming power—as " a mighty rushing wind."

But was there any thing in the character and the results of that Pentecostal occasion, which might not, and ought not, to be realized in the whole history of the Christian Church? It is a dispensation of the Spirit. There is no restraint with the Spirit —no restraint with the Father in giving the Spirit. He giveth not his Spirit *by measure.* A stronger assurance of God's readiness to give his Spirit to them that ask cannot be given; he is more ready to give his Spirit to them that ask him, than earthly parents are to give good gifts to their children. And whenever the same spirit of prayer prevails, are we not authorized to expect the same results?

If we may judge from the readiness with which men of all classes come together to pray—not excepting men of business— those the most burdened with life's cares and toils; and to business men, *the untimely hours* at which they assemble, and the frequency and fervency with which they pray, we are constrained to conclude that the present era of the Church is marked by an unusual spirit of prayer. Perhaps no age since the day of Pentecost has been, in this respect, so signalized and blessed. And is not this the very thing which, guided by prophetic vision, we have reason to expect as preliminary and introductory to a yet greater ingathering to the fold of the great Shepherd? And are we not authorized to expect yet richer effusions of the Spirit, and yet more wonderful demonstrations of his power in the conversion of yet greater multitudes to God?

One of the rich promises which remains to be fulfilled in the " last times," is: " I will pour upon the house of David, and upon the inhabitants of Jerusalem, the spirit of grace and of supplication." The Church of the living God shall become priests— intercessors before the mercy-seat, for a world that lies in ruins. They shall appreciate as never before the priceless value of the immortal soul, and lift up their hearts in agonizing prayer for their salvation. As we shall more and more witness abroad over the face of Zion, such a spirit of prayer and supplication, we may know that Zion's redemption draws nigh.

3. The present work of grace is no less signalized by *the readiness of God to hear prayer.* This identifies the present religious interest with the great turning to the Lord before the great and notable day. A striking characteristic of that period is to be, that " *whosoever calleth on the name of the Lord shall be saved.*" How delightfully, in the history of God's grace, do the multitude of extraordinary answers to prayer which have been recorded the last year, verify this declaration. I will cite a few—which are as only one in a thousand—and these perhaps not the most striking:

The son of a faithful minister in New England had fallen into evil ways—given his parents much solicitude—and had gone to the West to study law. A Revival commenced in his native town. A friend proposed in one of their meetings that they still pray for their pastor's son. Earnest and repeated prayer was offered. The first letter his father received, announced him greatly anxious for the salvation of his soul. Soon he returned home a new man. There was joy over him that was lost and is found. He returned to the west; has changed the course of his studies, and is determined to give himself to the work of the gospel ministry.

A stranger from City Island, a town of 400 inhabitants and only twenty professors of religion, appears in the Fulton Street Prayer-Meeting, and asks prayers for his native town. Prayers are offered; and in due time he returns home: when to his great astonishment he is saluted with the inquiry, "When are you going to come out on the Lord's side? we have been praying for you ever since you have been gone." "It went like a dagger to my heart. How strange! while I was here asking you to pray for them, they should be praying for me. The Lord has turned my sorrow into joy." He stands a witness for the truth amidst a goodly number of his fellow-townsmen into whose mouths the Lord hath recently put the new song.

In a prayer-meeting in Philadelphia, prayer is requested for the conversion of a son of an aged clergyman. A pastor, well stricken in years, who had long been praying that *his* own prodigal son might be arrested, rose and made earnest supplication "for this son of an aged clergyman." His own son, out of mere curiosity, had entered the room unknown to his father, and sat at some distance from him. There he heard his father praying for just such a son and just such a sinner as himself. He left the meeting in great distress—could not sleep, but walked the streets the whole night. In the morning he returned as a prodigal to his father's house—humbled before God, and ready to enlist in the service of Him who suffered on the cross for sinners. He is now daily at the prayer-meeting, and not without a word of warning to all who are out of Christ.

A profane, intemperate and generally irreligious sea-captain becomes the object of the intense interest and fervent prayers of his wife. She leaves nothing unsaid or undone to impress him with the importance of seeking the salvation of his soul. He goes to sea, setting all these things at defiance. She now re-doubles her diligence at a throne of grace, and besought others to pray for him.

This sea-captain was in the city of Antwerp, Germany, in a convivial party in a parlor. He had a glass of wine in his hand and was in the act of raising it to his lips—quick as a flash the thought came into his mind, " What is to be the end of all this ? " The arrow sunk deep. He put the glass down untasted—soon retreated to his ship—locked himself in his cabin and tried to pray. His distress was keen and pungent. He found no peace till, weeks after, he found it in Jesus. Alone, on his homeward-bound voyage, with his Bible and the great Teacher, he dragged heavily in making his peace with his God. But peace came. The hand that had arrested him in Antwerp, in that parlor amidst his jovial companions, never left him till he was brought to himself at the foot of the cross.

Having thus incidentally referred to the mighty hand of God as come down upon the *sea*, a further allusion to the extraordinary work of grace at present in progress among the class referred to, will not be out of place. There is perhaps no feature in the present Revival more promising of an extended influence, or more significant as a sign of the times, than the one in question. Though the number of seamen recently converted, both in the navy and in the mercantile service, is not inconsiderable, yet it is not so much numbers as the character, the position and the relations of these men to the conversion of the world, to which we refer. Sailors are citizens of the world. They visit every port, and bless or curse every city and nation under the sun. And such are the habits, the propensities, the nature of the sailor that he will leave his mark wherever he goes. He is true to his master for good or for evil. He exerts no neutral influence among the masses of the people wherever he may be. If he be a praying, pious, devout man, he will not fail to bear witness to the truth as it is in Jesus; as the wicked sailor is sure not to fail to corrupt and put to shame the very heathen who are so unfortunate as to come within the contagion of his example.

We may therefore confidently expect to hear good tidings of salvation, which shall gladden the heart of the American Church from the hundreds of seamen who shall soon go out from the Bethel churches of our principal seaports, and the scores that are already being detailed from the receiving ships of New York and Boston, and soon to be scattered through different ships of the navy and sent to different and distant ports. They will go, each in his own way, preaching the words of eternal life. Without charge to the Church, without any expensive agency of missions, every sailor, every officer of the vessel, may be a missionary, and in proportion to their fidelity, every nation and kindred may hear of the unsearchable riches in Christ. In no class of men has the Christian Church a more vital interest than in seamen. Let the leaven of genuine piety once pervade the mass of the five hundred thousand seamen who speak the English language, and we should at once have a class of representatives abroad among the nations whose influence would tell mightily on the conversion of the world to Christ.

There is something perfectly wonderful in this subject of prayer! I cannot understand it. "It seems," says some one, "as if God had disclosed the fact that he cannot withstand the prayers of his people." What means it that God could not destroy his rebellious people Israel, if Moses interceded for them? What means it that at the prayer of one man, the sun stood still? at the prayer of another, it rained not for three years and a half; and again he prayed and there was an abundance of rain? When Israel was invaded by an overwhelming army, one man prayed, and 180,000 of Israel's vaunting foes in a single night lay prostrate in death, and Israel was saved. Paul and Silas prayed, and their chains were loosed, and the prison-doors were opened, and the foundations of the prison were shaken.

If such be the power of prayer, and such the readiness of God to hear prayer, and there be, among the people of God, so greatly increased a spirit of prayer, then may we not take courage that God has risen up and made bare his arm to hasten his work on the earth? May we not take it as an evident token that he will soon set up his kingdom among men?

4. The same conviction is pressed on the mind again, from the fact that *men of all conditions in life so readily listen to the calls of mercy.* You will hear the claims of religion, as I have said, discussed in the saloon and the restaurant—on the pier and in the counting-room—among laborers in the field, and mechanics in the shop—among merchants, lawyers, physicians. Seamen, as they do duty on shipboard, or as they tarry at their land "retreats," or congregate in the Bethel, inquire after the chart and the compass of God's eternal truth, and seek to steer their course into the haven of eternal rest. Boatmen on our rivers and canals—a godless crew—are heard to ask after the way of life and plead for mercy. One hundred and fifty boatmen on the Mississippi River—a hardened race—have during the past year been gathered into the fold of the good Shepherd. For whom may we not hope now?

In one of our great cities (Philadelphia) there are eight or ten prayer-meetings among *firemen*, in as many different engine and hose houses. "A silent and effectual work is now going on among them." These meetings are largely attended, and promise rich results. "Some of the most striking conversions," says one, "that have ever come under our notice have been brought about by the Spirit of God brooding over these engine-house prayer-meetings." Scarcely is there a class of men so far removed beyond the limits of mercy that individuals of the class, at least, have not turned a favorable ear to the gracious calls of the gospel. They are, as never before, ready to hear.

And not only has there been such an unwonted readiness on the part of so many to give a respectful if not a *cordial* and saving attention to the things that belong to their eternal welfare, but there is no marked or conceited opposition. They who care for none of these things, nevertheless, seem secretly to concede that it is the finger of God, and that they "must let these men alone, for if this counsel or this work be of God, ye cannot overthrow it."

It is but a common testimony which comes to us from an important quarter of the great field, viz., that "those Christians who have been stimulated to make efforts for the good of their neighbors and friends, have been surprised that the mind was already prepared and open to impressions, and men are more than ever before *disposed* favorably to consider the subject when presented kindly but faithfully to their attention."

5. Another feature which gives the present religious interest an Apostolic, pentecostal, millennial aspect, is the *Christian union* which so greatly characterizes it. The Jachin and Boaz of the strength of this movement, is the *power of united prayer*. The apostles, as preparatory to the wonderful manifestations and works of Pentecost, were *waiting and praying*, with *one accord*, and *in*

one place. It is recorded by the prophet Isaiah, as a feature of the coming golden age of the Church, that *"they were enlarged and flowed together."* Nothing like the present movement has so completely annihilated denominational barriers, and made Christians of every name to *flow together.* Union prayer-meetings, in which Christians assemble, simply as the disciples of the same great Teacher and servants of the same Master, have been favored, honored spots which God has been pleased to visit, and the Spirit has loved to bestow his richest gifts. Union is the watch-word—union the talisman by which we conquer—union the love which binds together, the spirit of our religion, the badge of discipleship, "By this shall all men know that ye are my disciples because ye love one another." This should give strength and power, and secure progress to the religion of Jesus. This is an element in our religion which gives it a power that the enemy can neither gainsay nor resist. It is heavenly, and it will exalt the earthly and make it set in heavenly places.

6. We come to speak of the *results* of this work in their bearing on the future destinies of the Church. And what impresses us as particularly worthy of remark here, is the *number* and *the character of the converts.* The number probably may be safely put down at 500,000. This is a great number when compared with the results of any previous revival since the origin of Christianity; yet it is but a small number compared with the number that still remain unconverted.

But what more especially claims our attention here, is the *character* of the converts. Who are they? Do they belong to classes in society not so generally reached by spiritual influences; and who, if reached, are fitted to exert on community in general a deeper and more permanent influence? We make no comparison between the value of one immortal soul and another. What is most highly esteemed of man may be least esteemed of God.

Yet there is a very great difference to a community and to the world in the worth of the conversion of different men. While the poor man, and the ignorant man pray as fervently, and have as much power with God at a mercy-seat, and may illustrate the truth as impressively, and in every thing live as holily as the rich, the learned, or the man of influence and position ; yet the last may do all this and a vast deal more. The man who, in addition to a holy life and power with God at the throne of grace, conse- crates to the Lord a large amount of wealth, or brings talents and the acquisitions of learning, or the power of social position and influence, and lays them all down at his Saviour's feet, does more than it is possible for the poor and illiterate disciple to do. God has given him more, and he can consecrate more to his Lord. He comes into the vineyard of his Lord with weightier responsi- bilities on him, and with increased facilities with which to serve his Lord; and consequently, if he do his duty, his conversion is worth more to the common cause than his who comes in empty- handed. Just as the man who comes in a partner into some joint stock company. If he come with a good stock of capital and en- terprise, habits of industry and business talents of high order, and an irreproachable moral character, he is worth vastly more to the company than the man who comes with neither capital nor busi- ness aptitudes nor general intelligence.

Judged on this principle the converts of the past year consti- tute an unusually valuable accession to the Church. Never at any one time were there brought in so many business men—men of wealth—of learning, of influence—or so many *young* men, and so many of these setting their faces towards the sacred office. There has, in a word, been brought into the work an unusually large amount of *lay* labor. And the whole course of the late work has been to provide and employ for the general prosperity of re- ligion the labors of her lay membership. Long and grievously has the Church suffered for the lack of a feeling of individual responsibility in her members. Private Christians have for the most part, heretofore, embarked rather as passengers. The ship had been provided, furnished, and was sailed, they supposed, chiefly to give them a safe and gratuitous passage from earth to heaven. They were willing to share in its comforts and accommodations, and hoped to share largely in its benefits when safely landed on the heavenly shore. But they never understood that they had much to do in working the ship. They were passengers and not laborers.

Many are now beginning to learn that this is a ship in which the great Captain does not engage to take *cabin* passengers. All must work their own passage—help work and guide the ship, and bring her to a safe haven and a successful issue.

Now when we see so many *working men* brought into the Church —so many who come in with their loins girt ready for the work, and who from the very outset begin to work, and who have apparently buckled on the harness with the expectation and determination *to* work and to make a life business of it; and when we see multitudes come into the vineyard furnished largely with the qualifications and appliances for the work—with wealth, talents, learning and social advantages, can we be mistaken if we infer from all this that the master has a great work to do, and that he is about to do it?

Again, when we see a vast many already in the Church who have heretofore been but mere *passengers* in the ship, enjoying her protection and feeding on her rich stores, and hoping she may prove a safe and convenient vehicle to convey them to heaven— when we see many of this class rousing from their lethargy and betaking themselves to the work, taking in hand the laboring oar, we infer again that a new era in Immanuel's kingdom is struggling in birth. " Christ is about to reorganize the world;" and out of the ruins of the old, to bring the new heavens and the new earth.

And again, we are conducted to the delightful conclusion, when we see so many *young men* brought in and subsidized for the work. When a prevailing majority of *natural* births are *males*, human sagacity predicts a war ahead. In very truth we may predict that, when a decided majority born into the kingdom of Christ are males—young men—just putting on the harness and enlisting in the King's army, there is war in the no distant future.

God makes no vain preparations. The great Captain is not thus so greatly recruiting his army, and collecting the munitions of war—storing his arsenals—preparing the weapons of war— and appropriating to his service the silver and the gold—the time, talents and various services of all sorts of laborers, if he is not about to arise and enter on the warfare with renewed vigor and carry it into the strongholds of the enemy. We do not see a great nation—a wise and powerful king, greatly filling up the ranks of his army, and at work in his dock-yards and arsenals, if a great war is not expected. And the extent of the preparation indicates the extent and importance of the expected war. We may then very ligitimately infer, from the greatly increased numbers of men enlisted and the vast amount of resources engaged, that our Lord and great Captain is about to push the warfare to a final victory. And may we not judge something of the magnitude and grandeur of the approaching conflict by the vastness of the preparation ?

7. *Present appearances* indicate that the work of grace now in progress will become *more extensive* and *powerful* than it has yet been, and that it is but the first fruits of a glorious harvest which remains in reserve for all who wait for the appearing of the Lord. " At no time since the revival begun, more than a year ago, was

the spirit of prayer more earnest, never more confident of a blessing. The past week will be long remembered for glorious answers to prayer." And another says " the spirit of prayer, as indicated by such an attendance at prayer-meetings, inspires fresh
confidence in the continuance of the work." There seems an
increasing confidence and high expectation on the part of Christians of all classes that the work shall not cease. The undimin-
ished numbers that attend the daily meetings for prayer—the
unanimity of spirit which pervades those meetings—the multiplied
and urgent requests for prayer which are daily made to these
assemblies, and the remarkable answers to special prayer, all
seem pledges of a continuance of God's converting grace.

"Since the beginning of our meetings," writes one, "we have
never seen any thing more encouraging than the present. It is
felt on all hands that we are on the eve of great and blessed times.
Stand at the door and see the crowd as it disperses. These are
mostly business men. Some few hurry, but very few. A vast
majority seem in no hurry to leave the scene."

But we may not confine our observations to any narrow limits.
We ask after the signs of the times in different parts of our land,
and in other lands. "Watchmen, what of the night?" The
response comes from Ohio : "This is the time to favor Zion.
Many Christians," says the writer, "are believing that the revival
has but just begun. Never did I hear so much good news from
so many pastors as last Saturday." "The revival of religion,"
says the Maine *Evangelist,* "throughout our State seems to be
deeper and more earnest at the present time than at any time
previous. Nearly all our exchanges come to us laden with the
most encouraging reports. It is evident that our richest harvest
is yet to come." Tidings from Philadelphia announce that "the
work of grace is extending itself more and more in the city and
environs, and for thirty miles around." Never was there a time

when so many heard the word gladly; and so many others hear to be pricked in their hearts and anxiously ask, what shall we do to be saved? "God has come down in great power, anew, upon the prayer-meetings of this city and imparted a fresh baptism of his Spirit."

The English correspondent of the *Chronicle* says: "Signs of the presence and power of God are manifest, and I greatly mistake if an abundant reaping is not near the British Church. The conviction is deepening in the minds of multitudes, and the spirit of anxiety for it was never more powerful for years."

We hear the same good tidings from Scotland. "Within the month or two the interest has become more extended and intense. Within a very recent period there has arisen up a band of *lay evangelists* entirely from the ranks of society, who have not only done all the good they could in their own particular districts, but have rendered themselves extensively useful in the country generally."

And we are yet more surprised at recent intelligence from *Sweden*, in which we had feared evangelical Protestantism had almost died out. "There is scarcely a parish, if there be one, in which some persons have not been roused to an earnest concern about their salvation." And what is more remarkable, it is so even in parishes where a pure gospel is scarcely preached at all. The awakening is felt among all classes. "Not a few of the nobility have felt its power. Some of the principal families among the aristocracy are at the present time devoting the influence of their high position and adding to that their personal exertions to spread evangelical truth. Instances of sudden conversion are not uncommon. The Divine impulse has been in some cases so irresistibly felt in the midst of secular engagements and in the open streets, as to compel to the exercise of instant prayer, and behind the first gateway persons have been known to fall on their knees and cry for mercy. In other instances, in large and fashionable parties, congenial minds under a spiritual influence have retired into the adjoining boudoir, and the one sought counsel of the other, while big tears of penitential sorrow contrasted strangely with diamonds and plumes."

Five hundred thousand Bibles were circulated in Sweden the last year. Dr. Stearne of London says of this work : " It is, without exaggeration, one of the greatest spiritual phenomena of the times in which we live."

Our hearts are cheered, too, with good news from *France*. That land, once stained with the blood of St. Bartholomew's Day, has a few who have not " defiled their garments." Their prayers are heard. These " souls under the altar," are called to arise and stand up before the presence of the Lamb. The long deferred blessing has at length come down. Power is given to the word. Crowds assemble for prayer and praise, and multitudes are inquiring the way of life. The best spirit of the Huguenots is revived, and expectant piety hopes great things from that land so long overshadowed by the Hierarchy of Rome. A glorious revival is there begun which we fain hope will increase in power and purity till that great people and their mighty prince shall be gathered into the fold of the great Shepherd.

And, what shows the power and onward progress of this work of grace if possible yet more strikingly, *Ireland*, poor, priest-ridden, down-trodden Ireland, has become the theatre of the great power of God. " There is now going forward," says a gentleman from that country, " in the north of Ireland, and especially in the county of Antrim, such an amazing work of grace as the world has never seen since apostolic times." " Churches are opened for prayers, but so thronged that multitudes cannot gain admission. Not only individuals, but whole families whose members had encouraged one another in sin, are now rejoicing in holy peace and blessedness." In some places the mills are stopped, in others are "running on half time," so anxious and determined are the people to hear the gospel, and to attend upon places of prayer.

In one instance related, a funeral is passing by a mill or factory. An operative requests the accompanying clergyman to stop and preach a sermon. In a few minutes the mill was emptied, and the operatives all crowded into the street around the preacher; and "many souls were awakened and converted before the close of that sermon." In some of the towns the prayer-meetings have to be held in the streets, there being no churches or halls large enough to contain them.

A very pleasant incident is related. A clergyman from a distance is inquiring of a clerical friend he had met in the street about the Revival. To show the readiness of the people to hear the gospel, the resident clergyman said, "Preach right here in the street." "I can preach," said he, "but I have no congregation." "Open your hymn-book and we will sing." They had not sung more than two stanzas when hundreds were assembled. The Spirit of God came down in great power, and sinners were soon heard crying for mercy. And the same writer adds: "All through the north of Ireland are the same gracious and glorious displays of Divine Mercy in the salvation of souls."

And these same glad tidings from the frigid North are echoed back from the sunny climes of India. "All's well," says a revered Missionary; "the light is rising on India's obscurity, and her darkness shall yet become as the noonday. We are encouraged at the many indications that we see already of God's wise and gracious designs in connection with the late mutiny, and we look for a glorious work of grace in this land. And it may be nearer than we imagine."

And the Isles of the South, in cheerful notes, respond: "There is something wonderful," writes Mr. Baldwin, from Lahaina, " in the way God is moving among us. We have seen nothing like it in this part of the world. The greatest transgressors are those who seem most affected, and are the first to come out and declare their purpose to serve God. Two weeks ago I spent the Sabbath at a village seven miles south of this. The awakening there seemed even more universal than here. In Lahaina, nearly all our oldest and most hardened backsliders from the church have come of their own accord into our meetings; and as soon as liberty is given, they are on their feet, mentioning what they have labored all their lives to conceal, asking the prayers of Christians, and sometimes breaking out in prayer for themselves. It is the same also with the greatest sinners out of the Church. They seem to be pressing towards the kingdom of heaven, and our prayer is that they may not stop short of it."

These are some of the evidences that God is still moving on the minds of men without respect to race or locality, and is ready to convert and save. A very general impression is produced—a very general confidence and expectation exist that the way is prepared for a more general and extensive Revival than we have yet seen.

Truly we are living under the dispensation of the Spirit. We may expect great things. God is working wonders of grace, and gives no doubtful tokens that he will do greater things yet. Let the sacramental host come forward in the strength of their covenant God, and in the overcoming power of prayer, and our eyes shall yet see what our imaginations have never yet conceived. Never had God's people more for which to be unfeignedly thankful—never were they permitted to indulge higher hopes. It is a season of the richest spiritual blessing. Salvation has come near unto us. The good news of great joy has reached us from all

13

parts of our land and from other lands, proclaiming the Lord as nigh unto all that call upon him.

We have been praying and God has been answering our prayers, till now the world is literally opened and waiting for the gospel.

" This awakened and listening attitude of the nations, appearing at the same time with the outpouring of the Spirit, increased prayer, and the self-consecration of young men, in increasing numbers, to the work of the ministry, and the return of commercial prosperity—this concurrence of events all tending towards the rapid and effective diffusion of the kingdom of Christ, is a sign from heaven that the higher dispensation for the world's salvation is opening upon us."

I may appropriately quote here the words of the venerable Mr. James of Birmingham, England: " Are we not authorized to expect some richer effusions, some more wonderful manifestations, some more convincing demonstrations, of the Spirit's power than we have been accustomed to witness or receive ? Is this Divine Agent confined, and ought our expectations to be confined, to routine, formality and fixed order and measure ? Should we not look for times of refreshing days of power, intimations of the coming Millennial glory ? Are not these awakenings the very things we have prayed, longed for, waited for? Are they not, too, the subject of inspired prophecy ? Are they not given to support our faith in Divine prediction, and animate our languid hopes of the coming glory of the Millennial age, when a nation shall be born in a day ? "

Another word, in closing, upon the *time* of this wonderful manifestation of the Spirit. This revival begun "just at the time when the exulting note of defiance and contempt from the infidel school, of which the *Westminster Review* is the organ, was raised to its highest pitch." The infidel had been saying, and beginning half to believe that " the world had advanced far above and beyond Christianity ; that Christianity had lost its power— had become obsolete, and would have to be abandoned for some new religion that would have power to meet the necessities of mankind."   The enemy was exultant in consigning God's word to the fossil remains and huge debris of past systems and schools. He was loud in calling for a new revelation, a new religion because the " old was worn out, effete, and no longer able to satisfy the human heart or intellect."   This most timely visitation from on high has confounded Infidelity and put to shame the vaunting wisdom of man.

CHAPTER XIII.

No year since the Christian era has been more remarkable for great and far-reaching events than 1858. We receive these events as unmistakable signs of the times. They have thickened upon us the past year in such quick succession that before the marvel of one had passed away another trod on its heels. It is not too much to say that this single year has given birth to more great, influential events which shall tell on the future destinies of the world and hasten the long expected golden age than centuries were wont to do in the past history of the world. These events, while they have nothing in common in their character, and are brought about by agencies so entirely different, and impelled by motives so unlike, and transpired in localities so remote, the one from the other, yet all seem converging towards a common object, and that object appears to be the overthrow of Idolatry, Infidelity, and every form of false religion, the speedy and universal diffusion of the ever-blessed gospel, and the final establishment on earth of the kingdom of our glorious Lord.

Never before were we made to feel, as now, with what a glorious rapidity God is hastening the great crisis of the world's conversion, and the enemy's discomfiture. We shall do well briefly to review the leading events of the year, and contemplate them in their probable bearing on the great and final crisis.

The year was rendered memorable by the Revolution in India —the peace with China, and the opening of that great and populous country to free-trade and a free-gospel; negotiations and the opening of commercial relations with Japan; the exploration of Central Africa, and the new field of commercial and religious enterprise there opened; the laying of the Atlantic Telegraph; and the great financial convulsion and the remarkable religious interest of the year. Having already disposed of the latter two, a brief review of the other events may constitute a suitable appendix to the foregoing chapter.

III. The early part of the year was distinguished by *the revolution in India*—the commencement of a series of movements which we confidently expect shall be for the more perfect Christianization of that great and *populous* country—for the breaking down the institution of *caste*—the annihilation of the Hindoo and Mohammedan prestige, and the introduction of a new order of things in government and religion.

I have had occasion elsewhere* to speak of the never-to-be forgotten SEPOY MUTINY; and of what God seems to be bringing out of it. Yet I may not, in this review of the year, omit so significant an item in the year's history.

We believe the time is at hand when God will give to his Son that great heathen land. Its stagnations of forty centuries shall be broken up—its idolatries shall be abolished—its superstitious abominations and oppression shall be exposed and done away, and on their ruins shall be reared the beautiful superstructure of

---

* See "India and her People," by the Author.

a pure religion and good government. We believe the renovation of India is now hastening on with more rapid strides than ever before; and that the late appalling revolution was but the earthquake, the fire and storm, which go before when God is about to take some signal step in the advancement of the Redeemer's Kingdom. We believe it to be a marked sign of the times—a not doubtful token of what God is about to do for that great and populous land.

India contains a sixth part of the population of the globe; and she only needs good government, a Christian civilization and a pure religion to make her one of the fairest portions of the globe. But the god of this world has had almost undisputed possession there for four thousand years. It has been a land of the most systematic and inveterate idolatries—of wars and foreign conquests the most ruthless and bloody—of rites and superstitions the most senseless and degrading. All the activity and shrewdness of a class of men, by no means lacking in these qualities, have been employed from time immemorial to bind the yoke of bondage on that great people. Sin has there had its perfect work —the man of sin has been revealed. Under various forms and systems has Idolatry had its day and development, and shown what it can do to deliver man from the curse of sin, and make him sit in heavenly places. Moslemism has done what it could and as signally failed, and a half-Protestantism, succumbing to Mammon, and Moloch, and to all the Dagons of the land, has played its ignoble part. During a full century an unchristian Government has done little for Christianity but to bring scandal on the Christian name. The natives were left in doubt whether their Christian governors preferred the religion of the cross or the Crescent, of Brahma or of Boodh.

Heaven could no longer tolerate the indignity; and in wrath he rose to vindicate his cause, and dreadful was the wrath ; yet there was mercy in that wrath.

We have no need here to repeat the dreadful details of the Sepoy Mutiny. The annals of man's history scarcely present a more appalling array. It is enough for our present purpose that God has done it, and done it for a great and final purpose. It is evidently one of those great revolutionary struggles which ever and anon shake terribly the earth. We are less concerned with the *causes* of this dreadful insurrection than with the *results ;* and not so much concerned with the *immediate* results, as with the great and final purposes which Providence seems about to accomplish by it.

It matters little here whether "impatience," on the part of the natives, of foreign rule and a remembrance of past exactions and cruelties ; or " hatred of the Christian Religion " and a growing apprehension of its speedy triumph, and the not distant overthrow of the Religions of the country ; or whether it were " misgovernment and the unchristian example" of European office-holders in the country ; or the long-continued disaffection, and unheeded grievances of native princes ; whether it were a calamity sent to humble England and to rebuke the Church ; whether any, or all, or none of these be the real causes, it matters little in our present inquiry. This inquiry is, what indications do we discover, in this awful outbreak of violence, of the rapid, onward progress of the Redeemer's kingdom ?

India may, in an important sense, be taken as the great *central nation* of Heathendom. The day seems fast approaching when the whole of this great heathen empire, consisting as it does of not a few of the nations of the earth, shall be subdued and given to Christ, its rightful owner. And the late Revolution in India seems to present more of the character of a war which shall strike a death-blow to the great central nation, than any warfare

of modern times; and which shall at the same time enlarge the
borders of that western race which seems destined to act so important a part in the future regeneration of the nations.

No previous event has ever done so much to make India, her
wants and her woes, her religions and superstitions known—what
has been done for her, and what advances she has made in ameliorating her condition, and what ought to be done for her.   Nothing
could have so strikingly revealed the real character of the present race of heathen.   We are startled at such exhibitions of cold-
blooded ferocity.   If such yet be the character of the unevangel-
ized, what an argument to send them the gospel.   If such be the
character of the semi-civilized Hindoos, whom we had supposed
to be a very quiet, inoffensive people, what may we expect, when
their turn shall come to rise, will be the strength and malignity of
the more ignorant and savage portions of the heathen world?
All Christendom will now see that in self-defense, if not as a
matter of Christian duty, she must convert the heathen.

And nothing has done so much to humble the British Government in that country, and rebuke the Christian Church for her
apathy in not having ere this Christianized a people so completely
thrown into her hands.   The world would then have been saved
from witnessing one of the most appalling warfares which has ever
disgraced the annals of our race.   Had England and the Christian Church done their duty during the century which has elapsed
since England has had possesion of that country, that great and
noble nation had escaped this scathing rebuke, and the world had
not been shocked with the details of a war barbarous almost beyond comparison.

And nothing, it is believed, has struck so deadly a blow on the
native prestige of the country.   What of governmental power
remained in the hands of the natives is probably gone forever.
The native *regimé* has doubtless departed no more to be recalled.

Caste, that ruthless tyrant which has, unresisted and unquestioned, from century to century, controlled those numerous millions in all things social, secular and religious, has no doubt now received its final doom.   Superstition has lost its power to charm and blind men in its iron chains; and religious systems, hoary with age, and which have controlled uncounted numbers for twice twenty centuries, are become weak as the fallen Dagon before the ark of the Lord.   And not only do we believe that the civil and religious prestige of that great nation has now met an overthrow from which it can never recover, but the population itself, already doomed to dwindle away before a superior race, has been left to call down upon their heads the vengeance of British arms, to hasten their own destruction.   Like all other pagan races they seem, as a mass, destined to extinction.   Christianity shall interpose and stay the hand of the Destroyer, and rescue a multitude not small, of such as the great Shepherd will gather into his fold. But ask you, after another century shall have rolled away, *where are those numerous tribes*, echo will answer, " WHERE?"

They who watch the stately steppings of the King of kings in his onward march to victory, see that a " sword goeth before him." The destruction of his enemies, especially of the heathen, has always held a prominent place in the movements of Providence. And why should it not be so in reference to this great nation of heathen?

And, again, while the rebellion has done much to advance the final renovation of India by taking out of the way, or annihilating *obstacles*, it has done more by testing the faith of the native Christians, and arousing the whole Christian Church to renewed exertions for the conversion of India.   Never was the very heart of the whole British Church so moved as now to come up to the help of the Lord against the mighty.   And America is delightfully and earnestly responding to the call of her elder sister to come to her aid in the great work.

The martyr spirit has been revived. We feared that, in the day of temptation, these little ones would fall away. But they have stood the fiery trial like men in Christ; they met death like martyrs. Offers of exemption from prison and death could not draw them from their allegiance to their Divine Master; tortures the most inhuman could not make them deny the Lord that bought them. And not only have members of Mission Churches manfully met death rather than abjure Christ, but others have avowed themselves Christians and since united with the Church, although assured of the determined vengeance of the mutineers.

And we are daily confirmed in this favorable view of India's not distant evangelization by the late reports of the progress of Christian missions there since the partial return of peace. Numbers in different parts of India have since been received into the Christian Church; and what has not failed to attract the grateful and admiring regard of the Christian more than any thing else, is the very encouraging report from MERUT, the spot which had been marked as the place where first a native Sepoy was discharged from the English army because he had become a Christian; and distinguished again as the spot where, in dreadful retribution on a time-serving, unchristian Government, the late rebellion burst forth in retributive vengeance; and not the less distinguished as the place where the good seed, sown in less troublous times, is taking deep root, and the golden sheaves are already being gathered in.

And mark the finger of God here. A native Christian in his flight leaves behind his Bible. That Bible falls into the hands of a native who is disposed to peruse it. He was impressed with its truth, convinced that it taught the only true religion. He read, and persuaded others to read. God saw it, and was pleased to act on their hearts, and turn them from the vanity of their idols to the living God. Late intelligence announces a Church founded at Merut of sixty members and not less than two hundred inquirers. Never perhaps were the friends of missions more hopeful for India than at the present moment.

And never was evangelical Christendom more thoroughly and universally moved to send the gospel in the shortest possible time to that benighted land. Loud is the cry of every Missionary Society for men and money—earnest the appeal of every Bible and Religious Book Society for means to send the word of life to the aid of them who are perishing. The dying experience of many of the native Christians, especially when outraged by the mutineers, has had a wonderful influence on the Hindoo mind. " The blood of martyrs " in India is literally becoming " the seed of the Church." Where the mutiny was the worst and the atrocities the greatest, at the present time seems to be the deepest religious interest and the most earnest inquiries about the truth. The submission and patient sufferings of the Christians is doing its work silently and surely.

The watchmen on those distant walls, respond, " THE MORNING COMETH." The dark cloud of war is receding, and with it, the thick moral darkness which has so long settled down upon that unhappy land.

God has doubtless large and benevolent purposes to answer through these commotions and this bloodshed. When all parties shall have been humbled and duly punished, British pride rebuked and the Birtish and American Church humbled and roused to the importance of the conversion of India, we believe a glorious future awaits that long-forsaken, ill-fated nation. Hushed shall be the din of war; the carnage of the battle-field shall be forgotten. Immanuel shall there unfurl his peaceful banners; and those nations, no more inured to the devastations of war, shall become the willing subjects of the Prince of Peace. Faith contemplates these luxurious climes as all vocal with the praises of our King. Their idol gods cast to the moles and the bats, and the waning Crescent sunk into the abyss whence it came, all these populous nations shall bow before the cross, and serve the one God.

It is the voice of faith that proclaims there shall be yet another invasion, and yet another conquest of British India; and the fame of the Clives and the Wellesleys, the Lakes and the Havelocks, the Wilsons and Neills, shall yet be surpassed. The conquest is to be achieved by railways and telegraphs, by power-looms and steam-engines—by just and equal laws, by schools, by the active promotion of every good word and work, by the practical exemplification, from the Himalayas to the Indian Ocean, from the Birmese frontier to the banks of the Indus, of all those Christian principles and virtues, which have the promise of the world that now is, and of that to come. To this course the British people are impelled by the strongest motives of self-interest, as well as by the purest impulses of philanthropy. And we rejoice to see that they have become so deeply sensible of the fact. The rebellion, terrible as it has been, will prove a signal blessing, and no misfortune, if the sense of responsibility and spirit of duty which have been awakened shall bear their appropriate fruits in practical action.*

It is thus that we regard the Sepoy Mutiny as a sign of the times, betokening the no distant downfall of Idolatry in all nations, and as hastening that blessed consummation which we hail as the coming of Christ's kingdom on the earth.

IV. Another event worthy of notice which has distinguished the year just closed, is the peace recently concluded with *China,*

* " India and her People," by the writer of this work.

and the opening of that great and populous country to a free trade and a free gospel.

China is an ancient nation. When Europe was a wilderness, and America was unknown, China was in the vigor of her manhood—matured, rich, civilized—more advanced in the arts and sciences, more consolidated, more systematized in her religious faith than perhaps any nation then known. But China has from century to century strangely and determinedly isolated herself from all foreign intercourse. Though in dimensions the largest, in age the oldest, and with her teeming multitudes of people the most numerous, and in the exhaustless resources of her soil, her mines and her mechanical skill the most wealthy, she has proudly and selfishly stood aloof from the great family of nations. She has refused her shoulder to bear international burdens, or to contribute her share of influence to international prosperity. No foreigner might enter her bolted gates.

British cannon, a few years ago, in a war which we have no necessity to attempt to justify, battered down some of her strongholds, and forced a treaty which opened some of her ports to foreign trade and intercourse. But this did not long serve the rapidly unfolding plans of an ever onward marching Providence. Commerce demanded more. Literature, science, civilization, Christianity demanded more. Nations no more than individuals, may longer be allowed to live to themselves. Consequently in the ever restless, never retrogading movements of human affairs, another war transpires. Now France and Russia, as well as England and America, have demands to make of China. She can no longer be allowed to coil herself up in her own selfishness. She must now live and let live among the nations of the earth. She is at length forced to yield to these demands and to throw open her gates and let the nations come in.

The late war with China has, we trust, forever settled the question of her exclusiveness. The terror of French and British arms, on the one hand, backed by the urgent and oft-repeated demands of Russia and America; and the resistless and ruthless invasions of the "Rebels" on the other hand, forced the trembling emperor and a weak government to yield to the demands of the four great western nations. The treaty embraces all they could have asked or could desire. "This haughty and isolated power has thus been humbled, and forced to open its doors, which have heretofore been rigorously closed, to the nations of Christendom. Its great river, the Yang-tse-kiang, is to be opened from its mouth to its source, a distance of three thousand miles through the very heart of the great empire. Six more ports, eleven in all, are opened to commerce. Missionaries are to be allowed to diffuse Christianity throughout the empire without persecution or annoyance, and the Chinese are allowed to embrace it without any injury to their persons or property. Foreign ministers are to have free access to the imperial court at Pekin, whenever necessary."

This we claim to be one of the great events of the year, an event, which, in its relations to the world's future, can scarcely be overrated. It has, as if in a day, introduced into the great family of nations a new member, of full age, of huge dimensions, laden with wealth, and rich in mechanical skill and in all the resources, which, if rightly directed, cannot fail to make a nation truly great. But this new sister comes into the great sisterhood of nations with but a heathen civilization, and a Pagan religion— wise, yet ignorant of every thing which pertains to the great end of this life, and to the realities of the life to come.

China is the last great nation that remained to be opened to the ameliorating influences of Christianity. And scarcely any event could just now more distinctly betoken the speedy coming of the long looked for day when the kingdoms of this world shall become the kingdom of our Lord. Chinese Idolatry seems more completely intrenched in the strongholds of civilization, learning, wealth, numbers, and national pride, than any other system. The charm is now broken; the death-blow is struck—the strong governmental arm which has been so long nerved for the defense of that religion, is now paralyzed; her strong intrenchments are prostrated; and the formidable obstacles to the free and universal evangelization of China seem removed. The chief solicitude now in reference to the conversion of that great nation to Christ, relates to the ability— rather to the willingness of the Christian Church to put forth the adequate Christian effort, and to make the needed sacrifice to accomplish the great work. Heaven is willing—Providence has the most significantly and effectually moved in the matter. Heaven's aid is ready—and now it would seem that heaven waits that man should do his part.

The missionaries in China are looking with anxious expectation to see what will be the effect of this great event upon Christians at home. Especially are they turning their eyes to this country with the hope of being strengthened by the fruits of the great revival with which our churches have been blessed. In removing the last obstacle to the introduction of the truth into that vast empire, God in his providence has opened a door, which those who pray for the extension of his kingdom should be ready to enter.

"It was a remarkable and delightful coincidence" says one, "that while the first dispatch sent across the Atlantic cable was the chorus of the angels proclaiming glory to God and peace on earth, the first *news* telegraphed from the Old World was the unexpected intelligence, 'Peace with China,' and a report that the mutiny in India is being rapidly quelled. Under the terms of the treaty of peace, the Chinese empire is open to the trade of all foreign powers. *The Christian religion is allowed in all parts of the empire.*

Foreign envoys are to be received at the capital, and France and England are to be indemnified for the expenses of the war.

"Sixteen years ago, August 29, the war between Great Britain and China was closed by the signing of a treaty, by which five ports were thrown open to foreign commerce. Three years after, a treaty was ratified between China and the United States, by which our citizens were admitted to the same privileges. This new treaty greatly enlarges these privileges, and gives the promise of opening to the gaze of the world the political, commercial, and social life of that most exclusive people. The importance of the commerce of China can hardly be estimated. It is stated that the tonnage used in the navigation of its rivers and canals is larger than the aggregate tonnage of all the other nations of the earth; that ten thousand imperial barges collect and carry to Pekin the duties in kind imposed on grain, and an equal number on salt; that the annual revenue of the government amounts to about $120,000,000; that there are over four thousand walled cities and towns, and not a creek or haven on which there is not a town of commercial importance, and that its great river Yang-tse-kiang opens up the trade of a hundred millions of people.

"But this treaty concerns the Christian still more than the merchant. That vast empire, containing one-third of the population of the world, is now open to the spread of the religion of Christ. Instead of being confined to a few points on its borders, the missionary may now penetrate to the heart of the kingdom. A still greater load of responsibility is thrown upon the churches. The gospel must be given to the four hundred millions of Chinese. Men and means must not be wanting, now that the door has been providentially opened."

And we must not overlook, in the review of the providential opening of China, the terrific agency of the present *Insurgents' war*. Like the first Mohammedan conqueror of India with his fearless, half-barbarous Afghans, they spread devastation and death wherever they go. They fight, they pray, they plunder and rob, and break in pieces idols and demolish temples; and are the fierce champions for the unity of God and the religion of Christ. They seem sent before as a scourge, to break down and put out of the way what God is about to destroy—the rod of heaven's anger to weaken, and then annihilate the prestige of the native government, and finally to batter down the great colossus of Chinese Idolatry. This idea is confirmed by those most conversant with the condition and prospects of China. A missionary recently writes: "The rebels in the country are reported to have committed dreadful enormities, in some places, in revenge for what was done to them last year, when they were driven away. I would hardly like to have them regarded here as Christians; I fear they would do little honor to the Christian name; and yet I may say, in regard to this rebellion, whether in this province or elsewhere, that if there is not a single individual among all the "insurgents" who is a true follower of Christ, I think it is a great step, preparing the way for the gospel in China, to have an army of natives marching through the country destroying the idols and ploclaiming that there is but one God. By this movement, which at present brings countless miseries upon this nation, God may, in his wonder-working providence, be preparing the way for speedy and most wonderful displays of his grace in this dark land."

We think we see, in the present aspect of the Chinese Empire, and especially in the results of the late war and in the prospects of the successful diffusion of the gospel there, a glorious hope for China, and, in that hope, a delightful anticipation of the coming of the universal kingdom of our Lord. The Christian Church is now earnestly asking, "How shall we best evangelize India and China?"

14

V.   The next important event of the year, and one kindred to the last, is the late commercial *Treaty with Japan*, and its opening to receive the gospel.

The eagle-eye and the all-encroaching spirit of commerce have for a long time been directed towards Japan.   That rich and populous, and in many respects, highly civilized yet idolatrous people, have most sternly and hitherto most successfully resisted all the overtures of commerce and intercourse with foreigners.   They have at length yielded to the demands of human progress and thrown open their doors.   Soon shall European science pervade that hitherto isolated land.   Modern inventions and discoveries, improvements and facilities for intercourse and communication with other nations, shall now bless that land.   Railways, steam-ships, telegraphs, shall henceforth become so many agencies and resources for progress and profit to the improved and highly improvable people of Japan.   A great and promising field is there open to the agency of the Christian Press.   No people are perhaps better prepared to profit by the introduction among them of a Christian literature.

Since writing the above the Japanese Embassy have arrived in this country to ratify the treaty alluded to.   The manner the embassy have been received ; the universal interest excited in the event throughout the country ; the very gratifying attentions paid these distinguished strangers, are all significant events, and signs of the times.   It encourages the hope, so animating to Christian faith, that the last formidable barrier to intercourse with any considerable nation, is at length removed, and, having embraced, as we now hope, this interesting but hitherto isolated people in the fellowship of nations, we would fain receive it as a token that the King of nations and the King of Zion is about to gather that people into the fold of Christ.   The event is truly extraordinary and hopeful, and, though the hope may be deferred, yet we wait to see this to be but the beginning of a most interesting series of events.

The extraordinary reception of the Embassy in New York on the 16th (June, 1860), seems to the reflecting mind, to foreshadow the coming importance of the event, as the shrewd people of that great commercial city seem to interpret it. Scarcely any previous event has ever called forth so enthusiastic a demonstration. It was a grand and whole-hearted welcome of Japan into the fellowship of nations. Broadway for miles was thronged with the eager multitude. Flags of all nations, at different points, greeted the imposing cortege. Some index of the public feeling seemed signalized in the numerous mottoes which appeared in the windows. I transcribe one as a specimen. It appeared at Nos. 320 and 322 Broadway. Numerous flags were flying, and there was a motto in each window. The following were the most striking:

WELCOME—JAPANESE EMBASSY—WELCOME.

JAPAN AND UNITED STATES. FRIENDLY NATIONS.

UNIVERSAL BROTHERHOOD.

GATES OF ALL NATIONS THIS DAY OPENED.

WALLS OF TYRANNY AND OPPRESSION MOULDERING TO DUST THE WORLD OVER.

FREEDOM FOR THE WORLD. THE TRUMPET-BLAST OF THE NINETEENTH

CENTURY.

LIBERTY, EQUALITY AND FRATERNITY.

1860 — PEACE, PROGRESS, PROSPERITY.

ONE BLOOD—ALL NATIONS.

ALL NATIONS—UNION FOREVER.

THE JUBILEE OF THE WORLD NEAR AT HAND.

But we here refer to the Treaty, the Embassy and all the interest that attaches to it, as an event principally challenging our admiration and Christian gratitude, because of its hopeful and prospective relations to the spread of the gospel among that interesting people, and their final Christianization. The great obstacle seems now removed, and henceforward the friends of

Christian Missions may arise and in the name of Immanuel take possession of the land.   A wide and effectual door seems there to be opened, and it is truly delightful to witness the readiness of our Benevolent Societies to enter in.   Already meetings have been convened, and consultations held, and measures adopted for the speedy evangelization of Japan.

Truly God seems to be hastening his work on the earth.   India, China and Japan, the great nations which Satan hath bound, lo these twice eighteen hundred years, are now disenthralling themselves from the bondage of ages—are bursting the chains of their darkness, and are coming to the light and liberty of the children of God.   Half the population of the globe, as embraced in these three great nations, are now, in the wonder-working providence of God, laid at the feet of the Christian Church, waiting the voice of the gospel trumpet, bidding them that are dead, to arise to a new national, social and religious life.   Never were the responsibilities of the Christian Church so fearfully increased ; never did the conversion of all nations to Christ appear so near.

But there is yet another great Missionary field beginning to loom up from the dark abyss of Paganism, which we may not here overlook.   When the great Asiatic field shall have been occupied —when the teeming millions of India, China and Japan shall be added to Christ's heritage, then we may expect Zion's conquering King will turn his victorious sword towards the long neglected, the long afflicted children of Ham.   Africa shall become the object of his next great conquests.   Ethiopia shall stretch out her hands to God.   We need not then be surprised that,

VI.   The *fourth* great event of the year relates to movements in AFRICA and in respect to Africa.

The last year's explorations of Livingstone, Bowen and Barth into the interior of this almost unknown continent, have formed a new era in the history of Africa.   Starting from different points on the coast, each of these travelers explored different portions of the interior, and all essentially for the same general purpose. They have laid open to the world great and interesting fields, which invite the labors of the philanthropist and the Christian. Those inland tribes and nations are found to be far more intelligent, industrious, enterprising and hopeful than the people on the coast. They have a better country, a more salubrious climate—show themselves not the less accessible to foreign influence, and decidedly favorable to the introduction among them of the gospel.

A new impulse is consequently given to the friends of Africa to redouble their diligence and zeal for the renovation of that long oppressed and abused continent, with fresh hopes of success. Africa, we may expect, shall henceforth become a most interesting missionary field. In proportion as she has been the scene of oppression and cruelty, of neglect and abuse, by other nations, shall she receive at the Lord's hand "double" for all her afflictions.

But we should quite fail, rightly to estimate the recent opening of Africa as a promising field for the spread of the gospel, if we did not take a cursory view at least of the peculiar character of this field, and the prospects of a rich and speedy return for all labor bestowed. We shall therefore briefly refer to a few features in the present condition of Africa, which are especially hopeful.

1. The native Africans are a *settled* people—not migratory—moving from place to place, and never at home, so that what should be done one year should be undone the next.

2. They are a domestic people—formed into families, and appear capable of strong domestic affections. There is not a more promising basis for the success of all religious instruction. And to this we may add, they are naturally kind, affectionate, generous and benevolent. No people appear by nature to be more richly endowed with all the gentler virtues of humanity. Love, grat-

itude, obedience, docility, are traits of moral character most easily developed in the African, and altogether promising of success in all our attempts for his moral improvement.

3. But, what is yet more promising, the African race, more than any other race, are *readily impressed with religious truth.* The religious instinct is ever prominent. I know of no one trait of which travelers and missionaries have more frequently spoken than the unusual susceptibility of the African to the religious sentiment; and certainly there is not a more hopeful trait. No race has received the gospel with so much eagerness and docility. And the reason assigned by the missionary is that there seems in their very nature a principle of *reliance and unquestioning faith* which has not been discovered in any other race. "It has often been found among them that a stray truth, borne on some breeze of accident into hearts the most ignorant, has sprung up into fruit, whose abundance has shamed that of higher and more skillful culture." African races form an exception to all other races, in their readiness to embrace the gospel as soon as it is offered. And more especially has this been found to be true of the more highly civilized tribes of the interior. They make the missionary welcome—provide houses for them, and do what they can to facilitate their work.

4. Another hopeful feature of this great field is, that there is in Africa less to be *undone* than in any other portion of the heathen world. In India and China the ground is *preoccupied* with a sturdy, inveterate growth of error, to eradicate which, and to prepare the ground for the good seed, is for years the great work of the missionary. The greatest obstacle to his immediate success lies in the preoccupation of the Pagan mind with false systems of philosophy and religion, which are stereotyped in a false literature. In Africa there is very little such rubbish to be removed. Books, science, philosophy, they have none. They

are a people for the most part without a written language—they have no literature—no long established and venerated systems of religion, to be contended with and overcome, before truth can be received and established. They are without a history. Their crude Religion has neither system nor law, nor any very strong hold on the mind of the people. They are, compared with the old Asiatic nations, without a religion. This they virtually acknowledge in their anxieties that the *bookmen* may come among them. And as the missionary goes he has nothing to contend with but ignorance and common depravity—nothing to do to remove the rubbish of wrong systems, before he may build the superstructure of the right. A people without a literature or religion are in a much more favorable state to be acted on. Vast indeed, in this respect, is the difference between the native of Africa and the superstitious, conceited Hindoo, or the no less bigoted *Romanist*. So completely is the latter ensconced in his impregnable fortresses of error, which are all a matter of the book, written and engraven on his mind as with a pen of iron, that the well aimed arrow will sarcely reach him.

What immense facilities for good, then, do *they* possess, who have it in their power to give a people their literature—to begin to write *their history*—to make their books—to have the control of their education—to teach them philosophy, and to give them their religion! They have very much thrown into their hands the control of the native mind. They secure at once the three great elements for reforming, civilizing, and Christianizing a people; education, the Press, and a preached gospel. Such facilities has the missionary enterprise now in Africa. No other field probably presents so few obstacles to success.

5. Another feature in the present condition of Africa relates to her *commerce*. This potent agent which Providence is pleased largely to employ for the amelioration and final Christianization

of a people, has hitherto done little for Africa. Aside from the direct agency of divine truth, there is not perhaps a mightier element at work. In Africa this agency has but just begun to be operative and make its power felt. Her vast resources are now being developed—all the great staples of commerce are there indigenous to the soil—all the various and rich productions of the Indies, East or West, are found there, and these are the articles of exchange which are so much in demand by the two great branches of the Anglo-Saxon family. African commerce must consequently fall chiefly into the hands of these two great Protestant, Christian nations. This will throw the destinies of Africa very much into the hands of these two nations. An interchange of commodities and easy facilities of intercourse will here bring Africa into contact with the literature, the science, the philosophy and the religion of England and America. It will, on the one hand, bring poor, bleeding Africa into direct communication with the great heart of the Protestant Church. It will open the channels through which the waters of salvation shall flow over that great moral desert and make it as the garden of the Lord.

And more than this: commerce promises to extinguish for Africa her cruelest *curse*. The *Slave-Trade* is the blighting curse of that unhappy land. Africa wants the commodities of other lands, and they have wanted her human chattels in return. But let her once understand that her cotton, indigo, coffee, sugar, and the great variety and abundance of her native productions will be accepted in exchange for what she wants, think you that she will, amidst cruelties direful as death, make merchandise of her sons and her daughters?

With such tokens for good—with such facilities and resources for successful action, can we otherwise than opine no distant, no stinted good in reserve for poor Africa? The explorations of the last year and the unwonted preparedness of the people of the interior to receive the good tidings of great joy, betoken the speedy approach of Africa's gracious visitation. We will thank God and take courage. May the Lord hasten his work and bless that captive race.

VII. The only other great event of the year which I shall notice. is the laying of the transatlantic TELEGRAPH CABLE. We cannot just now speak, as we gladly would, of the final success of this great enterprise. The mere fact that the cable *has* been laid and communication *has been had* from continent to continent would seem honor enough for one year. The principle is established—the practicability of the enterprise is no longer questionable. And now it only remains to complete what has been begun. All probably now needed, in order to realize the enthusiastic hopes of a few months ago, is time and further experiment, the opportunity to remove difficulties and to supply defects, and perhaps the application of yet more skill and enterprise. Though our rejoicings over the work as if complete, were premature, yet they were neither premature nor overabundant, as designed to commemorate an event which shall undoubtedly in the future accomplish all, and more than its most sanguine projectors have yet conceived. Though there be at present a lull in the loud jubilations of a few months ago, and we are in danger of overlooking the importance of this great event of the year—though the éclat of the event is less enthusiastically celebrated, its real importance and prospective utility are scarcely diminished by the mere failure, or rather the delay of sending messages from one continent to the other. The indomitable enterprise and scientific skill which have already done so much, are our best possible pledge that they will not give over till they shall have accomplished what they have begun.

Even should the whole matter end here and what has been done should remain merely as an exploit of science and human enterprise, never to be repeated, the mere fact that, in the year 1858, a chain cunningly wrought of copper, gutta-percha and steel was stretched across the bed of the Atlantic Ocean, and that messages were transmitted along it instantaneously from the Old World to the New, will remain a marvel for all ages. It will gather new lustre as each generation transmits it to its successors, and may fill, in the poetic chronicles of some future age, or unborn civilization, a larger space than *our* "ancients" allotted to the labors of Hercules or the voyage of the Argo.

But we wait with confidence the realization of all our former hopes of the final and complete success of the Atlantic Telegraph. We do not believe its important bearings on the social and moral condition of the world have been overrated. It no doubt has a most important part to play in the renovation of our world and the establishment of Christ's kingdom on the earth.

The year in question was truly a notable one. It was crowded with great events, each of which seemed but the beginning of a series which presages the speedy revolution of the world and the introduction of that golden age for which we wait. All are hastening on the great conflict between truth and unrighteousness. The whole heathen world is thrown open to the labors of the Christian Church—the numbers and resources of the Church have within the same short year been greatly increased—unwonted facilities have been provided for easy access to the heathen world—distances have been annihilated—national alienations been unexpectedly removed, and they that were afar off have been brought near. Truth approaches her triumph.

But we may not pass from a review of that eventful year without associating with it another event, of later date indeed, but which seems in a sense to belong to the same year. We refer to the "Great Eastern," the Mammoth Steam Ship. This seems but a prognostic, kindred with the last, of the coming auspicious age. No reflecting mind can look upon this leviathan of the deep, comparing it with the ordinary craft that lies in the harbor about it, and not be impressed with the idea that it foreshadows a future order of things yet to be revealed. No present commerce, no carrying trade, no migrations of mankind, no existing system of warfare, requires any such stupendous craft. It no doubt belongs to an age yet future; to an age of unprecedented enterprise, of heretofore unknown prosperity and magnificent achievements.

Its very name may be significant of its future destiny. The GREAT EASTERN—shall it have any special relations to the "kings of the east?" when by the drying up of the waters of the Euphrates—the gradual decay and destruction of the Turkish Empire—the power of the Moslems shall fall and the great obstacles to the restoration to their land of the Jews, the royal priesthood, the kings and priests of God, shall be prepared? May not this be a precursor of the "ships of Tarshish?" which means by eminence, a ship of the ocean, a palace of the deep, a great ship. These "ships of Tarshish," the prophet says, shall bring "the sons and daughters of Israel from afar, their silver and their gold with them, unto the name of the Lord, the Holy One of Israel." And not only shall they return with their own great wealth, but kings shall minister unto them and they shall bring the riches of the nations. And what more likely than that extraordinary modes of conveyance should be provided for so extraordinary an occasion? All is mere conjecture. Or shall the ordinary pursuits of commerce, as in human progress they shall enlarge, demand so extraordinary a mode of conveyance? Be it enough that the heretofore undeveloped advancements in human affairs, whatever they may be, shall require correspondingly extraordinary modes of transit and conveyance.

Truth, I said, approaches her triumph: yet in her triumph we

descry a gathering storm which shall for a time spread " desolations " over the earth.

This is that which was spoken by the royal seer : " The heathen
raged ; the kingdoms of the earth were moved ; he uttered his
voice, the earth melted."`

And then men and angels are summoned to survey the great
battle-field and behold the dreadful displays of incensed Omnipotence on his enemies. " Come, behold the works of the Lord,
what desolations he hath made in the earth." " But," says a con-
fiding Church, " the Lord of hosts is with us ; the God of Jacob
is our refuge." The great conflict passes over ; the Church triumphs. Her Lord " maketh wars to cease unto the end of the
earth. He breaketh the bow and cutteth the spear in sunder ;
he burneth the chariot in the fire." And then in view of the dreadful desolations which have covered the earth, and the signal discomfiture of the enemy, and the triumphant and glorious vindication of his people, heaven and earth are charged to bow in
reverential fear before the God of the whole earth, and to submit to his sceptre : " Be still and know that I am God : I will
be exalted among the heathen ; I will be exalted in the earth."

CHAPTER XIV.

The great American Crisis; or the Conflict of 1861—Its causes, character
and results—The hand of God in it.

WE have already treated of civil commotions, wars and revolutions, as the sure precursors of that coming kingdom for which
we look, and the efficient agents which shall hasten it on. We
have seen how India, China, Italy, and the Crimea have, each
in its turn, been made the battle-field, on which to decide, in some
of its forms, the great question of the age—the question between
liberty and despotism, between human freedom and bondage.
The great centre of conflict is for the present transferred to
America; and here the next great blow shall be struck in the
name of human freedom. The light of the nineteenth century;
the course of human events; the onward march of an irresistable
Providence; the latent workings of liberty in the great mind of
the whole civilized world; the pulsations of the great heart of
humanity, and the outspoken conviction of all Christendom, have
decreed that man shall be free, and especially have they decreed
that man shall no longer buy and sell his brother, and thereby
disown his manhood, and reduce him to a mere chattelship.

It has been a long conflict in this world of ours—an "irrepressible conflict," which has at length gathered strength and reached a crisis. The wise and patriotic framers of our Constitution felt the incongruity of incorporating a system of human bondage into an instrument which should stand before the world as the magna charta of our liberties. Yet, in the hope of its early extinction, they extended to it a present *toleration*, contemplating it as an *existing evil*, to be *tolerated* only till it could be peaceably terminated. Hence the "compromises of the Constitution." The northern portion of the original confederacy continued to treat the institution of Slavery as the framers of the Constitution evidently intended it should be treated, and consequently State after State gradually terminated the relation till at length all these States became free; and having tried the experiment, first of slavery, and since of freedom, found the last state better than the first. The southern portion of the confederacy pursued an opposite course, and established and perpetuated slavery.

These two antagonistic elements have been in active conflict (though suppressed), and gathering strength for more than four score years, and have now burst forth into open hostility. The one strikes for freedom; the other wages an uncompromising war for the extension and perpetuation of slavery. For a long time it was a war of opinion, of the ballot-box, of the pulpit and the rostrum. At length the appeal is made to the sword; and we wait in awful suspense the result. Each contending party, confidently, appeals to heaven for the justice of their cause. We wait to see whom heaven will favor; whether the just, the good, the merciful God will smile upon and bless a confederacy confessedly founded on negro slavery as its corner-stone; or whether by giving success to our arms, he will vindicate our cause and establish us such a nation as, in his providence, he indicated he would establish in this Western world.

If the finger of Providence ever pointed out a land "as the

land of the free and the home of the brave," it was the United States of America. Early in our national existence was the tree of Liberty planted upon this soil; and under its shadow have sprung up and grown all those civil and religious institutions which had made our land the glory and envy of all lands. But engrafted on this sightly tree was a bitter stock, which has borne nought but a bitter fruit. That stock was African slavery—permitted, as we said, by the wise and patriotic framers of our Constitution, but cordially adopted, cherished and perpetuated by all the Southern portion of our confederacy, until it threatened to overtop the whole tree and to blast its entire fruit.

The North, though slow to believe and slower to act, were at length aroused to withstand the steady determined and persevering encroachments of the South; and the South were yet more determinedly aroused for the defense ef their darling institution, and for its extension and nationalization. Apprehensions for the security and the perpetuation of slavery, arising from the more determined conviction of the North, and an equally strong conviction on the part of the whole civilized world that every system of human bondage ought to be done away, gradually led, not only to drawing tighter the bonds of the system, and of adopting a course of strong justification of the system, making that to be a good which they once conceded to be an evil, but the same apprehensions, united with a strong self-interest and a feudal pride, rapidly fostered a sentiment of hostility to the North.

The agitating process produced the general conviction throughout the entire South, that the institution of slavery was no longer secure in the hands of men who recognized neither its divine right, nor its economic or humane policy. Hence it had become a necessity, with all such as felt *slavery* to be with them a necessity, that the *administrative power of our government should be in their hands.* They did not feel that their institutions were secure in any other hands. Such a feeling has in a measure prevailed at the South from the beginning, but it has from year to year gained strength, till at length it is demonstrated in an open resistance to the ballot-box, and we are plunged into a direful war because a fair majority declared in favor of a Northern President. Of the seventy-two years which has elapsed from the inauguration of George Washington, first President of these United States, in 1789, to the inauguration of Mr. Lincoln, in 1861, Southern men had occupied the Presidential chair fifty-two years.* And not even this undue proportion measures the share of governmental power and patronage, which, in other respects, have been accorded to Southern men. Such undue balance of power in their own favor have they deemed it needful that they should hold in the halls of our National Legislature and in the Presidential Mansion in order to preserve intact and inviolable the peculiar institutions of the South.

But even this would no longer do. The opposing tide from the North, backed by the united sentiment of the whole civilized world, still rolled on. It seemed to carry in it the portentous decree of universal emancipation. And it must and it should be resisted. And as no other government on earth would lend its support to the system, the Government of the United States *should.* Hence the uncompromising determination to force our own government to a virtual nationalization of Slavery. And hence the *necessity* felt that the friends and supporters of Slavery should hold the government of the country at their own control. Identified as they have chosen to make the institution with their

---

* And we must not overlook the fact here, that of the five Northern men who have occupied the White House during the twenty years in question, two or three of them were but "Northern men with Southern principles," or proclivities, extending an unduly liberal patronage to the South. Indeed we are not quite sure of the loyalty of any but the two Adamses, though sure that the last of these Northern incumbents of the chair was as arch a traitor as ever escaped hemp.

very social and civil existence, the wielding the powers of government becomes a matter of life or death. When, four years previous to the late Presidential election, a strong apprehension existed that the sceptre might pass from the hands of the Southern Oligarchy, there was a determination to resist scarcely less marked than at present. Had the election terminated in the choice of the non-slaveholding candidate, war was then equally inevitable. Under another like contingency war has come—but with a four years' accumulated vengeance.

It is a war for *power;* generally for the love of power, and because men, inured to despotic rule in their social and domestic relations, have a feeling that they are the most suitable if not the legitimate rulers of the nation; but, specifically, it is a war to secure the prestige of American Slavery.

It is a war, not against the form of Republicanism, but against its very soul and spirit. And it is waged on the part of the insurgents with an uncompromising determination and virulence, and an unscrupulousness, which seem to proclaim "rule or ruin" to our whole land. Appearances at present seem to force upon us the conclusion that the war shall settle the long vexed question of slavery or no slavery, through the length and breadth of our land. There is indeed a prevailing conviction on the one hand, and a fearful foreboding on the other, that the war now so fearfully raging shall strike the death-blow to the last great system of human bondage which now afflicts our world.

The present war is the great conflict of eighteen hundred and sixty-one. With so wonderful acceleration do events now hasten on the great and final consummation of the Divine purposes among men and nations, that each revolving year presents some great decisive conflict, and wins some signal victory for truth and righteousness. Civil despotism is overcome; or Papal Rome is cast into the crucible of war and her dross burnt out;

15

or Pagan Idolatry is put on its last trial, and its fate decided on the battle-field. And finally, in the present war, the last great scheme of human bondage is summoned to answer before the high tribunal of justice and humanity, for its long-protracted and relentless depredations on human rights and all the dearest interests of man. Every dictate and prerogative of Christianity declares man to be free. Every step in the progress of the light and liberty which distinguishes the middle of the nineteenth century from the darkest period of the dark ages, demands that man, of whatever nation, lineage or color, shall own in fee-simple both his body and his soul. Our Declaration of Independence proclaims the right of every man to life, liberty, and the pursuit of happiness; and to all this the spirit of our age most unhesitatingly responds a long amen.

Our present conflict is eminently a war for human freedom; for Republicanism in the purest form it has ever yet been able to exist; for the emancipation of man from the thraldom of his fellow-man. It is the last great blow struck for liberty. If successful, it shall proclaim liberty to the captives, and the opening of the prison to them that are bound. If unsuccessful; if they who offer to the world as a "model Republic" for the times—a Republic founded on negro slavery as its corner-stone —shall succeed, then we are thrown back into a barbarous age; the tide of human progress is arrested and turned back a century, and hopelessly may we look soon again to see the fair form of Liberty rise and attain its present stately proportions.

And what would the nations of the earth say—those nations, and their potentates and rulers, who have looked on with evil eye and predicted, and more hoped than predicted, our downfall? Shall they hold us in derision, and rejoice over the downfall of liberty as fallen to rise no more? Shall they rejoice over her, and make merry and send gifts one to another, because she that tormented them is no more?

Such being the *cause*, and such the *character* of the war which now afflicts our land, we come to inquire after the probable *results*—what may we expect God will bring out of this war?

War is one of the dread agencies of Providence, used more commonly than any other form of agency, to break down and remove out of the way the great hindrances to human progress. It is the millstone more usually employed to grind to powder the great systems, organizations, or confederacies, which the arch enemy of man erects as the stronghold of his empire. And we may expect to find that all wars, but more especially modern wars, are more or less directly overruled for such a purpose. What, then, may we expect as the issue of the present war?

1. We may expect an *expensive* war, possibly a protracted war, and certainly a war that shall *sorely afflict us*. As a nation we have grievously sinned. Our pride and extravagance; our Sabbath-breaking and intemperance; our ingratitude and general forgetfulness of God, and, more especially perhaps in the present case, our past complicity with the system of human bondage, which has at length cried to heaven for righteous retribution, have come up in remembrance before a righteous God, and we must not think a strange thing has happened, if God should reward us according to our doings. In all the afflictions which an expensive and bloody war shall bring upon us, we only recognize the righteous judgment of God. And we need not expect this war shall close till we shall be thoroughly purged from our national and social sins. God will turn away his wrath from us, when, having forsaken our sins, we with repentance and contrition turn unto him.

God hath dealt so with no other people. He hath made us his modern Israel—hath seemed to choose us as a peculiar people—hath made his goodness to pass before us as he did to his Israel of old; and yet in many respects, more abundantly. In our origin, and growth, and rapid maturity, we most distinctly discern the mighty hand of our God. But our ingratitude and forgetfulness of God, and especially our failure to stand up before the nations of the earth as a model nation, to exhibit to them the beauty and glory of free institutions—of a self-governed people—a great moral fountain whose fertilizing streams should go out to bless a desert world; these and a long list of our national sins, have provoked our Lord and King to subject us to his chastening hand. But he has not cast us off. If we turn unto him he will turn unto us, and again make his face to shine upon us. He will not cast off his people, nor give up the heritage, which he has cherished and watched over with such parental tenderness and care, to spoiling and final desolation. Yet he may afflict us still more severely; for deeply indeed have we been compromised in the sin that now makes us mourn. Our statesmen, our army and navy, our ships and capital, have all done homage to the great Moloch of our nation; and now we are made to participate in the awful retribution that has overtaken us. We are made to drink to the dregs the bitter cup we had mingled with our hands. This we may expect as the first and most obvious result of our present conflict. And we may be yet more sorely afflicted. But though cast down and sorely chastened, we shall not be destroyed. For,

2. We may expect a *final victory*. Yet this expectation we do not predicate on the fact that, in money and men, and in all the munitions and resources of war, we have the advantage of our enemy, but on the confidence that, with all our sins and ill-deserts, God is on our side. They that have risen up against us, fight that they may, without let or hindrance, bind the yoke on the oppressed and never let them go free. We, on the other

hand, have raised the banner of freedom. It is a strike for liberty and the institutions of our Puritan fathers; and our confidence is that, however dark the cloud that overcasts our hemisphere may be—however fierce the assaults by which these dearest interests may be assailed, they can never be destroyed. They are interests dear to humanity—dear to God. And whatever checks or seeming retrogressions may, from time to time, betide, God and humanity will be sure to vindicate these interests. They are vital to human progress—essential to the carrying out of the gracious purposes of heaven towards our degenerate world.

We have only to cleave to these interests, and heaven is surely on our side and we cannot fail.

A brief retrospect of our past providential history is full of encouragement here. The *time* of the first settlement of this country; the *character* of the early settlers; the peculiar *training* they had for their mission in the new world; the peculiar institutions which they brought with them and established here; the peculiar prosperity which has attended these institutions; the great success and efficiency which has here been given to the Puritanical element and Anglo-Saxon type of our people;—these are some of the features in our history which encourage the hope, and give unfailing confidence that, however sorely we may first be scourged for our sins, we shall not be overcome or destroyed. We are sure that heaven is on the side of the *principles* and *institutions* which brought our fathers to this land, and which have had the smiles of heaven from the beginning of our national existence. And we cannot for a moment entertain a doubt that what has been so propitiously begun and so far prosperously conducted, shall go on to its glorious completion. Progress is the law of Heaven; and strange indeed would it be if the wheels are now to be stopped and rolled back into the dark ages; if the great, the modern idea of self-government is to be exploded; Republicanism to prove a myth; feudalism to be restored and perpetuated; the African slave-trade reopened in all the horrors of that odious traffic, and men again barter in the souls and bodies of their fellow-men :—if such things are to be; if such a melancholy retrogression is to blight and turn back all that modern enterprise and improvement have done, and all that the most sanguine friends of progress have predicted and hoped for, then may we expect failure in our present struggle. Our confidence of final victory is predicated on the assurance we feel that God is just, and therefore will not allow oppression to riot forever; that God is the friend of freedom, of light, of progress, and therefore he will not retrace his stately steppings, and allow the sad retrogression which the triumphing of our enemies would entail on the world for ages to come.

That we have formed a just estimate of the feelings of the South on the subject of social and civil freedom; that such are their prevailing sentiments, and such their determination and real design in waging a ruthless war against us, and such our hopes or fears in victory or defeat—at least that the views above expressed harmonize with those of persons who have had ample opportunities to form a just judgment, we take the liberty to transcribe a paragraph or two, from a writer who seems to know whereof he affirms, and who affirms what tallies but too well with what we know from a great variety of other sources. The article from which we copy is entitled "The Spirit of the South," and headed with a sentence from a Southern paper, in these words:

"'We claim to be the superiors of the Northmen in every respect, and we are.'—*Augusta (Ga.) Chronicle and Sentinel, Aug.* 18.

"Allow an old subscriber to your paper, and a son of a soldier of the Revolution, to state two reminiscences that came under his own observation, for the consideration of those who are aiding the insurgents in this wicked rebellion by their cry for 'peace!'

"In the fall of 1839, twenty-two years ago, the writer returned to this country from Europe. During his residence abroad, he made the acquaintance of several gentlemen from the South. Soon after his return to America, he was present at a large dinner party which was composed almost altogether of Southern gentlemen, many of whom, at the time, were high in office under the General Government. The conversation was mostly on Southern men and Southern matters;. and, after a circulation of the wine, the conversation became quite free and outspoken, and made such an impression on my Northern ears, that its nature has been distinctly remembered ever since. It was on the subject of the government of our country, and on the superiority of the Southern over the Northern people! It was emphatically declared by these gentlemen, that 'no man born north of Mason's and Dixon's line' should ever have any thing to do with the government of the United States;. or should hold, under government, any office of trust or importance. And it was as emphatically declared that an arrangement would be brought about, sooner or later, when the entire government of these United States should be in the hands of the men of the South—as they only were the race *par excellence* fitted to govern the nation! They claimed then, as now, 'to be the superiors of the Northmen in every respect,' and that the people of the North must, and should be, under the dominion of the men of the South!

"The other reminiscence is of more recent date. Twenty-one years later—in August, 1860—the writer met, at the White

Sulphur Springs, in Virginia, several hundred of the very men, many of whom are now among the leaders, and who were the fomenters of this wicked rebellion. There were present some of the leading men from every one of the Slave States. Their meeting at this time was for the purpose of planning this rebellion; and they were then as much determined on breaking up the Union as they have ever been at any time since. The writer knew personally many of these men, and the declaration was made to him repeatedly, that if the 'Black Republicans should elect any man as President, the Union would be dissolved.' Governor Letcher, of Virginia, was there, and on that occasion reviewed the first volunteer company which was formed at Richmond, and, in addressing this company of F. F. V.'s, the writer heard him make this declaration: 'You, young gentlemen, are the nucleus of five hundred thousand Southern men, who will yet be called together to repel the invasion of the Black Republicans of the North!'

"These statements are given to show what we have long believed to be true—that the plotters in the present outrageous rebellion have been for more than a quarter of a century maturing their plans to destroy this government; and that, during this time, they have never for one moment intended, nor do they now intend, to listen to any terms of 'peace' or of 'compromise,' short of the entire subjugation of the North to their will! No, gentlemen of the 'white feather' 'peace' negotiators! Know, assuredly, that one of two conditions must take place in our country—*the North must conquer the South, the rebellion must be 'crushed out;' or, we and our children must take our position only one degree above the slave, and be prepared to hoe the corn of our masters!*

"A SON OF ONE OF THE SOLDIERS OF THE REVOLUTION."

Because we believe God is the friend and abettor of liberty, the friend and avenger of the oppressed; because we believe he will finish in our country the work he so nobly begun, and which, without let or hindrance, he has thus far so effectively carried on up to the present day, we believe the final victory shall be ours.

3. We expect as another issue of the present war, the final triumph of free principles—a signal vindication of Republicanism—and the unloosing of every yoke and letting the captives go free.

Republicanism is now on its trial. The lovers of liberty the world over—all who expect that such a boon shall yet be the inheritance of man, and that the nations that have heretofore sat in darkness and in the shadow of civil despotism, and sighed for deliverance, shall see light—and all, wherever found, who hope yet to taste the sweets of freedom and to repose under the shadow of her wings, look on, with irrepressible anxiety, to see how the battle will go with us. Shall we succeed and liberty triumph; or shall the rising hope of millions set in darkness to rise no more? Must they yield in despair that such an heritage shall ever be realized on the earth? The war now so fiercely waged, is as truly a deadly blow aimed against civil liberty, as it is against the personal liberty of the four millions of colored men already held in bondage. And as the American Republic has stood before the world as nearly the sole representative of civil liberty, we may expect the nations of the earth will regard our success or failure in the present conflict as decisive of the fate of liberty for years to come, and perhaps forever. If self-government cannot be maintained under the favoring auspices of its present existence, we should seem to look in vain for it elsewhere.

But who for a moment will believe that a retrogression in

human affairs so disastrous and disheartening as the one implied in our failure in the present struggle, awaits our world? Most wistfully do the friends of freedom throughout the world, now hope for and expect a signal triumph of free principles—a manifest vindication of civil liberty.

And not only this; but there is an equally confident expectation that the present war shall not end but in the entire emancipation of our whole enslaved population. Though not entered upon by our government with such an intent, and though there be still the greatest reluctance on the part of both the government and people of the North to make the war a war of emancipation, yet the conviction is every where and every day strangely gathering strength that it will be so; that it must be so; that heaven has decreed it, therefore it must be so. In every form and mode, unmistakable utterance is given to the feeling that the day of redemption to our captives draws nigh; the year of Jubilee is at hand. Thousands who were silent a few weeks since, now give unequivocal expression to the sentiment in question. A writer this very day, signing himself "A Veteran Observer," may be taken as a representative of the sentiment. "We may dodge the point," he says, "as much as we can, but slavery *is* the cause of the war, and the war will be the *commencement de la fin* to slavery. The time has come when the problem of the day, beyond all others, will be: 'What shall we do with the negro?' Any general, senator or editor who tells you this is not the case, may be written down either a blockhead or a hypocrite."

That the war on the part of our assailants means the *defense*, the sure *establishment* and the *perpetuation* of Slavery in our land, and the no distant reopening of the slave-trade, there can be no doubt, and consequently success on their part, means the compassing of those ends. And so, we believe success on our part will finally mean universal emancipation ; and consequently the utter and final extinguishment of that odious traffic. The mighty of God shall do it.

To show that we have not mistaken the designs of our Enemy in this conflict—at least that we are by no means alone in entertaining such convictions, we may quote the opinions of others. An intelligent observer of the great events now transpiring in our nation says:

"To a looker on, in the extreme South, this rebellion has so many curious phases, it may be a matter of interest to the inquiring mind to analyze the mutiny in all of its forms, throughout the Southern States.

"It is, doubtless, a well understood fact, that the perpetuation of Slavery, and the revival of the slave-trade, were the chief incentives to this unholy revolt against the laws of civilization. It is a fact easily susceptible of proof, that with the first outbreak of this revolt, the slave-trade *was reopened.* Aye, notwithstanding the cunningly devised clause in the rebel constitution—devised for the purpose of deceiving Europe—notwithstanding that clause, the slave-trade was reopened, by the equipment of many vessels for the coast of Africa, some of which, it is believed, have landed cargoes on the Southern coast, recently."

Or would we know how the great philanthropic heart of England pulsates on this subject—not how the aristocracy, or the cotton-spinning oligarchy, or the government feel, but how the mass of the people feel—what the popular voice of philanthropists and Christians is, we may quote a paragraph from the British *Standard*, of London. While the editor doubts our ability to cope with the South in arms, he does not conceal his horror of an empire founded on slavery. The reader will see that "he grows quite sulphury over the fate which he thinks the chief conspirator richly merits."

We quote the following rather to show that the heart and conscience of modern Philanthropy, and the living spirit of Reform, have decreed the downfall of the last great system of human servitude which yet mars the fair face of modern civilization. If the language is caustic it is not the less emphatic. The *Standard* says:

" Let none of our friends think that in thus speaking (expressing a fear that the Government cannot put down the rebellion), the wish is father to the thought; nothing can be more contrary to the fact. Our aversion to the Rebels, their cause, and their object, is intense, extreme, unutterable. They have avowed their purpose, in the face of the world, to found an Empire upon Slavery. Ten thousand execrations on the hideous project! The thing is of Hell, and worthy of its origin! We hold President Davis to be vicegerent of Beelzebub! If he succeed in his unholy enterprise, Slavery may exist for centuries in the States of the South ; and not only so, but overrun the entire territory of South America, after the way shall have been cleared for it by the sword. Slave-breeding will go on as now, but that will not suffice; and to meet the necessities of the Satanic Confederation, the slave-trade will once more be reopened with all its horrors in Africa, on the Middle Passage, and in the New World!

" These are the grounds on which we deprecate the success of the Rebel arms, and invoke defeat, confusion and destruction on the Rebel Chief, his Congress, and his Army, while we pray and agonize for universal triumph to President Lincoln.

" Such are our desires ; but, alas! fear preponderates over hope. Our sole remaining consolation arises from the fact that the Lord God Omnipotent reigneth! In season due, He will avenge the oppressed and break in pieces the oppressor."

And not only at home and abroad has a strong impression possessed the mind of the friends of freedom that the day of general emancipation is at hand—that the present war shall secure a consummation so devoutly to be wished; and are we mistaken in our belief that there is also, throughout the dark domains of Slavery itself, the same longing hope and confident expectation that the tocsin of freedom shall soon be heard through all their fields and cabins, and the long oppressed tribes shall rejoice that the day of their redemption has at length come?

How these things shall be we may not be prepared to explain; but that such is the purpose of God in the war, and that such shall be the result to the slave, we can entertain little doubt. Whatever disasters may first betide and try our faith, and humble our pride, and rebuke our extravagance and self-dependence and boasting, we fully believe the issue of the war will be such as abundantly to vindicate, in the eyes of the world, the strength, stability and superiority of our free institutions, and to proclaim a year of Jubilee to all that are still bound.

4. And yet more than this do we expect as an issue of the war. We look that it shall inaugurate a new era of development in connection with the whole Africa race. The enslavement and general debasement of that race is one of the great facts of history. Great results have already been brought out of it. And what has been is, probably, but the beginning of the end. God's designs are but beginning to be developed in connection with that race. So important an item, as their singular transfer to, and their long bondage in America, cannot but have a connection with their future history of stupendous interest. What it shall be we can scarcely more than conjecture. The shrewd observer of human affairs 3,300 years ago, might have predicted with some degree of certainty, from the peculiar dealings of Providence in conveying the *children of Israel* into Egypt, subjecting them to bondage there, giving them the peculiar training and experience which they were made there to acquire; from the deliverances he wrought for them in the land of Ham, and the judgments he

inflicted on their enemies and oppressors; from these things it might have been predicted that the future history of that people would be signalized in a manner corresponding to their singular training. This is precisely what we expect, at least of that portion of the African race which has served in " durance vile " in America. Their bondage here has been their school-master, to train them for the position they are yet to occupy among the nations of the earth—for their nationality wherever that shall be; and to train them for the Church and the peculiar type of Christianity and civilization which they are to illustrate. No people of the present day present a more interesting study for the philosophic historian, and none present a more interesting field for honest conjecture.

The providential history of the children of Ham has, from the first, been a very singular one. God in the beginning chose the seed of Shem as the favored race, where he would choose his Church and place his name, and whom he would first use as his instruments in carrying out his purpose on the earth, and through whom religion, and civilization, and all human progress should have their first development. The Patriarchal and Mosaic dispensations were confined very much to the race of Shem. And Christ came of the same race. But with the fading away of the glory of the Jewish Church and nation, and the introduction of Christianity into the world, the sceptre passed from the descendants of Shem to those of Japhet, and it is through this race that, for nearly two thousand years, religion and liberty, intelligence and human progress in general, have, from generation to generation, grown and matured. And poor Ham has, all these long centuries, been made the servant of servants. Abused, debased and made the prey of the worst passions of man, he has sorely suffered the malediction of heaven, doubly intensified by the malediction of man.

The descendants of Ham, as represented by present African races, have seemed, in the great army of the King, to be kept as a *reserved corps.* No conspicuous part have they yet taken on the great battle-field of human advancement. Ever and anon has African intellect, or skill or bravery, risen above the low lever of African degradation, towering aloft and yielding in eminence to the capabilities of no other race—just enough to vindicate to the world their real, though for the most part latent capabilities, but not enough to serve their turn in the great mission of life.

The query now is, shall not the *reserve* yet be brought up— brought upon the great field of human activity, and act a part in the last great drama?—a part not the less conspicuous, not the less effective and honorable in the eyes of the great Captain and of the world, than his elder brethren have acted. We think so; and we think we need not be careful to give but a single reason for such a belief. And that reason is, that *God is unfailingly and forever the friend of the oppressed.* On no other principle of the Divine government can we rely with a positive certainty. He *will* take the part of the down-trodden and oppressed, and break the arm of the oppressor. Yet were we to assign another reason, it would be the peculiar *susceptibilities* of African races, of a higher type of Christianity, and, perhaps, of civilization than the world has yet witnessed.

The religious instinct of the Negro is every where remarkable. He seizes the good seed of the word with an avidity common to no other race ; and his rude soul offers a ready soil to its acceptance. As in coming ages the spirituality of our Religion shall become yet more developed, the negro races, if we mistake not, will be found the happiest mediums of its exhibition. Their moral susceptibilities, or their susceptibilities of exemplifying the purely moral elements of our Religion, seem quite peculiar to themselves. There is, in the religion of the negro, a simplicity, a pathos, an absorption, a lifting up of the soul to God, a bringing of heaven and earth to meet, which we discover in the religion of no other people. They will understand what I mean better than I have been able to express it, who have had the privilege to join in their worship, and especially to lift the heart in the sacred song, in some colored church at the South. Such a scene not only illustrates the point in question—the susceptibilities of the negro for a higher order of spiritual worship, and a religion of a type better suited to that future and higher condition of Christianity which we hope and pray for—but it brings to our minds a delightful evidence of the great condescending love of God, in vouchsafing to them so richly of heaven's treasures, as a compensation, to the lowly and humble, to the outcast and down-trodden.

But it was to the other reason that we gave the precedence. The first and the chief ground of hope we find is in the long, low and extreme oppression of the African. Herein they have the unfailing promise of God, the guarantee of heaven, that the down-trodden shall yet sit in the high places of the earth. God will surely lift up the heads that hang down; "give them rule over them that hated them," and "reward them double" for all the dishonor which has been put upon them. God will surely take the part of the oppressed, and put to shame the pride of the oppressor.

5. There is a wide-spread conviction in the minds of reflecting people in all parts of our land, that the present war shall prove a great *moral agency* for the advancement of the higher interests of our nation—the interests of the Church and of a pure Religion. We have great confidence in these presentiments, or general expectations among men. They seem but the foreshadowing of the things which are about to transpire. It is a revelation from on

high, an inspiration of the Almighty, which, in a way we cannot account for, takes possession of the mind and creates a confident expectation of the coming event. Such a feeling in relation to the moral results which shall follow the present war is already finding expression in every part of our land. We may take the following as examples of such a persuasion, or presentiment. Writing from Ohio, one says:

"It is worthy of note, that Christians almost universally express the conviction, that God is about to work a great work in our land, for the vindication of his power and the advancement of Christ's kingdom. There is no complaint, no murmuring at the stagnation of business and the hard times, but on the contrary, a quiet disposition to 'stand still and see the salvation of God.'

"When I remember what blessings have followed some of the most grievous chastisements with which God has afflicted his people, I cannot but hope that, notwithstanding the portentous appearances, God has great things in store for his people. If the Church of Christ shall be found in her lot and place, near the mercy-seat, I cannot but hope that, although the heavens blacken, the thunder mutters and the lightnings flash, yet, in due time the rain—the refreshing rain of righteousness—will fall."

Another, writing from Pennsylvania, utters a similar sentiment, in expressions like these:

"This war is but the work of the Lord. He has this nation in the crucible of affliction, to burn up the dross. If I was ever thankful for any thing, it is for this; and my prayer is, that the fires may not cease to burn until the gold of this nation shine in righteousness, clear and bright, reflecting the image of our Saviour. I am willing to suffer with the people all that may be necessary to this end. Nay, it would be a pleasure, if it were necessary, for me to pour out my blood, with our noble Ells-

16

worth, to sustain our government, and our much loved country. I do hope our government will not draw back—I believe it will not. God is in this work."

We await the issue with a solemn awe, and yet with a confident hope. The cloud through which we are passing may become yet darker. The thunders may roll and the lightnings play yet more terrifically, yet our confidence wavers not; the end shall be well. It is but another of those great and terrific moral earthquakes which ever and anon shake terribly the earth. It is a thunder-storm which for the moment shrouds the earth in darkness and portends only desolation; but as the storm soon passes away and the sun reappears with healing in his beams, and the earth smiles with new beauty and fertility, so, in like manner, we contemplate the passing away of the present fearful crisis. It is one of the last mighty strides of Providence towards the goal of humanity's final and high destiny.

A few more such strides, a few more such terrific struggles and travail-pains among the nations; a few more such convulsions and revolutions, that shall break to pieces and destroy what remains of the inveterate and time-honored systems and confederations of sin and Satan, and the friends of freedom may then lift up their heads and rejoice, for their redemption draweth nigh. THE DAY OF VENGEANCE HAS ALWAYS PRECEDED AND BEEN PREPARATORY TO THE YEAR OF THE REDEEMED.

CHAPTER XV.

The Scripture view; or several Scripture representations of the Great Conflict.

HAVING in previous chapters shown that the characteristics of our age indicate the no distant approach of the final and universal triumph of the Church, preceded by a great and terrible conflict, it remains now, that, in confirmation of the foregoing views, we should present the Scripture argument; and also the argument derived from the ANALOGY of the Divine mode of working.

The Scripture view of our subject will occupy our present chapter.

Were we to divide the eventful history of our race into but three grand periods, the *first* should reach from the fall of man to the establishment of Christ's reign on earth, of a thousand years. This is the empire of sin. The *second* should be the "thousand yéar's reign," the conflict still going on, yet righteousness, during this indefinitely long period, being in the ascendant. The *third*, after a short interval in which Satan shall be loosed for a little season, shall be the final, complete and eternal triumph of righteousness, and the final and everlasting overthrow of sin.

It is the closing scenes of the first of these periods that now claims our attention. And if, as I have endeavored to show, the events of our times seem to identify them with the period in question, it invests them with a new interest.

We are not, however, ignorant that it is a favorite theory with some that the Millennial morn has already dawned, and that its consummation will be no more than a continuation and increase of what we already experience. I see gleams of light streaking the eastern horizon, which no doubt are the sure harbingers of the day soon to burst upon us in all its glory. Yet I see a dark and threatening cloud gathering. It increases and spreads itself athwart the whole horizon, and soon will obscure the rising light. Though it may obscure it for a little time, it cannot extinguish it. It shall burst through that cloud, and, scattering the darkness, reveal a glorious day. Everywhere do the sacred writers couple the "year of the redeemed" with the "day of vengeance of our God." When ye shall see "these things" (tribulations and conflicts, sore as death), then "lift up your heads, ye saints, for your redemption is nigh."

I shall call attention, first, to a class of scriptures which describe the "*great battle*" of Gog and Magog: of which we have a full account in the 38th and 39th chapters of Ezekiel, and reiterated and confirmed in the 20th chapter of the Revelation. Gog is believed to designate the king, and Magog the people, who shall make war upon the Church and seem to have overcome her. What people are here intended, seems not easy precisely to determine. Nor do I suppose *any one* people is designated. The prophecy which predicts the invasion of this numerous and mighty host, and their apparent victory, but their final and signal overthrow, commences thus: "Behold, I am against thee, O Gog, the chief prince of Meshech and Tubal."

The word here rendered "*chief*" is *Rosh*, which, if taken as a proper name, as many commentators do, is the name of a portion of the *Scythians* from whom the modern *Russians* have their origin. *Magog* was the son of Japhet, from whom the Scythians are supposed to be derived. *Tubal* was the fifth son, and Meshech the sixth son, of Japhet. They are supposed to be the progenitors of the *Muscovites*, another large portion of the Russian empire. The Tartars, from whom descended the Turks, are of Scythian origin. The Mogul Tartars are to this day called *Magog* by Arabian writers. The people, therefore, here designated would seem to be (as national localities now are), the Russians, the Turks, the Tartars, and all those vast hordes of Barbarians that inhabit the north of Asia. In ancient times all these would have been called by the comprehensive and indefinite name of *Scythians.*

I, therefore, understand the terms *Gog* and *Magog* to be general terms, used formerly to denote those hordes of northern Barbarians that used to make their bloody and desolating incursions on the more civilized portions of the south. Hence these terms come in time to mean any barbarous, cruel, invading army. It is in this sense, I apprehend, that the prophets used the words Gog and Magog, in reference to the enemies of the Church. *Sennacherib*, with his fierce, blood-thirsty army, was the Gog and Magog of that period. The heartless and ferocious *Antiochus Epiphanes*, whose whole heart seemed intent on his bloody design of exterminating the people of God and blotting out their name forever, was the Gog and Magog of his dark period. He raised his foot and had well nigh crushed his prey, when a hand from on high snatched them as from the paws of the Lion. In like manner the Romans were the Gog and Magog of that disastrous period, when, in the destruction of the Holy City and the overthrow of the Jewish nation, God allowed his elect people to be scourged for their sins.

These terms are used, alegorically, for any princes or people that set themselves up to oppose the true Church; and the instances to which I have alluded, may be taken as primary though not principal fulfilments of those prophecies which predict the general invasion of the Church by some strong, combined and cruel enemy, and as emblematical of that *great and final conflict* to which our attention is now called.

The conflict described in Ezekiel, 38th and 39th chapters, is confined "*to the latter days.*" The substance of the prophetic description is this: that a powerful and fierce army shall be arrayed against the people of God—shall put them in great fear, and well nigh overcome them, yet they shall be signally discomfited by the special interposition of the Almighty. Their defeat is described thus: "My fury," says God, "shall come into my face; for in my jealousy, and in the fire of my wrath have I spoken (saying), Surely in that day shall there be a great shaking in the land—so that the fishes of the sea, and the fowls of the heaven, and the beasts of the field, and all creeping things that creep on the earth, and all the men that are upon the earth, shall shake at my presence; and the mountains shall be thrown down, and the steep places shall fall, and every wall shall fall to the ground. And I will call for a sword against him throughout all my mountains, saith the Lord God: every man's sword shall be against his brother. And I will plead against him, with *pestilence* and with *blood*; and I will rain upon him, and upon his bands, and upon the many people that are with him, an overflowing rain, and great hailstones, fire and brimstone." Then follows a survey of the battle-field. The weapons of war lie mingled with the dead—shields and bucklers—bows and arrows—hand-staves and spears—cover the wide and bloody arena. For seven years they take no wood out of the field, nor cut down any out of the forests, for they shall burn the weapons for fuel—and seven months shall be occupied in burying the dead bodies, or in gathering up their bleaching bones from off the face of the land.

They came as a mighty, vaunting, countless host—they came over the whole land as a cloud, and darkened the whole face of the earth—nothing seemed wanting to ensure them a complete victory—they are about to shout their triumph, when in an unexpected hour pestilence, and the fiery flying dragons of divine judgments come down upon them, and they are as the stubble before the devouring flames. And the "Lord magnifies himself," and makes known "among the nations that he is Lord."

Here we have, "*in the latter days*," a great and confederated assault of the enemies of godliness against the true Church, and their final overthrow, and the triumph of the Church.

There is also a prediction of this same thing, as it seems to me, in Isaiah, 66th chapter, 15th to 24th verses. A very similar scene of conflict is here described with the additional fact, that after the great battle and the temporary overthrow of the righteous, the remnant that shall "escape" shall flee to the *Gentiles*, to *Tarshish*, *Pul*, and *Lud*—to *Tubal* and *Javan*, and the isles afar off—countries which, in the minds of the ancients, occupied the places of what we term *heathen nations*—and "they shall declare my glory among the Gentiles." That is, the conflict will become so severe that many will gladly make their escape to the heathen world where they shall preach the good news of the kingdom, and exemplify the glory of the cross, to those who know not God. Their fall shall be the rise of many.

The *result* of the great conflict as here described is, first, a great overthrow of the wicked, and, secondly, a great ingathering of the saints. The enemies of the Church are now all prostrate : "And they shall go forth and look upon the carcasses of the men that have transgressed against me; for their worm shall not die, neither shall their fire be quenched; and they shall be an abhorring to all flesh." The overthrow shall be complete, signal and disgraceful in the extreme. But, on the other hand, the people of God are strengthened and multitudes of all nations added to their number: "And they shall bring all your brethren for an offering unto the Lord, out of all nations, upon horses, and in chariots, in litters, and upon mules, and upon swift beasts, to my holy mountain Jerusalem, saith the Lord." That is, great multitudes of converts shall come from all parts of the world and shall be conveyed to the Holy City or the central place of worship, by all the facilities which the different modes of conveyance can afford. There seems something here to favor the idea that, during the Messiah's reign of one thousand years, not only the Jews shall occupy the Holy Land, but Jerusalem shall be made a kind of religious capital for the whole world—that not the twelve tribes alone, but *all* that be the true seed of Abraham or heirs according to the promise, shall, by their representatives at least, go up to Jerusalem to worship.

I would next direct attention to the scene as presented in the *Revelation* given to the disciple at Patmos. Here I would make a remark or two concerning the thrillingly interesting subjects brought before us in that extraordinary portion of the Sacred Volume. Its general subject is *the condition of the Church*, in the different ages of the world, up to its final triumph. There are seven *seals*, seven *trumpets*, and seven *vials* of the last plagues. The first, or the seven seals, are taken by the most approved commentators to be a representation of the Church and her persecutions under the pagan power. The seven trumpets represent the same under the iron rule of Popery and Mohammedanism. And the seven *vials*, or the seven last plagues, symbolize the destruction of these mighty and long continued antichristian powers. The pouring out of the *first four vials*, describes the successive stages of the destruction of these antichristian powers. The fifth and sixth symbolize the final downfall of the Romish and Mohammedan powers. And the seventh, the grand overthrow of the *combined* powers of Satan on earth. It is with these three last with which we are at present more particularly concerned.

" The fifth angel poured out his vial upon the *seat of the Beast;* and his kingdom was full of darkness, and they gnawed their tongues for pain, and blasphemed the God of heaven, because of their pains and their sores, and repented not of their deeds." " *The seat of the beast* "—the centre of *Papal power,* or Rome itself. The proud and cruel, the persecuting and usurping hierarchy of Romanism shall wane more and more, till there shall come some terrible interposition of divine indignation. He will send " darkness " into their kingdom. He will confound their counsels and bring their cunning craftiness to naught. But this shall not bring them to repentance, but shall only the more call forth the venom of sin, and nerve their arm the more madly against the God of heaven—whom they shall more wickedly blaspheme—and " gnaw their tongues for pain."

Bear in mind now for a moment the state of high excited feeling and of mad and irrepressible frenzy into which this portion of the enemies of the Church are now brought by the judgment of Heaven and the insupportable apprehension that their cause is now desperate, and we will turn to the next, or the *sixth vial.* " And the sixth angel poured out his vial on the great River Euphrates, and the water thereof was dried up that the way of the kings of the east might be prepared."

Here we have the extinction of the Turkish power and the Mohammedan Religion. It is symbolized, as before shown, by the River *Euphrates.* And the drying up of the waters of that river is an apt illustration of the extinction of that mighty flood of oppression to the true Church. " That the way of the Kings of the East might be prepared "—that the mighty obstacles thrown in the way of the conversion and return to their native land, of the Jews, who, by the special divine favor, are princes of the

East; or it may mean that the way for the conversion to Christianity of the nations of the east with their nobles and kings, might be prepared. For Mohammedanism is the grand barrier between Paganism and Christianity.

The Crescent is no doubt waning, and soon to cease to cast its sickly light over the nations. But it is not with its *waning*, or with the means, or the precise time of its overthrow, that we are at present so much concerned, as with the results of that much-to-be desired catastrophe. We have seen into what a state of demoniac madness the correlative power of the beast was thrown by the many encroachments of the kingdom of light into his dark domains. As soon as he sees his empire in peril he maddens like a chained tiger—" gnawing his tongue for pain " and " blaspheming the God of Heaven." And if you will read on from the 12th verse of Chapter 16th, you will see that the adherents of the Papal Beast are not alone in waging a dreadful warfare against the saints of the Most High. After the drying up of the waters of the Euphrates and the consequent ingathering of many eastern nations, and the glorious progress and triumph of Christianity, then shall come the great battle of *Armageddon*. The vision of the man of Patmos, describing this mighty conflict, was this: " And I saw *three unclean spirits, like frogs*, come out of the mouth of the dragon, and out of the mouth of the beast, and out of the mouth of the false prophet. For they are the spirits of devils, working miracles, which go forth unto the kings of the earth and of the whole world, to gather them to the battle of the great day of God Almighty. And he gathered them together in a place called in the Hebrew tongue Armageddon."

Mark here the origin and the character of the hostile invaders. They are all " unclean spirits "—the first is an emanation from the " Dragon," the personification of Paganism ; the second is the embodied spirit of the Beast (or the Papal Power), and the third of the False Prophet. An unholy confederacy of these three, it would seem, is to compose that last great enemy against which the Church of Christ is finally to contend. Hitherto the warfare between the powers of light and of darkness has been carried on *sectionally*. Formidable *divisions* of the enemy have from time to time made their deadly assaults, and never are they absent from the field, yet never before have they *united* their inglorious destinies and fought for the common interests of a sinking cause. It is not said, nor are we to suppose, this combined foe to God and man, that shall wage so fierce and exterminating a war against the saints, shall, in *form*, be either *Pagan*, *Mohammedan*, or *Papal*. It may, in name and dress, be altogether another thing; yet it shall possess the *spirit* of the Dragon, the Beast and the False Prophet. Its spirit shall be a disgusting compound of the abominations of Idolatry, of the bigotry and blasphemy of the Papacy, and the delusion, the cruelty and haughtiness of Mohammedanism. It shall be literally an *antichristian* power—a grand confederacy against a pure Religion. However at variance they may be on other points they shall agree to unite all their powers, and put forth all their fury against the people of the Holy One. That this shall be altogether a conflict with carnal weapons I do not assert. No doubt it will be a spiritual warfare—a war of words and of principles, and opinions such as the world never yet witnessed, yet I see not what reason we have to believe it will *not* be a *war of nations and of blood.* There is every appearance of it both in the prophecy and in the present signs of the times.

The place of this great battle is said to be *Armageddon.* This is a place in or near the great plain of *Esdraelon*, not far from Mount Carmel. It had become proverbial as a place of blood and slaughter—more than a *Waterloo* of modern history—a place of *many* fights. It was the battle-ground of King Josiah against Pharaoh, King of Egypt—of Gideon with the Midianites—of

Saul with the Philistines—of Judas Maccabeus with Tryphon—and in later times, of the Tartars with the Saracens. Hence the term *Armageddon* is probably merely a proverbial expression for a great and bloody slaughter, in whatever part of the world it may be. I think, however, there is much which leads to the expectation that this great conflict will be in or near the Holy Land.

The 15th verse, which I omitted in the above quotation, contains an admonition to all, to be prepared for the great day of trial: "*Behold I come as a thief. Blessed is he that watcheth, and keepeth his garments, lest he walk naked, and they see his shame.*" He shall come as he did to vindicate his cause in the overthrow of Jerusalem, unexpectedly. He shall take the world by surprise. The language of warning, therefore, is, "WATCH, for ye know not in what hour the Son of man will come." Keep your lamps trimmed and burning, for He will come as a thief in the night.

Let us now turn for a moment to the *result* of this mighty combat. Nothing, as we have seen, can exceed the fierceness of wrath by which the aliens shall be urged on to the battle-field. They gnaw their tongues in their rage. They seem now determined to crush their long-hated tormentors and to cast their bonds from them forever. But they know not against whom they contend. The Lord of hosts, the God of armies is there; and, with all their power and their wrath, with all their vaunting and prowess, they are as chaff before the wind. Their overthrow is described in the pouring out of the next vial.

"And the seventh angel poured out his vial *into the air;* and there came a great voice out of heaven, from the throne, saying, *It is done.* And there were voices, and thunders, and lightnings; and there was a great earthquake, such as was not since men were on the face of the earth, so mighty an earthquake, and so great. And the great city was divided into three parts, and the cities of the nations fell; and great Babylon came in remembrance before God, to give unto her the cup of the wine of the fierceness of his wrath. And every island fled away, and the mountains were not found. And there fell upon men a great hail out of heaven, every stone about the weight of a talent; and men blasphemed God because of the plague of the hail; for the plague thereof was exceeding great."

Though highly figurative, yet nothing could be more awfully descriptive of an irrecoverable overthrow. The vial is poured out into *the air*—on the prince of the power of the air. It is aimed at the very principles and outbreakings of sin. It struck a *death-blow*. Angels saw it, and a song of triumph and of praise issued from the Temple above, saying, " *It is done;* " the great battle is fought and victory won. And this is echoed back to heaven by nature's spontaneous bursts of joy :—voices and thunderings and lightnings and a great earthquake. The mystic Babylon fell. It was a great commotion. " Every island fled away, and the mountains were not found." The whole earth shall be shaken in this mighty convulsion. A dominion of six thousand years shall now be domolished, and on its ruins be established the empire of the Messiah. Men, who shall " blaspheme God," shall still exist, yet they shall not, as now, sit on the high places of the earth. The leviathan shall then have a hook in his nose.

The seventeenth and eighteenth chapters are taken up in a more detailed account of the great slaughter and of the magnificent victory of the saints, together with the bitter lamentation of the wicked over the downfall of their great Babylon. The nineteenth chapter begins with a beautiful and sublime ascription of praise to Him who has avenged the cause of his elect—overthrown the powers of sin and hell and, as the Lamb of God, made ready the Bride for the marriage-supper. " And to her was granted that she should be arrayed in fine linen, clean and white, for the fine linen is the righteousness of the saints. And he said unto me, Write, Blessed are they which are called unto the marriage-supper of the Lamb."

The latter part of the nineteenth chapter seems but a prophetic description of the same great conflict which we have seen to be foretold in the sixteenth chapter. He that is called "Faithful and True," whose name is called "the Word of God"—and the ensign of whose authority is written on his vesture and on his thigh, KING OF KINGS AND LORD OF LORDS, whose eyes are a flaming fire, and on whose head are many crowns, and out of whose mouth proceedeth a sharp sword, he leadeth forth the hosts of heaven. While, at the same time, an angel summons the fowls of the air to come and feast on the flesh of kings, and on the flesh of captains, and the flesh of mighty men. So sudden, so signal and so complete should be the overthrow. And the kings of the earth, with their armies, headed by the beast, make war on him that sitteth on the white horse and on his army—and the result is that they were "cast alive into a lake of fire and brimstone." "And the remnant were slain with the sword of him that sitteth on the horse—which sword proceedeth out of his mouth: and all the fowls were filled with their flesh."

And here we must drop the curtain and leave this most awfully interesting scene. Christ has conquered; the Church is triumphant; the empire of sin is demolished; angels shout the victory; hell trembles; heaven rejoices.

It behooves us, then, seriously to reflect how puny, how unavailing is the rage of man. He may speak great swelling words and mouth the heavens, but his breath is in his nostrils—his arm is in a moment palsied. In vain does he contend with the Almighty. Men may combine their counsels and their might—nations may confederate and speak stout words against the God of heaven—

the heathen may rage, and the kings of the earth set themselves and the rulers take counsel together against the Lord and against his anointed—they may defy the majesty on high, and think to cast off his law; their attempts are but presumption and madness.

How solemn, then, to occupy, as we now do, a position where, either as a matter of history, present experience or of prophecy, we see the steady, the onward and the irresistible movements of Providence, accelerating as they advance, and drawing along with them events more and more momentous; and leaving behind them consequences more and more magnificent; and we ourselves associated with and expected to take a part in the affairs of a period like the present. What a responsibility rests upon us to live worthy our times!

CHAPTER XVI.

The Day of Vengeance and the Year of the Redeemed.

> " Ye princes, potentates, and men of war,
> And mitred heads, associate now yourselves,
> And be dispersed; embattle and be broken.
> Gird on your armor, and be dashed to dust.
> Take counsel, and it shall be brought to naught.
> Speak, and it shall not stand."

INCIDENTALLY having alluded to the fact that the sacred writers are wont to speak in the same connection, of the day of the Lord's vengeance on the wicked and the year of the redeemed, or the great and final deliverance of God's people, as contemporaneous events in close juxtaposition, it may seem proper to sustain this position by a reference to a few passages of Scripture. These will go to support the position we have assumed, viz., that the clearing away of the smoke of the great battle-field, shall reveal the dawn of the glorious Millennial morning. The sun of right-eousness shall arise upon the darkest cloud that ever brooded over the face of our sin-smitten earth. The great conflict shall be the dying struggle of the Dragon, the Beast, and the false Prophet. It shall shake terribly the earth, yet shall be the immediate pre-cursor, yea, the efficient agent to bring in that reign of righteous-ness of which we speak.

I shall call attention to a class of scriptures which describe as contemporaneous events the day of the Lord's vengeance, and the year of the redeemed. Of the many which might be adduced I shall select but a few.

The first description of the great battle which I shall cite is taken from the 34th chapter of Isaiah, summoning all the tribes and nations of the earth to come and behold what the Lord hath done.

" Come near, ye nations, to hear ; and hearken, ye people ; let the earth hear, and all that is therein ; the world and all things that come forth of it. For the indignation of the Lord is upon all nations, and his fury is upon all their armies ; he hath utterly destroyed them, he hath delivered them to the slaughter. Their slain also shall be cast out—the mountains shall be melted with their blood. And all the host of heaven shall be dissolved, and the heavens shall be rolled together as a scroll ; and all their host shall fall down, as the leaf falleth off from the vine, and as a falling fig from the fig-tree. For my sword shall be bathed in heaven ; behold, it shall come down upon Idumea, and upon the people of my curse, to judgment. The sword of the Lord is filled with blood ; for the Lord hath a sacrifice in Bozrah, and a great slaughter in the land of Idumea. For it is the day of the Lord's *vengeance, and the year of recompenses for the controversy of Zion.*"

What we would have more especially noted here is, that the dreadful conflict described above, and which we verily believe is at hand, is a conflict which, while it shall bring disaster and in-evitable defeat on the aliens, shall end in the triumphant deliv-erance and the final enlargement of the Saints of the Most High God.

Edom or Idumea, the land of Edom, is used in the passage cited, as the prophets are wont to use it, to denote the enemies of Zion, or the true Church. Being an ancient, prominent, and inveterate enemy of Israel, it is taken as a representative of Zion's enemies in all after-ages. In its general import it does not seem to differ greatly from that of Gog and Magog. In modern phrase, both may be taken to represent the great modern antichrist, which, after having stood as the enemy of the Church from generation to generation, shall, in some more concentrated form, and in the spirit of a more confirmed and inveterate hostility, make war with the saints of the Most High, and overcome and kill them. Bozrah was the chief city of Edom—the Rome of the ancient Church, and a living type of modern Rome.

But we should quite fail to discover the force of the Prophet's prediction: "My sword shall be bathed in heaven; behold it shall come down upon Idumea and upon the people of my curse, to judgment; the sword of the Lord is filled with blood—the Lord hath a sacrifice in Bozrah," unless we admit that the prediction, in its principal and final import, remains to be fulfilled in the coming conflict with the modern Edom, the Antichrist of the present day.

But lest the reader should think the attempt to identify Edom and antichristian Rome, fanciful or far-fetched, we may remind him that history has identified the two in a manner he may not be aware. What we have intimated is that the terms Esau, Edom, Idumea, representing as they did the ancient enemies of the Church, have, in prophetic language, descended to us as the representatives of the modern foes of Zion. Yet more than this is true. There is a historical connection of some interest here. Rome was founded by the Trojans; Troy by the Tyrians; Tyre by the Edomites, and some historical records claim a yet more direct lineage of Rome from Edom; viz., that the earliest colonists of Rome were actually *Edomites*. And others think they discover veritable marks of consanguinity between Papal Rome and Edom, not the less significant or interesting, making one a type of the other.   Esau or Edom means *red*.   Rome is delineated in prophecy, and largely characterized in all history as a woman arrayed in *scarlet*—as a woman on a scarlet beast—and she is denominated a great city clothed in *scarlet*.   Rome is Edom—Red—the scarlet city.   And it is upon this Idumea, this land of Edom, that the unsheathed sword of the Lord, bathed in blood, shall come down, and dreadful shall be the sacrifice upon the altar of the Divine displeasure when he shall arise to be avenged on his enemies.

But this " day of vengeance " shall be the " year of recompense for the controversy of Zion."   The Lord shall interpose when the foe shall appear the mightiest and the most boastful; and " great shall be the slaughter."

Did the above view need verifying we might call to our aid another vision of the same prophet.   The 63d chapter of Isaiah represents a terrible conflict and a dreadful slaughter of formidable enemies; and the period at which this occurs is characterized as the time when the " year of the redeemed is come."   The description is that of a warrior returning from an awfully destructive battle.   " Who is this that cometh from Edom, with dyed garments from Bozrah? this that is glorious in his apparel, traveling in the greatness of his strength?   I that speak in righteousness, mighty to save.

" Wherefore art thou red in thine apparel, and thy garments like one that treadeth the wine-fat?

" I have trodden the wine-press alone, and of the people there was none with me; for I will tread them in mine anger, and trample them in my fury; and their blood shall be sprinkled upon my garments, and I will stain all my raiment.   For the day of vengeance is in my heart, and the year of my redeemed is come."   " And I will tread down the people in mine anger, and make them drunk in my fury, and I will bring down their strength to the earth."

It is the day of the Lord's vengeance—a day of dreadful slaughter—of unparalleled carnage, yet the day of deliverance to God's people—the usherer in of the "year of the redeemed." Then follows a state of quietness, peace, and blessedness, which puts into the mouth of every saint the song of triumphant praise: "I will mention the loving-kindnesses of the Lord, and the praises of the Lord, according to all that the Lord hath bestowed upon us; and the great goodness towards the house of Israel, which he hath bestowed on them according to his mercies, and according to the multitude of his loving-kindnesses."

In view of such a triumphant deliverance, the evangelical prophet elsewhere utters the same voice of hope and encouragement: "Strengthen ye the weak hands, and confirm the feeble knees. Say to them that be of a fearful heart, Be strong, fear not: behold your God will come with vengeance, even God with a recompense; he will come and save you." Then follows the happy time which prophets and kings have desired to see: "The eyes of the blind shall be opened, and the ears of the deaf shall be unstopped. Then shall the lame man leap like the hart, and the tougue of the dumb sing. For in the wilderness shall waters break out, and streams in the desert." The same Mighty One, who shall come in vengeance on his enemies, shall come with a recompense to save all, and to be honored in all whose names are written on the palms of his hands.

Again, in that great and notable day of the Lord, the day of sore consternation and rebuke, when the Lord shall arise to shake terribly the earth and to be avenged on his foes, he utters to his people the warning voice: "Flee out of the midst of Babylon and deliver every man his soul: be not cut off in her iniquity; for this is the time of the Lord's vengeance." But Zion shall not be forsaken of her God. "He will render unto her a recompense."

And since I have taken in hand to cite a few of the passages which sustain the position assumed, I will adduce a few corroborative passages from the New Testament.

In the 21st chapter of Luke, the same idea is not the less distinctly announced. The evangelist alludes to the commotions and afflictions which shall precede and accompany the last great conflict. There shall be "wars and commotions; for these things must first come to pass." Nation shall rise against nation, and kingdom against kingdom, and great earthquakes shall be in diverse places, and famines, pestilences; and fearful sights and great signs shall there be from heaven. They shall lay their hands on you and persecute you. There shall be great distress in the land and wrath upon the people. And then shall there be "signs in the sun and in the moon, and in the stars; and upon the earth distress of nations, with perplexity: the sea and the waves roaring; men's hearts failing them for fear, and for looking after those things which are coming on the earth; for the powers of heaven shall be shaken."

These strong figures, describing as they do a most appalling series of events which accompany a great and general conflict, had, no doubt, a primary though not principal or final fulfilment when our Lord came to be avenged on and to destroy Jerusalem, and the people who had by wicked hands crucified and slain the Lord of life, and to give enlargement to his Church. The great conflict of that eventful period was but a type of the one of which we speak. This shall be the signal and final overthrow of the powers of darkness; and the great and final victory of the saints. The sun of that glorious morning—the morning of the "latterday glory," shall arise out of, and shall scatter that cloud of "blood and fire, and vapor of smoke," with which the last great battle shall envelop the earth. Or, as the evangelist has it: "When these things begin to come to pass, then look up, and lift up your heads, for your *redemption* draweth nigh." "When ye see these things," these dire calamities, these scathing judgments "come to pass, know ye that the kingdom of God is at hand."

We cannot look abroad over the face of the earth and behold the commotions which at the present moment disturb the nations—the wars and rumors of wars—the popular outbreaks of political furor—the internal smoulderings of suppressed liberty—the explosions of anarchy and usurpation—the ebullitions of insubordination and discontent, and more than all, the illy-suppressed and the irrepressible rage of a half-suppressed infidelity and the ominous festerings of public corruption and wickedness, and suppress our most serious apprehensions that "that great and notable day of the Lord" hastens on apace: a day as great and notable for the deliverance and enlargement it shall bring to the saints of the Most High God, as for the disaster and overthrow it shall inflict on their enemies.

The appearance or revelation of our Lord Jesus Christ, spoken of by Paul in his second epistle to the Thessalonians, teaches the same thing. And it matters not here if it be claimed that this passage refers more particularly to our Lord's second coming to judge the world. The coming of which we speak is at least typical of that second coming; and the general design and results of the two comings are the same, viz., to vindicate himself, to take vengeance on his enemies, and to accept, honor and bless his friends: "The Lord Jesus shall be revealed from heaven with his mighty angels, in flaming fire taking vengeance on them that know not God, and obey not the gospel of our Lord Jesus Christ—and to be glorified in his saints, and to be admired in all them that believe."

"Christ's coming," whether taken in the higher sense, or in some subordinate acceptation of the term, is a period of righteous discrimination between the wicked and the righteous, exalting the one and humbling if not overwhelming the other.

Another of these characteristic passages which describe the coincidence in question, occurs in the eleventh chapter of the Revelation. The Beast that ascendeth out of the bottomless pit makes war against the saints, overcomes them, and kills them. So completely prostrate do they seem to be that their bodies lie dead and unburied three days and a half in the streets of the spiritual Sodom, in contempt, and triumphed over by the victorious foe. Then follow a series of judgments—and then a most remarkable resuscitation, vindication and exaltation of the prostrate saints, and the most unexpected and complete overthrow of their enemies. The seventh angel sounds—the last great woe is inflicted—and the Revelator, without stopping to detail its awful contents, hastens to tell us of the grand consummation; the result educed by the Divine Hand from that terrific event. It is that "The kingdoms of this world are become the kingdom of our Lord, and of his Christ; and he shall reign forever and ever." The four and twenty elders (representatives of the Church) fall on their faces and worship God, praising him for his judgments and his mercies, "who is, and was, and is to come, the Almighty;" and that he has taken to himself his great power and established his reign on the earth. And having seen the temple of God established among men, in which is "the ark of the testimony"—the New Jerusalem come down from heaven, they revert again, that the contrast may appear more marked and the mighty hand of God more visible, to the tumultuous condition of the world at the time of the introduction of this blessed period—to the "lightnings, and voices, and thundering, and earthquakes, and great hail," which were employed and overruled to the bringing in of this better condition of the world: "And the nations were angry, and thy wrath is come, . . . that thou shouldest give reward unto thy servants the prophets, and to the saints, and to them that fear thy name, small and great; and shouldest destroy them which destroy the earth."

The great and notable events which shall prove so disastrous and overwhelming to the one party, shall be joy and righteousness and final redemption to the other.

But we need not perhaps pursue our subject further in this direction. Yet we may, partly by the way of recapitulation and confirmation, and partly for the sake of additional thoughts on the same general subject, ask attention to two other somewhat extended descriptions of the last great conflict. The one we meet in the prophecy of Joel, and the other in that of Zephaniah. The first is announced by the sound of a trumpet and the marshaling of warlike hosts, such as "hath not been ever the like, neither shall be any more after it, even to the years of many generations." The description is contained in the second and third chapters. We need not quote the whole, yet our quotations may exceed our usual limit.

The first quotations which I shall make (from chapter second), seem to describe the shaking and commotions, the wars and rumors of wars, which precede and prepare for, the great and decisive battle—in connection with which, and commotions going on at the same time and often favored by them, is the diffusion of the gospel, the extraordinary outpouring of the Spirit, and the revival and extension of a pure religion—the conversion of all nations to God. That is, the *taking out* of all nations a people to serve God—the bringing in of the " fulness of the Gentiles." The prophet announces the approach of the stirring events of the latter days, thus:

" Blow ye the trumpet in Zion, and sound the alarm in my holy mountain ; let all the inhabitants of the land tremble: for the day of the Lord cometh, for it is nigh at hand: a day of darkness and of gloominess, a day of clouds and thick darkness, as the morning spread upon the mountains; a great people and a strong; there hath not been ever the like, neither shall be any more after it, even to the years of many generations. A fire devoureth before them, and behind them a flame burneth: the land is as the garden of Eden before them, and behind them a desolate wilderness; yea, and nothing shall escape them." "The earth shall quake before them; the heavens shall tremble; the sun and the moon shall be dark, and the stars shall withdraw their shining."

Such is a description of the formidable martial forces that shall be rallied at the period under review; and of the unprecedented commotions and slaughter which shall follow. "Nation shall rise against nation, and kingdom against kingdom: and there shall be famines, and pestilences, and earthquakes in diverse places." And "all these are" but the "beginning of sorrows." They are not the Great Battle, but preliminary and preparatory to it. They are the rallying and the adjusting of forces, and the natural collisions into which the warring elements or strife are, in the nature of the case, brought. And of the same general character are the *moral* convulsions of that period—the persecutions, treacheries, betrayals one of another, apostasies, and the singular abounding of iniquity. These do but correspond with the *civil* commotions that shall then agitate the world. And both these series of terrific agencies that shall shake terribly the earth, are controlled by the Omnipotent Hand. They are the dread agents of Heaven which shall bring a sure and gradual yet a complete and final destruction on the wicked; and the happy emancipation and the final beatification of the righteous. Hence it is announced of the King the Lord of Hosts: "The Lord shall utter his voice before his army; for his camp is very great: for he is strong that executeth his word: for the day of the Lord is great and very terrible; and who can abide it?"

And in connection with this, and in strange contrast, the gospel is preached and great multitudes out of all nations are converted. And as things wax warm—as the two series of antagonistic agencies gather strength and wax valiant, and become more and more aggressive, uncompromising and determined on conquest, the great and final conflict is hastened on apace. Yet before this, and while the opposing powers of the aliens are rallying yet more strongly and becoming more bold and vaunting, the rival powers of truth and righteousness are rising and entrenching themselves more and more firmly in the strongholds of the sanctified hearts of God's people. The Spirit is now poured out upon all flesh. Religion is now signally revived. Great numbers are now gathered into the fold. The graces of God's people are quickened—their energies for useful activity are roused. Whosoever now "heareth," says to his brother, "come." New agencies for usefulness are created, and old ones are quickened. "Your sons and your daughters shall prophesy, your old men shall dream dreams, and your young men shall see visions: and also upon the servants and upon the handmaids in those days will I pour out my Spirit." All classes, old and young—men in all positions of life, shall, each in his own sphere and according to the measure of his grace and gifts, become witness for his Lord, and a living teacher of righteousness and the way of peace.

And wonderful in that day shall be the *power of prayer*. All may then prove the Lord that there is "deliverance in Zion." For now "whosoever shall call on the name of the Lord shall be delivered."

Very appropriately is there interposed here an exhortation to the Church that she be fortified to meet the *trials* that await her, and be prepared to receive the unwonted *blessings* in store for her, and to do the *duties* which the times and the privileges of the times devolve upon her.   First of all they must turn—repent—return to duty.   But how shall they turn?—with what temper of mind? Their repentance must be sincere and hearty. "Turn ye to me with your whole heart, and with fasting and weeping and mourning.   And rend your heart and not your garments."   And this is with the assurance that if they repent and turn and do their first works, they shall be accepted: " for he is gracious and merciful, slow to anger, and of great kindness, and repenteth him of the evil."   Hence the Church is directed to humble herself before her God—" to sanctify a fast, to call a solemn assembly, to assemble priests and people—to weep between the porch and the altar—to pray, " Spare thy people, O Lord, and give not thine heritage to reproach, that the heathen should rule over them: wherefore should they say among the people, Where is their God? "

And what *encouragements* have the children of God, that if, in these troublous times, in these times of apathy and rebuke, they hold fast their integrity, and turn with full purpose of heart to the Lord, and challenge the fulfilment of the great and precious promises of a living interest at the throne of grace—the full realization of the actual power of prayer—followed up and clothed with power by a holy activity and an acting faith which makes religion a mighty, living reality—what encouragements, I say, are here held out that the children of God shall find these very untoward circumstances to be preparing them to realize a security and prosperity, a spiritual plenty and unfailing stability never before enjoyed?   These are (vs. 18, 27) shadowed forth in temporal blessings, but not the less on this account real in their possession. " Ye shall eat in plenty and be satisfied, and praise the name of the Lord your God, that hath dealt wondrously with you, and my people shall never be ashamed."

And then shall follow the glorious period predicted, an earnest of which was experienced under Peter's preaching at Pentecost, the grand consummation of the earthy state of the Church. Through the dark cloud of that eventful day—"the wonders in heaven and in earth, the blood, fire and pillars of smoke," the darkening of the sun and the moon turned into blood, as preliminary to the coming of the "great and terrible day of the Lord"—the glorious sun of righteousness shall arise and shine. "And then shall follow the wonderful outpouring of the Spirit upon all flesh;" of which I have spoken.

Two features of our present times seem to be furnishing a fulfilment of the above quoted prophecies. The first is the extraordinary *military preparations* of the present day, together with the occasional terrible outbreaks of war; and the other is the no less extraordinary outpouring of the Spirit, and the extensive and powerful Revivals of Religion of the present time.

Never were the states of Europe so much on the alert in preparing all the defenses and munitions of war. France, England, Austria and Russia, they scarcely know why, are creating a material for offensive and defensive warfare never before known. Skill, ingenuity, science in its present advanced state, is now singularly made to contribute to the perfection of the art of war. Other European states are following on in the same course; and America is not a stranger to that "distress of nations, with perplexity, the sea and the waves roaring," which has led the nations of Europe to arm and fortify themselves against some apprehended danger. Men's hearts fail them for fear of the things that are coming. And what these things may be we seem to have some fearful foreboding in the late outbreak of violence and insurrection in India; in the carnage and slaughter about the walls of Sebastapool; and the unparalleled bloodshed at Montebello, Magenta, and Solferino.

And in happy contrast to this the Spirit is poured out from on high, and Revivals of Religion, unsurpassed for power, extent and frequency, have blessed Zion in all lands.   In America, in Ireland, Scotland, and portions of England; in Sweden, France, and in various localities where Rome bears rule, and where the Crescent wanes; and where Idolatry still has its shrines, the ever blessed Spirit has come down in unwonted effusion, and great numbers of all callings and conditions, have turned unto the Lord. The ranks of business have been happily invaded; the walks of learning and the halls of science, and the whole arena of common life, have been pervaded by those blessed influences.   The abundance of the sea has been converted to God, and the forces of the Gentiles, as never before, have been brought in.

I shall refer to but one other of these characteristic sketches from the Prophets.   It is from the first chapter of Zephaniah. And there is perhaps nowhere else a more graphic, vivid and terrible description of the great and terrible day of the Lord for which we look.   One will scarcely fail to notice a great similarity of the terms used by this Prophet, and those used by the other writers who have described the same scenes.   He says, "The great day of the Lord is near, it is near, and hasteth greatly, even the voice of the day of the Lord; the mighty man shall cry out bitterly.   That day is a day of wrath, a day of trouble and distress, a day of wasteness and desolation, a day of darkness and gloominess, a day of clouds and thick darkness, a day of the trumpet and alarm against the fenced cities, and against the high towers. And I will bring distress upon men, that they shall walk like blind men, because they have sinned against the Lord; and their blood shall be poured out as dust, and their flesh as the dung. Neither their silver nor their gold shall be able to deliver them in the day of the Lord's wrath; but the whole land shall be devoured by the fire of his jealousy: for he shall make even a speedy riddance of all them that dwell in the land."

Then follows an exhortation, not unlike what is common with the prophets—an exhortation to repentance and a sincere return unto the Lord; if, peradventure, they may escape in that great and terrible day. "Seek ye the Lord, all ye meek of the earth, which have wrought his judgment; seek righteousness, seek meekness: *it may be ye shall be hid in the day of the Lord's anger.*"

The prophecy last quoted and the exhortation which follows doubtless has its primary and partial fulfilment in the general destruction of Judah and Jerusalem by the Chaldeans. But the similarity of the language and the thoughts, to those used to describe the destruction of Jerusalem at a much latter date—which latter description, it is generally conceded, is applied to describe the last conflict and destruction at the end of the world or the dispensation—seems to warrant the application we have made of it here.

We need only add, that already have we more than sustained our general position, that the final and glorious establishment of the reign of truth and righteousness in our world shall be preceded by a great "falling away"—that the prevalence of universal Peace shall come through grievous wars, and a great and final conflict—that Immanuel's reign on the earth shall be established in troublous times. The Sun of righteousness shall arise through clouds and darkness. Thunderings and lightnings, earthquakes and storms, shall attend the advent of that kingdom of Peace and righteousness which shall ere long bless the earth.

The conflict is ended; Christ has conquered. Great Babylon has fallen; her ruin is complete. "A mighty angel took up a stone like a great millstone and cast it into the sea, saying, Thus with violence shall that great city Babylon be thrown down, and shall be found no more at all." "And after these things I heard a great voice of much people in heaven, saying, Alleluia; salvation, and glory, and honor, and power, unto the Lord our God; for true and righteous are his judgments : for he hath judged the great whore, which did corrupt the earth with her fornication, and hath avenged the blood of his servants at her hand. And again they said, Alleluia, and the smoke rose up for ever and ever. And a voice came out of the throne, saying, Praise our God, all ye his servants, and ye that fear him, both small and great. And I heard as it were the voice of a great multitude, as the voice of many waters, and as the voice of mighty thunderings, saying, Alleluia ; for the Lord God omnipotent reigneth. Let us be glad and give honor to him, for the marriage of the Lamb is come, and his wife hath made herself ready. And to her was granted that she should be arrayed in fine linen, clean and white : for the fine linen is the righteousness of the saints. And he saith unto me, Write, Blessed are they which are called to the marriage-supper of the Lamb. And he saith unto me, THESE ARE THE TRUE SAYINGS OF GOD."

CHAPTER XVII.

I HAVE selected this chapter for the sake of considering, in the connection we find them, certain great events which we look for as future, and probably not distantly future, and which are the great events of prophecy. The chapter is a very extraordinary one. It clusters together, in the space of a few short paragraphs, a series of events of the most thrilling interest; events which seem hastening on apace. The wise will discern the signs of the times and prepare for the great and final consummation.

It is good to stir up our minds to greater diligence in the work of our Divine Master. If he is shortening the time and hastening his work, it behooves his people, as co-workers with him, to set their hearts to the work with a renewed diligence; to pray more earnestly, to give more liberally, and work more circumspectly, provoking one another to love and good works; and so much the more as ye see the day approaching.

I shall speak of these events in the order in which they here occur. And I shall speak of them as *future*. Whatever partial fulfilments they may have had, we feel shut up to the conclusion that the whole, at least in their principal and final fulfilment, are future.

(272)

I. The great Battle which shall precede and usher in the empire of peace and righteousness which shall follow. "Behold, the day of the Lord cometh, and thy spoil shall be divided in the midst of thee. For I will gather all nations against Jerusalem to battle ; and the city shall be taken, and the houses rifled, and the women ravished; and half of the city shall go forth into captivity, and the residue of the people shall not be cut off from the city. Then shall the Lord go forth, and fight against those nations, as when he fought in the day of battle."

We shall not add here to what has already been said of the great and coming conflict. The Prophet would here seem to determine its *locality*, in the Holy Land, in the neighborhood of Jerusalem. It shall be a dreadful conflict, and a decisive one. The Lord shall appear, in his great power and by mighty judgments, to discomfit the foe and to give the victory to his people. By what providential arrangements the two great contending armies shall meet in that locality, and there decide the great question which has so long kept the world at strife, we do not know. The oracle is silent—or at least speaks not in language sufficiently distinct. It may be that the present movements of Russian agents in Palestine, are laying a trail which ere long shall set on fire the warring elements of the nations and hasten on the final conflict. Gog, and the people of Gog, are said to be there industriously negotiating for lands, and forming settlements which may become matters of jealousy with the nations of western Europe, and lead to the concentration of hostile armies, and a final conflict in a land which has hitherto often been the "valley of Decision" to the nations of the earth. We wait the utterances of future events; when all shall be made plain and easy.*

* I have already quoted Dr. Macgowan, a resident at Jerusalem, as touching the extraordinary change which has already come over the Holy City, it having become the

18

Whether there are, as we believe, good reasons for assigning such a locality to the Great Battle, there seems no lack of allusions and declarations in the divine predictions, which imply that Jerusalem and the Holy Land are destined to occupy a position and to enjoy a prominence in the coming golden age of the world, the glory of which shall surpass any thing the world has yet seen.   Hence the next event alluded to in the chapter, viz.:

II.   The coming of the King to vindicate his friends, to decide the combat, and take vengeance on his foes.   "Then shall the Lord go forth, and fight against those nations, as when he fought in the day of battle."   The King does not come to the rescue till Jerusalem is environed with the armies of the aliens, and the "city is taken, and the houses rifled, and the women ravished; and half the city gone into captivity"—not till the encounter becomes desperate—not till their strength is clear gone, and from the depths of their helplessness they cry for succor.

What shall be the mode of this dreadful manifestation we do not profess to define.   Judgments, pestilence and disease are at his command, and he wields them as he will.   He may, as he did before the vaunting army of Sennacherib, pass before them as the angel of death; then an hundred and four score thousand were in a moment prostrated in death.   He has only to "breathe in the face of the foe as they pass," and they are no more.

Awful, indeed, are the visions the prophets had of this great and final conflict.   We will cite but a single one.   It is the vision of the son of Amoz.   He summons the world to come and see

resort of the wealthy and the great ones of the earth, and magnificent buildings being erected.   A correspondent from Syria, too, says:

"Jerusalem has been making rapid strides of late towards a new-born civilization, and its progress has been watched with interest the most intense, on the part of those who associate with the name of the Holy City ideas of the Millennium and the speedy return of the Jews.   Large buildings, convents, hospitals, and churches are rising in every direction, and thousands of Russian employees and Jews are becoming residents of the place."

what desolations the Lord hath made in the earth : " Come near, ye nations, to hear; and hearken, ye people; let the earth hear, and all that is therein; the world, and all that come forth of it. For the indignation of the Lord is upon all nations, and his fury upon all their armies; he hath utterly destroyed them, he hath delivered them to the sláughter. Their slain also shall be cast out—and the mountains shall be melted with their blood. My sword shall be bathed in blood; behold, it shall come down upon Idumea, and upon the people of my curse, to judgment. The sword of the Lord is filled with blood; it is made fat with fatness; for the Lord hath a sacrifice in Bozrah, and a great slaughter in Idumea. For it is the day of the Lord's vengeance, and the year of recompense for Zion." " For behold, the Lord cometh out of his place to punish the inhabitants of the earth for their iniquity; the earth also shall disclose her blood, and shall no more cover her slain."

III. There is something yet more remarkable in regard to the *manner* of the coming of the Prince, the Lord of hosts; and not only in the deliverance already wrought, but in the singular provision here made for the immediate protection of his beleaguered people. "His feet shall stand on the mount of Olives." Whether this be literal or highly figurative I am not sure. In either case it indicates an extraordinary if not a personal *manifestation* of Christ, for the discomfiture of his enemies, and the reassurance and triumph of his friends. The *place*—overlooking Jerusalem, the arena of the great and dreadful contest, and the spot where his feet last trod as he left the scene of his former conflict and ascended on high—and the extraordinary *physical change* which now takes place in leveling this mountain and producing a great plain, cannot fail to invest the whole scene with a singular significance and sublimity. " The mount of Olives shall cleave in the midst thereof towards the east and towards the west, there shall be a very great valley; and half of the mountain shall remove towards the north, and half towards the south."

By some extraordinary means or supernatural agency, this mountain was cleaved asunder and removed out of its place, and turned into a great plain; and this for the more immediate purpose, it would seem, of affording an asylum and protection to the people of God. For it is added, "ye shall flee to the valley of the mountains." They shall flee to this retreat as men flee from the desolations of an earthquake. Possibly this is to be understood as representing a refuge to which the women, children and the mass of the people shall seek, as an asylum in that day of dreadful carnage.

IV. We have the introduction of the new order of things which shall follow the triumph of the Church—what it shall be —and what relation Jerusalem, and the Holy Land, and the natural descendants of Abraham, shall hold to this new kingdom.

1. The "latter-day glory" shall not be "ushered in," as many seem to suppose, as if the fully risen sun should in an instant break in upon the midnight darkness. It shall come as the morning— shall have its dawn and twilight. In its incipient stages it shall exhibit no doubtful marks of the moral splendor which shall characterize that blessed period; yet that brightness shall be partially obscured. Clouds, generated from the putrid waters of bygone ages, and still partially surcharged with the miasma of the old corruption, shall, for a little time, mar the beauty of the new heavens. Yet by and by these lingering mists shall pass away, and the unobstructed, free-orbed Sun of Righteousness shall arise with unrestricted healing in his beams.

The description we have here, of this intermediate or twilight period, is worthy remark. As the "fire and hail and vapor of smoke," produced by the great battle, clears away, the eventful morning is thus described: "And it shall come to pass in that day, that the light shall not be clear, nor dark, but it shall be one day which shall be known to the Lord, not day, nor night: but it shall come to pass, that *at evening-time it shall be light.*" This mixed, transition period shall not be long; and the close—the evening of this short intermediate day, shall be an unobscured brightness. Its sun shall not set, but shall seem to be lost in the greater effulgence of the fully risen Millennial day.

2. We notice what is here said of some of the characteristics of this glorious period when it shall be fully revealed. The figure is now changed. The symbol is no longer *light*, but *water*, or the fertilizing streams: The great moral transformation we have seen effected—the regimé established—the kingdom of God, the reign of righteousness, begun. And now we are told what are some of its characteristics. But two are specified. These, however, are very comprehensive. The one relates to the *blessings* of that heaven-favored era; and the other, to the *universality* and *unity* of this coming kingdom, as under the supreme kingship of the Lord Jesus Christ—Jerusalem, the centre of all authority, and the grand fountain of divine influences for the rest, peace, and purification of all nations.

The blessings are represented by "*Living waters going out from Jerusalem; half of them towards the former sea, and half of them towards the hinder sea: in summer and in winter shall it be.*" These are the waters which Ezekiel saw "issue out from under the threshold of the house eastward"—deepening and widening as they go, carrying health and fertility in all their course. Trees of life grow on either side, yielding their fruit every month, and their leaves are for the healing of the nations. "Whithersoever the river cometh every thing shall live." These are, wherever they flow, the waters of life — the life-giving waters. John the Revelator, in describing the same thing, says: "And he showed me a pure river of water of life, clear as crystal, proceeding out of the throne of God and of the Lamb. In the midst of the street of it, and on either side of the river, was there the tree of life, which bear twelve manner of fruits."

The same waters which John saw proceed out of the *throne* of God and the Lamb, Ezekiel saw issue out from under the *threshold* of the eastern gate of the Temple. Zechariah saw the same "go out from Jerusalem." Joel saw the same living fountain "come forth of the house of the Lord, and water the whole valley of Shittim."* These are "the rivers of Judah," which flow down from the hills of salvation. "The mountains shall drop down new wine, and the hills flow with milk;" all beautifully descriptive of the living waters which flow out from the great Fountain of the Divine Beneficence.

The three grand periods in the history of Redemption are here described: viz., the Tabernacle or Wilderness state of the Church, the Temple or Millennial state, and the New Jerusalem or Heavenly state.

In the *first* of these periods, the living waters issue out from under the *threshold* of the house, and go down through the desert, and make all to live wherever they flow. And they pour their healing streams into the Dead Sea, and its stagnant, putrid waters are healed. It is the fountain that was open to the "house of David, and to the inhabitants of Jerusalem, for sin and for unclean-

---

* Shittim was a valley in the land of Moab (whose king was Balak), where the children of Israel a long time dwelt before they entered the Promised Land—where they fell into gross sin by committing whoredom with the daughters of Moab—where Balaam came to curse Israel, and went away blessing them—where Moses, having rehearsed the history of God's dealings with his people, and repeated, and re-enjoined upon them the law, went up into Mount Nebo and died—where Joshua received the command of the Lord's host, and thence led them into Caanan. It was to Israel an epitome of the world—where they had rejoiced, where they had suffered, where they had been humbled, where honored, where oppressed, where delivered. In relation to Israel, Shittim was an eminent spiritual desolation. Well, then, is it used here to represent the desert world over which should course the waters of life as they flow out from the Fountain open in Judah and Jerusalem.

ness." Wherever this river flows, trees of righteousness abound on its banks, green and ever laden with fruit. It is everywhere the signal of life, social, civil and religious. Industry, enterprise, thrift, give signs of coming prosperity. Mind is emancipated—thought set free, and urged on to the fulfilment of its mission in the work of human progress. Increase of knowledge, the pursuits of science, inventions, discoveries, commerce, a high type of civilization, all follow in their train. And more than all and better than all, civil freedom, a sterner morality, and a purer religion, are the statelier trees which flourish on the banks of these streams.

And this process of spiritual irrigation shall go on till this whole desert world shall become as the garden of the Lord—trees of righteousness shall everywhere flourish; "the wilderness and the solitary place shall be glad for them, and the desert shall rejoice and blossom as the rose. It shall blossom abundantly, and rejoice even with joy and singing." The River which Ezekiel saw issue out from beneath the threshold of the house, has widened, and deepened, and spread itself over the whole desert world, and now the kingdoms of this world have become the kingdoms of our Lord and of his Christ.

Here commences the *second* grand period. The Church is now emancipated—the usurper of the dominion of this world is vanquished—the rightful proprietor has "come to his own," and taken possession. The wilderness state is passed—the Jordan is crossed, and the Promised Land is entered—deliverance from the enemy and enlargement to the rightful heirs. Or, to resume our figure, living waters now go out from *Jerusalem*. "Out of Zion now goes forth the law and the word of the Lord from Jerusalem." And now it has come to pass that the Lord is King over all the earth: there is "one Lord, and his name one."

Already, in a subordinate sense and as prefiguring what at

the period in question is fully realized, " repentance and remission of sins had been preached among all nations, *beginning at Jerusalem*." From that appointed centre " the sound had gone out to the ends of the earth." And here too the Holy Spirit had come down, and entered on his Mission for the renovation of the world. Yet all this was but an earnest or pledge of what should be in the " last days." It was then *Siloam's brook* that ran fast by the oracles of God; but it is now the *River* that flows out from Jerusalem and bears on its current, to earth's remotest bounds, Heaven's richest boon to man.

From Jerusalem, the grand Repository of divine influences, the living waters go out toward the former, and to the hinder sea —*from sea to sea*—in one rich, unfailing current. " In winter and in summer they shall be." No summer's drought, no winter's cold can arrest or retard their generous flow. As the waters cover the sea, so shall the knowledge of God cover the whole earth.

But there remains another period in the dispensation of grace —or rather a period when grace shall be finished and glory be begun. It is the heavenly state; when " the pure river of water of life, clear as crystal, proceeds out of the throne of God and of the Lamb;" when from the grand metropolis of Heaven, the Mount Zion above, the throne of the Majesty on high, shall go forth the law, and all the thrones and dominions, the principalities and powers of the heavenly estate shall fall down and worship before him that sitteth on the throne and the Lamb for ever and ever. And a great multitude which no man can number, of all nations, and kindreds, and people, and tongues, shall stand before the throne, and before the Lamb, clothed in white robes, and palms in their hands; and they ascribe all honor and power, thanksgiving and praise unto him that loved us and washed us from our sins, in his own blood, and hath made us kings and priests unto God and his Father; to him be glory and dominion, forever and ever. Amen.

But there arises under this general head yet another inquiry: it is—

3. What relation shall Jerusalem, and the Holy Land, and the natural descendants of Abraham hold to the new kingdom? We have more than intimated that Jerusalem shall be the great religious metropolis of the world, the radiating point of divine influences—morally at least, the throne of the " King, the Lord of hosts," whom the nations shall " go up from year to year to worship."   As Jerusalem shall be the great battle-field, on which the last great decisive victory shall be won, so shall she become the great religious centre of the Millennial kingdom.   And, as might be expected, we have, in prophetic vision, certain intimations as to the dimensions and magnificence of the coming Jerusalem which demand attention.   Singular *changes* are intimated, both in relation to the present site of Jerusalem, and for several miles around.   We have seen one marvellous change effected in the cleaving asunder, and the removing to the north and the south of the Mount of Olives, and so forming a plain.   In like manner the Prophet says, " all the land shall be turned as a plain, from Geba to Rimmon, south of Jerusalem; and it shall be lifted up, and inhabited. . . . And men shall dwell in it, and there shall be no more utter destruction; but Jerusalem shall be safely inhabited."

Precisely what these changes shall be we may not conjecture. Most obviously the dimensions of the ancient city shall be extended beyond any former boundaries.   The whole of the Holy Land known as Judea, from Gibeah on the north to Rimmon on the south, a distance of several miles, shall be leveled and prepared for the purposes of building and a high order of cultivation, that it shall be, as it were, but one great, extended city, with its suburbs, over this large extent of country.   Whether these changes shall be effected by extraordinary or miraculous means, or simply by the skill and power of man, we cannot affirm. The way mountains are now made low and valleys exalted—the way man is already overcoming the most formidable natural obstacles, and harnessing to the chariot-wheels of human progress, some of the mightiest powers of nature, do but too plainly indicate the extent of any future changes we may anticipate.

The description before us indicates an extent and magnificence of the city, and a degree of security, comfort, elevation and general prosperity which the Millennial state at once presupposes. But the extent of the city, great as it is, does not seem improbable, when we take into the account the circumstances of the case. It shall be the great Metropolis—exceeding populous—and the spot above all others on the earth where the great and the good will choose the place of their habitation. Kings, princes, and the great ones of the earth will bring here their riches and their honors. In the vision of the Jerusalem of that day, the prophet saw the sons of strangers coming to build up her walls; and their kings to minister to her." "The Isles wait for her, and the ships of Tarshish first, to bring thy sons from far, their silver and their gold with them, unto the name of the Lord thy God, and to the Holy One of Israel, *because he hath glorified thee.*" It shall be the favorite resort of travelers, and a choice place of habitation, *because* God hath put such honor on Jerusalem and made it a delightsome place. A single, brief description indicates its extraordinary beauty and grandeur; "the glory of Lebanon shall be given to it, the fir-tree, the pine-tree, and the box together, to beautify the place of my sanctuary; and I will make the place of my feet glorious."

When we consider the exceeding populousness of the city, in connection with the wealth and taste, high civilization and the increased wants of the citizens, we shall not be surprised at the extent of ground covered by the city. The gardens, orchards, and ornamental grounds of a few, now occupy more space than thousands once did in their haunts of poverty and vice; in their dirt and degradation.

But the natural descendants of Abraham, what relation shall *they* hold to the new kingdom? Here we may not safely indulge in details. Restored again to the favor of their covenant God, and to the land given them for an everlasting possession, and to their position as the first-born of the Father, and to all the peculiar promises and privileges implied; and occupying, as they do, so advantageous a position as a central, metropolitan province of Immanuel's Empire on earth, the conjecture would seem safe that they will hold an honored, and a very prominent place in the new kingdom. This would seem but to correspond with the prominence assigned to them as *agents* in the work of bringing in this kingdom. "If," says Paul, "the casting away of them be the reconciling of the world"—if this were used as a leading, efficient agency in the early propagation of Christianity—"what shall the *receiving* of them be but *life from the dead?*" And we seem to have more than a hint of the future prominence of the ancient Seed in the visions of the Prophets. Isaiah speaks, but in clearer terms, the language of them all. When he sees the ancient Zion "rise" in her renewed splendor, and shine," because "her light is come, and the glory of the Lord is risen upon her," he saw the "Gentiles come to *her* light, and kings to the brightness of her rising." "Lift up thine eyes round about, and see; all they gather themselves together, they come to *thee*. . . Then thou shalt see, and flow together, and thy heart shall fear, and be enlarged; because the abundance of the sea shall be converted unto thee, the forces of the Gentiles shall come unto thee." And they shall come from Midian and Ephah, from Kedar and Leba (from different parts of Asia and Africa), and from the "Isles of the sea " (the present Europe and America) ; and they shall bring gold and incense, and they *shall show forth the praises of the Lord.*" The latter expression would seem to indicate the *object* of their gathering together, viz., the service of God, the worship of the King, the Lord of hosts : referring either to the occasional worship of the multitudes who, as representative worshippers, shall come up *from year to year* to worship the King and to keep the feasts of Tabernacles ; or to the more permanent religious services, and privileges which they shall enjoy who shall choose their habitations in or about the Holy City.

But I anticipate my next particular :

V. That the Gentiles shall largely participate with restored Israel in serving God at Jerusalem, as they shall, by their representatives, at least, come up year by year, to worship and to keep the feast of Tabernacles. "It shall come to pass that every one that is left of all the nations that come against Jerusalem, shall even go up from year to year to worship the King, the Lord of hosts, and to keep the feast of Tabernacles. And whoso will not come up unto Jerusalem to worship the King, the Lord of hosts, even upon them shall be no rain." A remnant of all those nations and great confederacies which fought at Jerusalem against the true Israel, shall be converted to Christ, and become the loyal subjects of the King. And the two great antichristian powers (the Roman and the Greek) being overcome and their regimé destroyed, the remnant that survive the slaughter, together with the Gentiles who shall be converted, shall go up from year to year to Jerusalem to worship the King, the Lord of hosts, and to keep the feast of Tabernacles.

Yet I do not understand that the whole body of believers in all parts of the world shall appear before the Lord to worship at Jerusalem at the time of this feast. But Jerusalem being the place where God has put his name, "the city of the Great King"

—"the city of Truth, the mountain of the Lord of hosts, the holy mountain"—"the joy of the whole earth," devout men of every nation will love to resort thither.   And when, as in the days of Millennial prosperity, opulence and leisure, men shall be abundantly able to travel, and when from the yet vastly increased facilities for locomotion and communication, and from the central position of Jerusalem, an excursion to the Holy City shall be both quick and easy, it is not difficult to believe that great multitudes will annually resort thither, drawn by the great natural, social, intellectual, and especially the religious attractions of the Holy City.   And ships of Tarshish, the Great Eastern, possibly, the first of the class, may convey them thither.

The idea here presented of a great religious centre in the days of earth's great blessedness, seems but a common dictate of natural religion—I would rather say a dictate of Divine Wisdom. Every great form of religion has had its centre.   As far back as history reaches, Jerusalem was such a centre.   Before Abraham was, Melchisedec brought his offerings, and worshipped at Salem. And yet earlier, Mount Moriah had been holy ground; and in all succeeding generations, Jerusalem has been the Holy City.   The Mohammedans have their Mecca, and the Papists their Rome. And in no one thing, perhaps, has the religious instinct of man more distinctly harmonized than in the idea of a religious centralization in some particular spot.

But here we need to say a word in relation to the Feast of Tabernacles.   Shall it be perpetuated? and why? and how?

This was the feast of ingathering, the annual thanksgiving occasion among the Jews, observed in commemoration of the sojourn of the Israelites in the wilderness.   It was typical of Christ dwelling in our nature—tabernacling in the flesh—and as such it was one of the most interesting and solemn feasts of the Jews.   It was at this feast that they expected the Messiah would appear   Hence the expression in the Psalm (118th) which was sung on this occasion: "Blessed is He that cometh in the name of the Lord." And Christ did in a special sense make his first public manifestation at the time of this feast.   He now entered Jerusalem in triumph, the multitude strewing branches of palm-trees in the way before him, and singing the triumphal song of that occasion, and applying to Him the words of the Psalmist: "Blessed is He that cometh in the name of the Lord; Hosanna in the highest."

What then can be more befitting the Church of Christ when she shall have received her King, and she shall appear in her glory, than the observance in all coming time of a festival which shall commemorate the incarnation of her Lord and his triumph and glorification in the redeeming work?   This shall be the great THANKSGIVING occasion of the CHURCH UNIVERSAL for the gift of that LIVING BREAD which came down from heaven.   And we can conceive of no possible occasion that might so properly and naturally draw out the universal feeling of the whole Church, and be such a bond of union to all, and to present motives strong enough to induce all men everywhere to assemble (representatively at least) in one place to observe such a festival; and we can see no place so suitable, or so probable as Jerusalem, the "city of the Great King," "the joy of the whole earth."

VI.   But the Prophet has not here overlooked the complete and dreadful overthrow, and the utter destruction of the finally incorrigible, especially of the army of the aliens, who fought against Jerusalem—i. e., all who in the last great Battle fought against the true Church—who acknowledge not the Messiah, and come not up to the Feast of Tabernacles: "And it shall be that whoso will not come up of all the families of the earth unto Jerusalem to worship the King, the Lord of hosts, even upon them shall be no rain."   "And this shall be the plague wherewith the Lord shall smite all the people that have fought against Jerusalem: their flesh shall consume away while they stand upon their feet, and their eyes shall consume away in their holes, and their tongue shall consume away in their mouth."

So complete and dreadful shall be the destruction of the wicked. When the time of visitation shall come, the Lord shall arise in his wrath and take vengeance on all that have lifted up the hand against him; and he shall destroy them with an utter destruction. But this, as has been shown, shall be the day of vindication, and recompense to the righteous.

VII. Then follows the consummation of the earthly condition of the Church. The earth, as by right, so now by allegiance, is the Lord's. He has come to his own, and his own has received him. All is now holiness to the Lord. Holiness is written on men's employments—it follows them through all the intercourse and all the avocations of life; chastens their pleasures; graces their conversation; and pervades all their dealings and associations of life. "Holiness unto the Lord shall be written upon the bells of the horses;" and on the "pots and the bowls of the Lord's house." Holiness unto the Lord shall be the order of every-day life in all its occurrences and avocations. The Temple is now finished— the earthly Zion is complete. Beautiful for situation, the joy of the earth, is Mount Zion, the city of the great King. God is known in her palaces for a refuge. Come, then, all ye nations from afar, come ye who are near, come all who would worship the King, the Lord of hosts, come, walk about Zion, and go round about her: tell the towers thereof. Mark ye well her bulwarks; consider her palaces.

But glorious as is the Tabernacle of God when thus pitched among men, this is not the final state of the Church. Jerusalem, the glory of the whole earth, shall have no glory by reason of the glory that excelleth. We look for another, and a better, whose Maker and Builder is God: the Mount Zion above, the city of the living God, the heavenly Jerusalem, the innumerable company of angels, the general assembly, and Church of the first-born that are written in heaven, and to God the Judge of all, and to the spirits of just men made perfect, and to Jesus, the mediator of the new covenant. And then shall our eyes behold the King in his beauty.

CHAPTER XVIII.

The argument from analogy—How is God wont to deal with his People;
and how with the Wicked?

THERE remains one other source of proof that a great conflict,
such as has never been known, shall precede the triumph of the
Church. It is an argument derived from *the analogy of the divine
economy,* or the ordinary mode of the divine working.

But before proceeding to the consideration of this argument,
we may just allude, at least, to some miscellaneous items which
have been slightly if at all discussed; and which we may in like
manner take as precursors of the coming of the promised era,
and as contributing no inconsiderable share to hasten on such a
period. Among these we may enumerate, progress in science
and all sorts of learning; progress in the arts; discoveries; inventions; the introduction and use of new substances, and, more
than all, the subsidizing in the service of human progress, new
forces and powers of nature; improvements in modes of locomotion and the means of communication and conveyance; progress
of liberty, both civil and religious, and in the science of government: and the recent remarkable increase of wealth, and the
conversion of seamen and men of business, as furnishing the substantial resources and agencies of commerce, and the means for

carrying out all those benevolent and philanthropic schemes befitting the age, and especially contributing to the speedy advent of

" The promised age of gold."

I had thought to make each of these topics a subject of separate consideration, and the whole the subject of a short chapter. But we must leave to the reflections of the intelligent reader the bearing of these things upon the coming of our Lord's kingdom. He will not fail to see that these things *have* a very important and direct bearing on our main question. They are agencies, facilities, conditions of the coming of that kingdom; and then they are the things which are preparing the people of God for the enjoyment of their Millennial age. That high order of civilization and elevated social and moral condition which shall then prevail—that populous and prosperous condition of the earth will require just that kind of advancement in the particulars above referred to, which we see now in so successful progress. But we need not go into details here, though such details would richly repay our researches.

In the prosecution of the subject of this chapter we may originate and answer two inquiries: the one, *How, in the carrying out of his purposes in the great scheme of redemption*, is God in the habit of dealing with his people? And the other, How is he wont to deal with the wicked?

In the adoption of any particular course of procedure towards his Church, God chiefly regards his own glory. This however is, in the result, but a regard for man's greatest good. As God is the source of all excellence, his exaltation on the throne of the universe, is the direct and effectual way of securing the good of his creatures. God, then, in his extreme jealousy for his honor (for the Lord our God is a jealous God), and in the undisputed supremacy which he claims over all his creatures, is chargeable with nothing which, in our dialect, is called *ambition*. He assumes nothing. He simply takes his own. And in doing this he pursues the most direct—the only direct course which can secure the happiness of his creatures. *Peace and good-will among men* can only exist where *glory in the highest* is ascribed to God. God's undisputed sovereignty and man's entire dependence and obedience are indispensable requisites to make a happy world or a happy universe.

These remarks, if just, give us some clew to the course of dealing which we may expect God will pursue towards his Church on earth. It shall be such as to leave unimpaired *his own glory.* He will not treat with man on any other conditions. He will in no case compromise his honor. Of this we have overwhelming and repeated proof in the brief history we have of God's dealings towards our world in respect to its redemption. An entire race had fallen and were now rebels in the divine government, and as such consigned over by the law to remediless woe. Not one of these could be redeemed—not one could be raised to heaven, till a full satisfaction had been made to the injured honor of God. There was the first breach to be repaired. Violence had been done to his government—his law had been trampled on, and not a step could be taken towards a reconciliation till a full satisfaction should be rendered to his violated honor. Hence the whole scheme of Redemption by Jesus Christ is such, from its foundation to its top-stone, as to exalt God and humble man. There is nothing about the gospel mode of salvation, either in its provision or its application, which does not give the whole glory to God. It is exclusively a plan of divine wisdom. It is carried on at every step by the divine hand; and its end is altogether a gratuity of the inexhaustible stores of the divine goodness. It is "grace for grace"—altogether of grace. Its song is "unto him that loved us and gave himself for us."

Consequently we find that, in accordance with such sentiments, is *God's mode of converting* and *sanctifying the sinner*, as well as his mode of dealing with his Church as a body.

The sinner is living in the galling bondage of spiritual death. He is bound fast in the adamantine chains of sin, and nothing this side of Omnipotence can break these chains and give the captive deliverance. But how is redemption brought to this captive soul? It might be done immediately—without any instrumentality—without the lapse of any time, or without any process of conviction, or any preliminary work whatever. The sinner might be converted in his sleep. The abstract power of God is sufficient to accomplish this. But this is not God's plan of working. Men have raised the standard of insurrection in God's empire, and first of all they must learn their folly and their guilt. Then they must be made to *feel* the wretchedness and ruin of their present condition. They must clearly see and deeply and distressingly feel that there is no help in themselves—none in man—none in any other but in God. And not till, like Peter, they feel themselves to be sinking and cry, " Lord, help or I perish ; " or like the returning prodigal they can say, from the most painful and heart-felt conviction, " I have sinned against heaven and in thy sight, and am no more worthy to be called thy son ; make me as one of thy hired servants ; " not till the soul has been brought to the very verge of despair, and their strength is clean gone and the last glimmering ray of hope seems about to go out forever, will they flee to Him who is the resurrection and the life. Now if favor be shown, it will be received *as favor*— as grace and not debt.

There is wisdom worthy of God in such an arrangement. The sinner is brought to see his own weakness; his own guilt; his own *ruin*, and withal, his own *dependence*. He *never can*—if he have really been brought into the deep and dark valley of genuine conviction of sin—he *never* can glory in any thing but in the cross of Christ. He will remember the wormwood and the gall, and confess, "it is of the Lord's mercies that we are not consumed." The one reason (if we were to give but one) why God raises the sinner from so low a depth, and sheds light into his soul in the midst of such thick darkness, is that his own arm may be made bare—that the Christian may begin his spiritual life with the conviction indelibly impressed—and never to be obliterated, that *God*, in the whole matter of his salvation, is *a Sovereign*—that God is the sole author of all his graces and of all his hopes, and that he is wholly and unreservedly dependent on God for the continuance of his graces and the consummation of all his hopes. Such a conviction, inwrought into the soul, will do more for the Christian's spiritual growth, and for his usefulness in his present bodily sphere of action, and for the perfection of his character for another state of being, than all other means of grace that can be used.

I have dwelt on this longer, because it is but analogous with God's whole course of dealing with his people. Whether in the natural world the proverb will hold I know not, but in the spiritual world it will, that "the darkest time is just before the dawn." Never was the Church of God more persecuted and afflicted, and cast down and trampled under foot, than when on the very eve of deliverance from Egyptian bondage. Every struggle they made only seemed to sink them lower in the deep waters of oppression. Every effort that was made for their emancipation seemed only to forge new manacles for the victims of thraldom, and to rivet their chains more closely than before. It was a dark day for the Church, and never did she seem so far from enlargement. But the day of her extremity was the day of her visitation from on high. Behind that dark cloud, which shut out from view the already risen light of the early dawn, the full-orbed light of day was about to rise.   Deliverance came in the darkest hour—and deliverance too in a manner to show both friends and foes that it was the finger of God.   All would now say, *his arm had gotten them the victory.*   It was for this that they were brought low and diminished and oppressed.   God would show his people where their strength lay—and this they would learn only when brought to see their own weakness.

And so it has generally been with the Church of God.   Her greatest triumphs have been immediately preceded by her darkest periods.   The waning of an old and decaying order of things, and the revolutions and convulsions incident to the introduction and establishment of a new dispensation, give to the general aspect of affairs the appearance of a mighty dissolution.   It is fearful to see the fountains of the great deep breaking up, and the mighty floods rolling over the earth, and the solid ground giving way, and no new earth on which you may place the sole of your foot. It was a dark period to Noah, when he looked abroad upon the wide expanse of waters, and saw the last summit of the sinking earth, sinking deeper and deeper into a watery grave.   But soon a new world arose, regenerated—washed from the sins of the old and made once more a fit abode for holiness.

And that was the darkest night of all when the body of Him, who was to be the bright and morning star, was entombed in the solid marble of the "new sepulchre."   No wonder that the heavens gathered blackness—that the sun was darkened.   In yonder sepulchre was entombed the *hope of the world.*   The rising star of Bethlehem, which had already begun to cast its light over the thick darkness of the nations, now seemed to sink again below its horizon, and no bow of promise gave signs that ere long it should rise again in redoubled splendor.   The rising hopes of saints were now in a moment prostrated.   Many had *trusted that it had been He who should have redeemed Israel,* but as the morning of the third day approached and all was still silent about the sepulchre—except as the stern sentinel of the Roman cohort, half determined by martial pride, half trembling for a fearful looking after those things that *may* come to pass, keeps his nightly watch and proudly walks his rounds about the spot where lay, bound in the icy chains of death, the hope of a hopeless world—how must the last ray of hope seem to be settling down into the dark abyss to emerge no more forever! How, to the faultering hopes of saints and disciples, must the flickering light of eternal life seem to be sinking into its socket, and the world seem bound over to the unbroken and universal dominion of spiritual darkness and hopeless death! How did this overpowering despondency which had seized on every anxious heart, find a response in the bursting grief of those female disciples who came early to the sepulchre: " *They have taken away our Lord, and we know not where they have laid him!* "

Never was there a darker hour. Hope lay dead and incased in the solid granite. Death had gotten the victory—the grave had the spoil, sin triumphed, and hell kept jubilee. But hark! I seem to hear a rumbling sound. The earth quakes—the rocks rend—the priests come rushing from the temple, and proclaim that the veil is rent asunder—the graves open, and their pallid inhabitants again walk forth among the abodes of men. And what does all this mean?

One company and then another company of women—and then one of the disciples, whose ecstasy in the tidings he brings, bears him apace before his brethren, come running back to the Holy City early on the morning of the first day of the week, and what strange tidings do they bring! They say—and who at this juncture of fell despondency can credit it—they say that *the Lord has risen indeed!* The gloomy night is passed. The morning of the Resurrection has come. The entombed hopes of his followers now burst forth into a glorious reality. Incased in that hopeless tomb was the germ of hope for a ruined world. On Calvary, in the very ignominy and agony of the cross, was done away one order of things and introduced another, which should bring life and immortality to light. It was the darkness, the dread, the *death* of that dismal period, which introduced the most illustrious period the Church ever witnessed. They not only preceded it, but were the very authors of it. The scene on Calvary was the great conflict. It was the hour and power of darkness. When the great Head of the Church was about to introduce a new and more glorious era of his grace, all the powers of the Pit were roused to smother the rising glory.

Hence the conflict of that period—and hence the conflict that precedes every principal step of *advancement* in God's dispensations of grace towards our world. It is not merely a thing, which, as a matter of *fact*, does precede a triumph, but which, as a matter of reason, should precede it.

It was so again only a few years after the ascension of our blessed Lord. All things were prepared for the diffusion of the gospel among the nations. The disciples had received the command —their number was sufficiently multiplied—the Holy Ghost had come upon them, and all things seemed ready for their mission. But they lingered, and at this very juncture the heavens over them gathered blackness—a deadly spirit of persecution broke out about Stephen, and the disciples were scattered abroad among distant provinces and nations; and wherever they were driven, they went preaching the word. It was to all human appearance a dark day. But it was a darkness that presaged a more glorious light than ever before had risen on this benighted world. And so it has been in God's ordinary dealings with his Church. He gives them enlargement by bringing them through a very narrow way. He gives them light by bringing them through a very dark valley. He gives them joy and rest and peace and glory, by first bringing them through the dust of humiliation, and oftentimes out of the furnace of affliction.

It has been well said that "the hour of preparation for a better order of things is *not a time of favorable appearances*, but the reverse; and that, nevertheless, at such a time, human affairs are actually tending towards the approaching change." While clouds and darkness settle down thick on the surface of events, and presage any thing but a favorable change, the undeveloped operations of an under-current are bearing away all obstacles before them, and preparing the way for some radical and momentous change.

We no doubt mistake in supposing we must look for the signs of the times in the quarter from which the light comes. We must look towards the dark quarter, where the clouds are lowering and the storm is brewing—look beyond the circle within which religion has reared her standard and morality shed her benign influence. We must look abroad upon the wide surface of spiritual desolation, if we would discern indications that some mighty convulsion is at hand, which shall break up the deep foundations of error and sin, and establish all things on a new and a better basis. We look towards the *illumined quarter* of the moral heavens, and we see the light gleaming up higher and brighter. The sun of righteousness is manifestly arising on the dark face of the waters. The Bible is making its way into the ranks of unbelief and idolatry—the gospel is preached—the messengers of truth go to and fro, and knowledge is increased; but *these* are not surer harbingers of a brighter day, than the swelling, heaving, boiling of the great ocean of moral darkness. "When the wicked are like the troubled sea which cannot rest, whose waters cast up mire and dirt—when there shall be signs in the sun, and in the moon, and in the stars, and upon the earth distress of nations, with perplexity, the sea and the waves roaring (great political convulsions), then may you know that some mighty conflict is at hand—some signal victory awaits the saints of the most high God. For the empire of sin will never yield without a conflict, and a conflict between sin and holiness will always enventuate in the overthrow of sin.

This, under the direction of a wise and gracious Providence, is the natural order of things. As the kingdom of light advances, the prince of the power of the air is alarmed for the safety of his empire. His anger becomes the more fierce and his efforts the more impetuous, as he sees the onward and irresistible advancement of that kingdom which shall fill the whole earth. While he supposes himself an equal combatant, he is comparatively at ease. But the moment he sees the victory going finally and forever against him, he will contend with all the desperation of an arch fiend. We are, therefore, to expect—indeed it is but analogous to the ordinary operations of the divine economy in conducting the affairs of his kingdom, that a mighty conflict will precede any very signal triumph of the Church.

There is on the part of God a wise and benevolent design that it should be so. He thus vindicates his own honor and makes manifest his own power. He shows to the Church and to the world that the strength of his people lies in the omnipotent arm. He teaches his people their *dependence*, and by this says to the wicked, " stand in awe and sin not," for He with whom you contend is God.

There are, then, the best of reasons for believing that God will not change his mode of conducting the august affairs of his government. What has been, shall be. If he has seen it wise to *prepare* his people for the successive onward developments of his grace and his glory in his earthly Zion, by bringing them into that state of humiliation and dependence—where they are prepared to understand the loving-kindness of their God, and to appreciate his power, and to be in a state to ascribe all the majesty and the glory, all the power and dominion unto God and to the Lamb forever, he will continue to do so.

And if such a day of darkness and despondency; if such a period of trial and self-abasement, and of emptying of all human dependence; such a day of overthrow and despair was necessary to prepare the Church for those lesser manifestations of grace and glory in former periods of Zion's triumphs, how much more may we suppose the Church will be prepared for her Millennial triumph by a most galling encounter with her inveterate foe! How much more may we expect that the sun of the Millennial Morn will arise on the darkest, deadliest, the most tempestuous night that ever lowered on this lower world! None shall see that morn but such as come out of great tribulation. It shall be a most striking emblem of heaven. A prominent characteristic shall be, that "here the wicked shall cease from troubling and the weary shall be at rest." So sore will be the conflict—so raging the fury of the enemy—so near did they seem to gain the victory— and finally so providential and miraculous the victory in behalf of the saints, that not a suspicion can lurk in a single breast that it was any other than the hand of Jehovah which gave them the victory. As in the case of the convicted sinner, when overcome beneath the weight of his burden and ready to perish, deliverance is the more precious, and the arm that plucked him from the horrible pit and the miry clay is more readily acknowledged; so in the deliverance of the Church from her low and oppressed state, when the foot of the enemy is raised high to crush her, she can sing of triumph, and ascribe all the honor to Him who hath done it.

I have answered, and somewhat in detail too, the first inquiry proposed, viz.: *What is God's ordinary course of dealing with his Church* in reference to those periods when he is about to make some new and more glorious display of his grace towards her?

And from this I have drawn a fair inference, I believe, that it is but analogous with what in a great variety of instances has already taken place, to expect a mighty conflict before the final triumph of the Church in the days of the Millennium. I must now return a brief answer to the SECOND inquiry, viz.: *What is God's ordinary course of dealing*, under similar circumstances, *with the incorrigibly wicked?* And we may here be able to deduce the same inference as before.

Two objects are here to be gained: the one, to demonstrate to the wicked how perfectly unavailing is the warfare they are carrying on against God; and the other, to confirm the faith of his people in the power and determination of God to support his cause, and vindicate his chosen against *any* assault which may be made upon them.

Hence we find that God exercises a *singular forbearance* towards sinners. He allows them time to *exemplify their wicked principles*, and to *act out their characters*—that the world—that the universe may have a fair opportunity to see what they are, and to what they tend. He does not hinder them from exhibiting the extreme pride, and ambition, and malice, and madness of sin. He does not keep the sinner *caged* in such a lattice-work of restraints that he cannot act out, freely, his own nature. He gives him length of chain, that he may sport and rage—that he may show what he *is*, and what he *would do* if permitted to have a still greater range. Hence it is that when sinners get madly set on their idols, and are determined at all hazards to pursue the vanities of their own choice, God allows them to do so. As the light increases and trenches on the confines of darkness, they madden more and more. God permits this. They are at length wrought up into a frenzy of madness against the people of God, and venture to raise the hand of violence against God's anointed ones. They may beat them low, but they cannot crush them.

They may trample on them, but they cannot grind them to powder.
No weapon formed against them can *prevail.* It may seem about
to prevail, but it can never strike the final blow. The strong
arm of God interposes at the very moment when the ponderous
foot of the enemy is about to crush his prey. So it was when
Pharaoh and his host, mad on revenge, pursued the people of
God to the very borders of the sea. The maddening tiger crouched
to pounce upon his prey; and when it seemed in his very jaws,
a hand divine laid prostrate the prowling beast, rescued his lamb,
and gathered it into a larger fold. And here is reared one of the
most singular monuments in the history of man. On one side
you read a record of mercy; on another side a record of judgment; and on all sides you read the inevitable fate of the sinner
and the security of the saint. And so it was as the great conflict approached, near the close of our Saviour's eventful life.
The clearness and pungency of his instructions, the pureness of
his life, had so irritated and galled the foes of truth, and so disgorged the latent fires of malice against a holy Religion, that
they could no longer suppress the outbreakings of their corrupt
hearts. The object of their hatred was the progress of the
truth. They saw their ranks thinning and their territory narrow-
ing, their respectability waning and their influence depreciating,
and they made one deadly struggle to save their sinking cause.
The more desperate their cause the more deadly the onset. And
so we may expect it to be when the truth shall have taken so
deep root, and have extended its branches so widely as to create
the alarm that its empire shall become universal. The moment
that the stone cut out of the mountain without hands is increased
to such dimensions that it shall seem to be jostling from their
foundations and removing from their places, and casting into the
midst of the sea, all the dominions and principalities of error
and delusion and falsehood, till no place shall be found for them,

that moment, you may depend upon it, a low grumbling sound will be heard among the nations. The lowest elements of iniquity will begin to heave and give signs of a convulsion, and at length the warring elements will burst forth, and the fires of the pit will burn from the lowest depths of hell.

In a word, when the truth shall have made so much progress, and yet before it can set up its undisputed empire among the nations, there will, in accordance with the ordinary operations of the divine economy, be a conflict of principle—of truth with error—a bloody conflict in all probability, such as has never yet been recorded in the history of man.

How inevitable then is the destruction of the sinner! He may boast himself for a time. He may speak great swelling words. He may lightly esteem the God of his salvation and affect to despise his commandments. He may think to break the cords of restraint and raise the standard of rebellion, yet how perfectly futile are all his attempts.

Nothing can be so consummately foolish and futile as the sinner's estrangement from his God. He voluntarily forsakes his best, his only Friend: his best Friend in time, and the only one that can befriend him when time shall be no more.

If the sinner be not reconciled to God, there is no power in the universe that can save him from a never-ending ruin. He *must* perish. Sooner might you think to roll back the wheels of time, or to change the ordinances of heaven, than to save a sinner who will not yield in obedience and love to the Lord Jesus Christ.

CHAPTER XIX.

THIS is the last topic proposed for discussion. And it becomes us to enter upon it with some befitting sense of our responsibilities and duties at such a time as this.

However much they who talk and think and write on these subjects may differ as to the signs of the approach of such a period, or the time of its commencement, or its character or duration, there seems a very general agreement among all evangelical Christians that the "good time is coming;" and that it is not far in the future. To say nothing of all the absurd and fulsome things, which, in our pride and self-gratulation, has been said on this subject, we are no doubt living in a very interesting period of the world. Events, big with interest to the Church, as we have shown, are now transpiring in quick succession. Thirty years now leave in their wake, as they pass, a consummation of more events which hasten on the glory of Zion, than three hundred—I had almost said three thousand years—did at some former period of the history of the Church. Who could have conceived, thirty years ago, the progress which has been made in science, in government, in civilization and religion? Into how many languages has the Bible, within that period, been translated, and given, in their own vernacular, to more than half the population of the globe! How have the messengers of the Churches gone to and fro in the world, and knowledge increased, till the good tidings of great joy, which shall be to all people, has been proclaimed, in greater or less perfection, and more or less extensively, among almost every people and nation! The Press has sent forth its healing leaves as widely as the tree of life has been planted. Never before was the march of truth so rapid. The science of government; liberal principles; the progress of the arts, have within the same period, made rapid strides towards perfection. Much remains to be done, yet what are these but the sure harbingers of better days? What is their language but this, that *the night is far spent, and the day is at hand?*

And we may, if we will, discover in the *untoward* circumstances of the Church, and of the world, indications that the day of Zion's deliverance and enlargement is not distant. The very outbreakings of sin—the ravings and ranklings of Satan, are no doubtful indications that his time is short; his days numbered.

A voice on every side seems to say to Zion, " Arise, shine, for thy light is come, and the glory of the Lord is risen upon thee. Lift up your eyes around about and see, all gather themselves together; thy sons shall come from afar, and thy daughters shall be nursed by thy side."

If such a period as has been indicated—if such events as have been described, lie but a little way before us, and if the character of that period and of those events be such as I have intimated, it becomes a question of very serious import, Are we prepared for such a state of things? Are we doing what devolves on us to hasten the wished for era; and are we prepared to live in and enjoy such a period? The prophet just quoted adds—and this includes the preparation needed—" then thou shall see and flow together, and thine heart shall fear and be enlarged, because the abundance of the sea shall be converted unto thee, and the forces of the Gentiles shall come unto thee." In other words, when the heathen shall be converted, and they that do business on the great waters, and see the wonders of the deep, shall yield a willing obedience to the God of heaven, then shall be developed in the Church, the character here described. *They shall see*, shall know, shall understand; the films of ignorance shall be removed, and they shall see clearly, and comprehend more of the ways of the Lord. *They shall flow together*—shall be of one heart and one mind—shall be bound together by the golden chain of love, and shall not only harmonize in feeling and affection and cardinal principle, but shall, as far as the nature of the great work in which they are engaged admit, *think* and *act* in harmony. *Their heart shall fear and be enlarged.* Self-distrust, and reverence for God shall pervade their innermost soul. While they walk carefully and humbly before their God, they shall have increased confidence in him, and more liberal and enlarged views of his character and kingdom. They shall *be enlarged*—shall be capable of understanding more—of feeling more—of doing more—and shall desire more. They will ask great things of God—and expect great things. They shall be capacitated to live in a higher and holier and more advanced state of things.

But is not this higher and holier type of Christian character, which fits for that higher and holier state of the Church in the time of her Millennial glory, the very character which will *bring about such a state?* Holy fear; profound reverence and love of God; increased holiness; a more liberal and diffusive intelligence; union and harmony of action; enlarged views of duty, and feelings, affections, and desires Christ-like and heavenly, are the characteristics and the sure harbingers of such a period.

Would we, then, be the instruments of introducing such a day, and when it shall be introduced, be prepared to welcome and enjoy it, we must have this character. And so we must, should

20

we be first called to enter upon the more perfect fruition of a yet higher state of glory. The spirit that would fit us to enjoy such a state of things is the very spirit that will make us instrumental in bringing about that state.

What then is the duty of all who love and honor our Divine Master? He is doing great things in our world. He is accelerating his chariot-wheels with a glorious and fearful rapidity—glorious to all who will acknowledge his right to reign and rejoice in his dominion, and fearful to all such as will not have him to reign over them. He would have his people coworkers with him. He has preordained that he will carry on his work *through his people*. If he is now hastening things on to the grand consummation, as I have supposed; if, as a King he is riding forth conquering and to conquer, he expects, as never before, that his people will put on the whole armor, and in this day of the great conflict and victory stand, every man at his post.

What is a befitting preparation for such a period? I name as the *first* in order and importance, a higher, holier, a more purifying and appropriating FAITH.

As, on the one hand, dangers thicken about the Church, and days grow dark, and the enemy strengthens himself and seems about to prevail, the people of God need a firmer hold on the promises—a stronger faith—a more implicit reliance on their covenant God. Like John when he had been cast into prison, there is danger that their faith will, in the hour of their tribulation, fail them. They will therefore need a faith which shall appropriate the divine promises, and bring home to the soul a clearer evidence of things unseen. In the day of rebuke and trial that shall precede that latter-day glory, the soul of the good man will need to be fortified against the spirit that shall work in the children of disobedience. He will be able to stand only as he has on the whole armor of God.

But he must not only be prepared to meet, and to pass unscathed through, the coming conflict, when the "Lord shall come out of his place to punish the inhabitants of the earth for their iniquity," but when the "indignation shall be overpast," he must be prepared to enter upon, and be able to live in and enjoy a moral condition which shall require a much higher type of religious character, and a purer and more appropriating faith than has been hitherto known in the Church. While this will still be an earthly condition, it will be more heavenly than has yet been seen on earth. The prevailing exercise of that faith which overcometh the world, worketh by love and purifieth the heart, will make heaven and earth meet, and men will again seem to converse with angels.

From what has already been said, it will be inferred that a *deep-toned piety* is an indispensable preparation both for the speedy bringing in of such a period, and for the enjoyment of it when introduced. "To him that hath shall be given that he may have abundantly." They that wait for the coming of their Lord will live in near communion with their God. They will seek to be more conformed to his image, and, as adopted sons, will have more of the filial spirit. They will be more humble, more hopeful, more Christ-like.

The kingdom that is to come shall be a kingdom of holiness, of eminent consecration to God. Human energies and influence shall then be, in a manner heretofore unknown, devoted to the service of the Great King. They, then, who will hasten a consummation so devoutly to be wished, and who would, if permitted, enjoy its blessings, must be eminently holy. Holiness alone is the power that is to conquer the world, and to give the kingdom to Christ. Men, money, learning, political power, facilities for rapid communication with all parts of the world, will not do it—though the Church may abound and feel herself strong in all such resources, nothing short of the resistless, the omnipotent power of holiness, can demolish the strongholds of the adversary, deliver man from the bondage of sin, and, by reinstating him in the image of his God, make him a fit denizen in the New Jerusalem come down from heaven.

I scarcely need name *united, fervent and effectual prayer* as another duty of those who wait for the coming of their Lord. Prayer, the heart's desire for things needful, and not inconsistent with the honor of God and the rights and happiness of man, is of divine appointment, and a necessary means by which to procure the thing sought. The Church may expect nothing—no progress, no increase of numbers or of graces, except in answer to prayer. Would she therefore have her Lord come speedily, and take out of the way all that hindereth his working, and set up his kingdom on earth, she must cry mightily to God that he would do this great thing for her. Encouraged by such hopes, and vitalized by such a faith, the people of God will pray always and with all prayer.

Another duty, and also a characteristic of the age that shall precede the Millennial period, is an unprecedented Christian *enterprise*, pervaded and vitalized by an enlarged, enlightened and diffusive *benevolence*. Our age is not lacking in bold enterprise— in adventurous schemes of discovery — in an active inventive genius—in gigantic investments of capital—in plans of human advancement. There is no lack of energy and enterprise in devising and executing great schemes for all sorts of worldly aggrandizement. The expenditure of property for these things is enormous. We are amazed at the millions, the hundreds of millions that are so readily invested in railways, in telegraphs, in mining, manufacturing and mechanical operations. And we see a presage in these very things that the "good time" is hastening on apace. The Millennium shall undoubtedly be distinguished by physical features which are preparing in our own age. That period will no doubt be characterized by great wealth ; but wealth made tributary to the improvement and happiness of man—to the real aggrandizement of the race. Works to facilitate internal and international communication shall then be perfect. Science and the arts shall have made their richest contributions to the well-being of man ; the earth be made to yield her supplies in an abundance before unknown ; and prosperity shall smile on every human enterprise. All capital so invested as to accomplish such ends, is doubtless contributing to, and hastening the desired era, though the actors in these scenes may have no such design. They are all made to contribute to bring in the *physical* Millennium.

But it is rather to the *moral* aspects of that period to which I refer, when I speak of *enlarged and diffusive benevolence* as an imperative duty of the present day.

An all-controlling Providence is wont to set one thing over against another. A few years past have been years of unprecedented prosperity. Riches have increased in a manner unknown in any former age : at least the professed people of God, have had more of this world's wealth thrown into their possession than ever before. Mines in the far West, and in the far East, have poured forth their golden treasures without stint. Commerce, manufactures and agriculture have filled the land with wealth. The Christian Church has, in this respect, shared her full proportion. To say nothing of the hoarded stores and the misapplied wealth of the Romish communion, there is found in the Protestant Evangelical Church immense riches. She can count her millionaires —and a great multitude who measure their wealth by the hundreds of thousands. We are no doubt to regard this singular worldly prosperity of the Christian Church as a significant prognostic of our times ; as an interesting link in the chain of Divine Providence, indicating in no doubtful terms the present duty of the Church. For, on the other hand, the same strong arm has been at work in discovering the nations one to another; bringing into nearer proximity, and preparing the way for the spread of the gospel. The door has been opened—obstacles removed—facilities provided—the Bible translated, and only needs the pecuniary means in order to give it an indefinite circulation—systems of education inaugurated, and only it needs the momentum of an actual Christian benevolence, to give them all the required efficiency. The field is the world; and that field has, within the few past years, been remarkably thrown open to evangelical efforts. The day has undoubtedly come when the gospel shall be preached, as a witness, to all nations. The angel is now expediting his flight; and soon, as a needful preparation for the great day of the Lord, shall the good tidings be proclaimed, and the Man of Nazareth be offered as the Saviour of all men.

Hitherto every effort of the Church has been sadly crippled for the want of funds. Compared with her present resources, she has been poor—yet her greatest inability has been in her spiritual penury. Her soul has not been enlarged to consecrate her pecuniary resources to her Lord. When her members shall make such a consecration, and at the same time lay at the foot of the altar of their religion their time, talents and influence, the world shall realize and acknowledge the Church to be the light and the life of the world. Never was there a time when the Church might so effectually make friends of the Mammon of unrighteousness. Never before could consecrated wealth do so much to bless a ruined world, and to bring in the day which prophets have sung and kings desired to see.

We may not expect that day till the Church of the living God shall arise in her strength, and let her light shine, and put forth an energy and enterprise, and practice a self-denial, and exhibit a benevolence nothing less than apostolic. She must devote to the service of her Lord all the agencies she can command—whether of money, or men, time or talents—she must make the honor and the progress of Christ's kingdom the great business and aim of life. She will then put forth the whole power of her piety: men will then live, labor, get money and spend it, as in their honest judgment, they shall believe, will the most effectually advance the kingdom of Immanuel. And then, when they pray, "Thy kingdom come," there will be a heart in it, a power, which shall move the powers of heaven, and soon unveil, in this lower world, the glories of the New Jerusalem. Our hopes of the speedy coming of that blessed day are in proportion to the consecration of the Church.

But activity and enterprise, and even pious consecration, are not all. A high standard of knowledge, intelligent views of duty, and a profound acquaintance with the Bible, are duties of a kindred importance. They who have themselves been enlightened and tasted of the good word of God and "the powers of the world to come"—the dispensation of grace of which we speak—will be moved to search more and more into the mysteries of godliness, and the character of the expected kingdom. They will be more intelligent—will seek to know more of God, of duty, of man and his character, his history and his destiny; and more of Divine Providence—how he has carried on his work in past ages—what he seems about to do—what devolves on man to do, and how he is to do it? As a sure precursor of that day, "knowledge shall increase." The divine predictions shall now especially possess new charms. Through them God has foreshadowed the things that shall come to pass. And as their fulfilment draws near, they will appear to all who are waiting for the consolation of Israel, clothed in a new interest. All who are looking for the coming of the long-ago predicted era, will, like the holy men who of old spake as they were moved by the spirit of God and prophesied of the grace that should come, inquire and search diligently, searching what, or what manner of time, the spirit of Christ which is in them doth signify.

If there be signs in the political and moral firmament that the great and glorious things foretold draw near their accomplishment, then what manner of men ought we to be in all holiness of life, in untiring activity, in singleness of purpose, in well-directed and intelligent benevolence.

And another duty of the Church as well as another characteristic of her coming glory, is *brotherly love.* Union of heart— harmony of action, will prevail to a degree never before known. Denominational differences will be greatly lessened, and, as to all practical purposes, annihilated. The harmony of feeling and principle which will then prevail will not fail to produce a corresponding harmony of action.

And here it seems but apposite and just, to express a conviction which has for some few years been gaining strength, that a most important movement is making in this direction by the " Christian alliance," which is hopeful beyond any similar movement of our time. Men of enlarged and liberal views, of different nationalities, and ecclesiastical connections—men of tried piety, of experience, of influence and position, and of a catholic spirit, have arisen in the strength of their religious principles and feelings, and, soaring above the straitness and selfishness of sect, have joined their noble energies in one grand, concentrated effort against sin wherever found, and in whatever shape, and for the upbuilding of the kingdom of righteousness, irrespective of nationality or narrow bigotry. Is there oppression, or persecution, the undaunted hand of this alliance is raised in stern remonstrance. Does some earthly potentate, clothed in " a little brief authority," attempt to desecrate God's day, or to arrest the mission of his holy word in its circuit around the world, by excluding it from his dominions; or does some giant wrong prevail, or some corroding evil prey on its human victims, these noble Philanthropists, bound together and energized by principles and feelings which exist only to bless and to bind together and make strong, step forward in the majesty of a righteous benevolence, and rebuke kings and teach nations.

Let this alliance be encouraged as it ought to be ; let the good and great of all nations be joined in one great brotherhood, and let them go on from strength to strength, carrying out their great and good plans, and they shall soon, under God, bring the world into a state that shall first stir up to rebellion and conflict all the opposing powers of sin, and then introduce the reign of righteousness on the whole earth.   Yet our confidence here lies not in the *men* who happen at present to be the leaders of this noble movement, but in the *principles* of action by which they are bound together and actuated.   Should these men prove recreant to their great trust, their principles, under other auspices and agents, will not fail to work out their benevolent mission.

CHAPTER XX.

Our Age—Troublous times—Safe to trust in God—The end of the wicked—
The people of God urged to renewed activity.

In the foregoing pages I have essayed to set forth, in as practical a light as possible, the long and anxiously looked for and the much prayed for event called the Millennium. It is the period predicted by ancient prophets, and looked for by ancient saints. While philosophers and Pagan priests were descanting on the beauties of some "Golden Age" to be realized in the distant future, when Mammon should reign and all sorts of physical and sensuous prosperity shall smile on the earth; holy men of old spake as they were moved by a Divine monition, of a Golden Age which should be yet more remarkably signalized by the beauties of holiness. It shall be the peaceful reign of Immanuel. Righteousness shall be in the ascendant, and sin, which is a reproach to any people, shall hide in caves and dens of the earth.

And I have as distinctly shown that there come "a falling away first"—the Man of sin shall be revealed—the last, great and most fearful struggle of man's arch foe shall precede and hasten on this day of Zion's glorious triumph. "These be the days of vengeance, that all things which are written may be fulfilled." But when these things begin to come to pass, then look up, ye saints, and lift up your heads; for your redemption draweth nigh.

In drawing our discussion to a close certain reflections very naturally press themselves upon us. And one of the most obvious if not the most important is—

1. *We live in a solemn age of the world.* Great events are transpiring, and greater yet are but a step before us. The great purposes of the divine plan are steadily and speedily accomplishing. Nothing can frustrate them. He will accomplish all his will, and none can stay his hand.

Every day is big with interest—every year brings forth its great events. Every wind wafts some intelligence which presages revolution. Soon we may expect to hear of the downfall of the proud and oppressive empire of the Moslems. They have scourged the Church, have vexed the nations, tormented the earth near twelve hundred and sixty years, and slain a third part of our race. And, as nearly simultaneous with this, we look for *the ingathering of the Jews, the overthrow of Paganism*, and *the downfall of spiritual Babylon.* And in connection with these things, partly growing out of them, and partly producing them, we look for the great Battle, the conflict of the joint powers of sin against piety, and the apparent victory, and the short triumph of the enemy, called the "slaying of the Witnesses." And we look, too, that, when the nations shall be exceeding angry—when sin shall have had its triumph and Satan filled up the measure of his iniquity, He that hath written on his vesture and on his thigh, *the Lord of lords and the King of kings*, shall come to the conflict—shall set up his standard—and soon it shall be proclaimed, *The kingdoms of this world have become the kingdom of our Lord and of his Christ; and he shall reign forever.*

Thus shall end the great Drama. He shall overturn and overturn, till He whose right it is shall come and reign.

These are things that may shortly come to pass. Events thicken upon us. We hasten to the grand consummation. Ten years may bring us into a period of intense interest. Are we prepared—is the Church prepared to meet it? Days of sorrow and of joy, of darkness and of sunshine, of persecution and of prosperity are before us—days of a short and galling thraldom, and of glorious liberty and enlargement as the sons of God. Never has there been a time when Christians needed more knowledge and grace, more firmness and courage,—the need of the whole *panoply.*

Associated as we are with, and bound to take a part in the vast affairs of a day like the present, what a responsibility is laid on us to live worthy our times? How misplaced and ill-timed to trifle—to live for naught! How urgently are we pressed to greater diligence. Never was a time when our prayers were so likely to be answered, or our activities would be of so much service in the world's emancipation.

2. *Troublous times are times of strength.* This the individual Christian often has occasion to feel and acknowledge. He grows and invigorates the most in the Christian life. Not when he dwells in inglorious ease, and is fanned by the genial breezes of prosperity, but when he is beaten upon by the merciless storms of adversity—when every moral muscle of his soul is nerved to action by the stern hand of necessity or affliction. The strong men in Christ have been made in troublous times. They have been made bold by the wicked resistance of the foe; their faith has waxed strong, and their hopes bright, and their love ardent, and their prayers importunate and effective, when dangers have beset them, and persecutions have assailed them, and deaths manifold and appalling, have awaited them. The apostles were strong men; they lived in troublous times. And of those mightiest, Paul was the mightiest. But the great apostle to the Gen-

tiles was hardened for his warfare, by a training severe in proportion to the valor he was afterwards to display. "In strifes above measure; in prisons more frequent; thrice shipwrecked and left to buffet a day and a night in the deep; thrice beaten with rods and once stoned; and in perils by land and by sea, in the city and in the country, from friends and from foes; from his own brethren and from the heathen; and in deaths oft—these are the things which had much to do to make Paul the strong man he was.

The early Reformers were strong men; and under God, they were made so by the troublous times in which they lived.

But we speak now rather of the Church collectively. In the time of her quiet—in the absence of persecution, and when prosperity smiles, and the world favors, and religion is popular, the life, the soul of the Church is then sure to languish. Worldly prosperity has always been the bane of the Church. Whenever she has been nurtured on the lap of wealth, or robed in the purple and fine linen of courtly favor, and fared sumptuously in the high places of worldly distinction, she has become weak and sickly; her energies relaxed, her spiritual strength extinct, her power to resist the world, the flesh and the devil paralyzed, and she helpless and impotent in the face of a wicked world, and quite unfitted to make aggressions on them that are without. When Zion is at her ease, she is quite at the mercy of the world.

But when in times of trouble she is compelled to act on the defensive, and struggle for her life, and is forced to lay hold on the Almighty arm for her strength, then she begins to be strong. She is always and only strong in the omnipotence of her God. It is only when in her troubles she is brought low, and made to feel her weakness, and her dependence on her Almighty Friend, that she is clothed with a power which the world cannot resist. She will then so humble herself, and exercise such a faith, and offer up such prayers, and illustrate in living examples such truths, doctrines and precepts, as shall engage all the resources of Heaven in her behalf. And when the great King shall make bare his arm to avenge the cause of his elect, how shall his people be made strong—how shall the enemy be discomfited and Zion arise in the strength of her omnipotent Leader!

As the great conflict of which I have spoken shall draw near, as the Beast, the False Prophet and the Dragon, shall arouse their hosts once in deadly combat with the saints of the Most High, Zion will again see troublous times. The days of persecution shall return—a martyr's crown may again be as dearly purchased as in the darkest day Zion ever saw. The witnesses shall be slain; the triumph of their enemies shall be more complete and universal than has ever yet been known. This shall be the hour and the power of darkness: and yet it shall be a period which shall give birth to great and strong men in Zion. Faith shall then plant her root deeper in the secret recesses of the soul, and, taking root downwards, it shall more richly than ever bear fruit upwards. The sons of Zion, inured to the trials, afflictions and persecutions of that day, will be strong in the Lord and in the might of his power.

That was especially the "hour and the power of darkness," when the disciples were scattered as sheep without a shepherd, because their Lord and Master was seized and taken away to be crucified and slain. Faith failed them and hope died within them. All seemed lost. They trusted it had been He who should redeem Israel. But the enemy had prevailed over him; and no human hope remained that he would overcome the foe and realize to them what he had promised. Yet this was a day of strength. Though it was the annihilation of all human hopes, the apparent frustration of all human agencies and the utter failure of all man's expedients, it was the very juncture of the most glorious and effective interposition of the Divine Arm. This was the day on which Zion was clothed with new power: the day when she put on her strength and went forth in the might of Heaven to the conquest of the world.

The dark cloud which we believe will yet overshadow the Church, the day of dreadful conflict and apparent overthrow, shall, in like manner, be a day of renewed, and of unprecedented power to the Church of God.

3. We infer *the safety of trusting in God.* He that, in the day of trouble, leans on the Almighty arm, though he stumble, he shall not fall. Though he fall, he shall rise again. His feet are placed on the Rock. God has ever had a people in the world whom he keeps as the apple of his eye. If opposed, persecuted or slain, he will vindicate their cause and avenge their wrongs. " When they went from one nation to another, from one kingdom to another people, he suffered no man to do them wrong; yea, he reproved kings for their sake; saying, Touch not mine anointed, and do my prophets no harm." If crushed and trodden down he will raise them up. No weapon formed against his Church can prosper. He will complete the work he has begun and crown his name with glory in spite of all the confederated hosts of sin and hell. All that trust in Him are safe.

The Church shall live and prosper. She will be assailed as she always has been. All sorts of devices will be formed against her; all sorts of weapons will be employed. Her hay, wood and stubble must be burnt out; yet she shall live and prosper and finally triumph. Sin in every form and disguise will assail her; learning, wealth, fashion, civil power, will combine their strength to undermine, if possible, and break down the walls of our Zion. Ignorance and vice conjoined, will calumniate her; philosophy will cavil; infidelity will rage or decoy—will attack her as an angel of light in the stolen robes of the sanctuary, or in the native ugliness of its own deformity. Hypocrites within may play the traitor, and zealots without, with a fire-brand in the one hand and honeyed words of gospel love in the other, may promise the world peace and purity and all good, if we will only follow hard in their wake, and just help them first demolish the fair fabric of Zion, that they may build on its ruins a more stately and resplendent mansion; yet the Church shall live and prosper.

The evangelical Church of Europe and America, corrupt as she may be—*human* in foibles, defections and sins as she may be, is still, in a moral point, head and shoulders above any other organization on the face of the earth; and simply as a *reforming society*, she is far, far in advance of any other reforming body ever organized. She is, and always has been the *sun*, in comparison of which all other reforming bodies are but *stars*—blazing stars —comets, it may be, which, sometimes in transient effulgence, threaten to put out the light of the sun. Yet the sun stands, shines, enlightens and enlivens, clouds or no clouds, blazing stars and meteors notwithstanding—and so she will till the end of time. Though she may for a little time be overwhelmed by the floods which the Dragon shall send out after her, yet shall she live and prosper, and be received and honored at last of her Master, while all who honor and love her not, shall be destroyed by the "brightness of his coming."

"Though hand joined in hand," the wicked shall not prosper. "Their covenant with death shall be disanulled and their agreement with hell shall not stand; when the overflowing scourge shall pass through, then they shall be trodden down by it."

4. We would not here suppress a reflection of a very serious character, which has so often pressed on our mind in the preparation of these pages. It is this: *What a final and total calamity, at such a time, not to be on the side of the Lord!*

If God be about to rise and shake terribly the earth—if he is hastening all things with such a fearful rapidity as we have sup-posed—if the crisis is rapidly approaching, and God has risen up to avenge the cause of his elect; and, after allowing his enemies a temporary triumph, if he will crush them forever beneath his dreadful power, and bind and cast into the Pit him that hath power of sin and death, how dreadful, how fatally hazardous not to be on the side of such a God! God has allowed the wicked for a little time to resist his law, to defy his power, to mouth the heavens, to despise his mercy, to trample on his goodness, to do despite to the spirit of his grace and reject the offer of his only Son. But the day approaches when his forbearance will cease, when his mercy will be clean gone forever. Who shall stand when he shall appear? He shall come in his judgments—in the pestilence, by the sword and by famine. By all the dreadful agencies of nature, and no less by the violence of man as armed against his fellow-man, multitudes on multitudes of a wicked race shall be destroyed, till the wicked shall cease to be.

But this dreadful destruction can harm none but the enemies of God. They whose names are written in the Lamb's Book of Life, though their bodies may perish in the great conflict, their immortal spirits are joined to God by ties that can never be severed. Heirs of God and joint heirs with Jesus Christ, noth-ing can harm them.

But another thought is here suggested. It is none other than *the Lord Jesus Christ* who shall come thus dressed in vengeance to avenge his people, and to punish and to destroy his enemies. The Lamb once slain for sinners—the Good Samaritan who came to pour the wine and the oil into the wounds which sin has made —who came to pity our low estate and to blot out our trans-gressions—who was touched with a feeling of our infirmities— who enters into the secret chamber of our grief and is afflicted in all our afflictions; it is He that shall come with his mighty

21

angels, revealed in flaming fire, to take vengeance on them that know not God and obey not the gospel of his Son. Now he is the dispenser of pardon to the penitent no more. He is the Executor of the divine wrath on the ungodly.

"Kiss the Son lest he be angry, and ye perish from the way when his wrath is kindled but a little."

Once his was the voice of love, inviting the sinner to turn and live, in accents soft and sweet as the breath of heaven. Now his words are as the thunder-tones of wrath, speaking eternal banishment from his presence to the guilty soul who would none of his counsels. "Fear not him who can only kill the body; but I forewarn you whom ye shall fear; fear him who, when he hath killed, hath power to cast into hell. Yea, I say unto you, fear him!"

Be at peace, then, with God. Make man your enemy if you will, engage against you all the resources of the mightiest earthly monarch; let the world arm against you. It is not much that they can do. They can but kill the body. But make God your Friend; secure a saving interest in the atonement and intercesion of his dear Son, and you are safe. You are prepared for those things which must shortly come upon the earth. Nation may be dashed against nation—the earth be shaken—the great and terrible day of the Lord may come, and the wicked be as chaff before the wind, if God be on our side, we have nothing to fear.

How unequal and unavailing then is the warfare of the wicked against the Church of God! They may boast themselves for a time and speak great swelling words. They may think to break the bands of restraint and raise the standard of rebellion, but their attempts are all futile. God will sorely judge all them that raise a hand against his Church. Yet he will use them as his scourge. He will chastise his people and bring them low, and bring them back to their allegiance, *through the instrumentality* of those, who, through the pretext of healing their backslidings, would overcome and destroy and kill them. But when these modern Assyrians shall have accomplished the purpose designed, God will put his hook in their nose and *his bridle in their lips*, and turn them back by the way by which they came.

And how inevitable, I repeat, is the destruction of the wicked. God may for a time give them the desires of their hearts. He may allow them the length of their line—allow them to *show off* their real character, and to exemplify their own principles to their disgrace and final ruin. He may make them fit subjects by which for a time to exhibit his extreme forbearance towards the sinner—or, in the swift destruction which comes upon them, to give to his saints renewed assurance, that he will avenge the cause of his elect.

If the sinner will not be reconciled to God, no power in the universe can save him. He *must* perish. Sooner, I say again, might you hope to roll back the wheels of time, or change the ordinances of heaven, than save the sinner who will not have the Lord Jesus Christ to reign over him. Flee, then, and take refuge in him. He is your Rock and your salvation—your strong tower in the day of trouble.

Trust in Him and you are safe—though the tempest howl and the floods come—though the sea roar and the fountains of the great deep be broken up—though the earth totter beneath you, and the heavens gather blackness over you.

There was never a time when it was so fearful a thing to rest in the *uncovenanted* mercies of God. God is now as never before riding forth to victory. He is accelerating his plans for the complete and final overthrow of sin; and if the sinner do not escape, he must inevitably perish in the general ruin.

5. At such a day as this Christians ought to stand abased

and rebuked on account of their apathy in the service of their Divine Master. How slow are they to believe, and how indifferently do they go about the business of their Lord. All things they see hastening to a fearful crisis. The wheels of Providence roll on with accelerated speed. The promises are fulfilling, the great purposes of God are fast accomplishing—his threatenings are executed—and all things are indicating that the present scene of the great Drama is fast coming to a close; and that, after the commotions of a short and terrific interval, another scene, more glorious, to the wicked more dreadful, shall follow. Never since Christ had a Church on the earth, were his people so loudly called upon to double their diligence—to stand forth as the humble, fearless champions of the cross—to throw their whole souls into the work—to lay body, soul, time, talent, wealth, influence, all upon the altar of their religion, and to serve the Lord Christ with an unreserved devotion and singleness of heart.

No plainer or safe rule of duty can be prescribed than that the people of God should work *where* and *when* God works. As, in his Providence, God leads the way, his people are to follow. Wherever he opens the door for the exercise of their benevolent feelings and Christian activities, they must enter and cheerfully employ their graces and activities. It devolves on the present generation of Christians not only to *diffuse* a knowledge of their religion, as Providence has opened a wide and effectual way, but on them devolves the duty of *defending* the truth against the insidious attacks of skepticism and irreligion. Never did the cause of our blessed religion need more humble and fearless advocates. The Church militant of the present day occupies a position not unlike that of a besieging army which has for a long time been beleaguering some stronghold of the enemy. At length, after incessant toil, suffering and expense, the day has come for the last grand attack. They are now to make a final, desperate onset, and the victory shall be theirs.   Now more than ever it will be expected that every man shall do his duty.   Delinquency, apathy, desertion, cowardice now would be doubly criminal.   Every arm must now be made bare for the fight; every muscle must be exerted; every needed sacrifice must now be made to strike the final blow.   Dangers have thickened—the crisis has come, and now as never before every man must stand at his post.

The people of the living God are about to besiege the army of the aliens in their last strongholds.   The hardest battle remains to be fought; the greatest victory to be won.   And never did the great Captain of our salvation more imperatively demand that every man, each in his own sphere and according to his ability, stand faithfully and fearlessly at his post, and EVERY MAN DO HIS OWN DUTY.

CHAPTER XXI.

In the midst of these troublous times, when nation is dashed
against nation and the " world is turned upside down," it will not
seem out of place to contemplate the emergence of this distracted
world of ours out of such a chaos, and its happy restitution to its
primeval beauty and blessedness.   We have said enough of tur-
moils, convulsions and overturnings.   We come now to inquire
if our earth have not a different destiny.   Shall her fair face be
forever deformed by wars and tumults, by violence and corruption? and then, after a respite of a thousand years, shall she come
to a violent death, the victim of a fearful conflagration?   The
direction given to the reader's mind in the foregoing chapters may
have created some interest to inquire after the final destiny of the
earth, and of its teeming multitudes of immortal men.   Its previous history has been sufficiently marvellous—the foregoing
drama wonderful enough, to justify the expectation, that, as the
plot thickens and the finale approaches, the end shall be grand
and enduring beyond human conception.

There are scattered through the Bible a class of texts which seem to contravene the more generally received idea that, after a few generations, this globe of ours shall cease to be the habitation of man. No doubt the earth shall undergo a change so radical and complete as to justify language being used to describe it which seems to imply its *destruction*. So complete shall be the renovation and remodeling of the earth that old things are said to have passed away and all things to have become new. Hence it is called a "new earth:" which, by way of implication, justifies the use of the term "destruction," as applied to the renovating and new-modeling process which this globe shall undergo, as a preparation for the future residence of the saints.

The texts referred to are such as these: " Blessed are the meek, for they shall inherit the earth." In the 37th Psalm a similar declaration is made no less than five times: "They that wait on the Lord shall inherit the earth." "The meek shall inherit the earth and delight themselves in the abundance of peace." " Such as be blessed of him shall inherit the earth." " The righteous shall inherit the land and *dwell therein forever*." The latter defines the import of the phrase "inherit the earth." Again, Canaan, the type of heaven, was given to Abraham and his seed, as an *everlasting* possession. And to Israel, restored and reinstated in the land, the promise is that " they shall dwell therein, even they and their children, and their children's children *forever*; and my servant David shall be their prince forever."

While all will concede that these texts teach, at least, that the righteous shall possess *more of the life that now is*—they shall enjoy more—shall live longer — shall have more name and memorial among men—have more of real life than the wicked; yet these texts teach more. They teach that this earth, when it shall have been renovated—purified by fire and fitted up for the purpose, *shall be the final and eternal residence of the saints.* It shall be their heaven: the New Jerusalem come down from heaven. The plain import of the scriptures already quoted would seem to teach this. Although true, in the sense explained, that they who fear God and love and work righteousness, live to a much greater purpose and realize more of this present life than the wicked do, we believe it likewise true that this earth shall be the everlasting possession of the children of God. The reason for such a belief we find,

1. In the class of scriptures already quoted.

There is not the least intimation that the meaning of these passages should be limited to the present life. Their plain, literal meaning is obviously what I have intimated. And the same idea is included in the song of the redeemed about the throne. They sing, "Thou wast slain, and hast redeemed us to God by thy blood out of every kindred and tongue and people and nation; and hast made us unto God kings and priests; *and we shall reign on the earth.*" Were it the design of the sacred writers to teach that this earth shall be the future and the final residence of the redeemed, we do not see that they would have used stronger language than we find already on record. And in corroboration of such a construction I remark,

2. This earth is as *likely to be the appointed habitation of the redeemed of God as any other planet or world,* which God has made. As heaven is undoubtedly a place, a local residence for material bodies, it must be some one, or more of the worlds which compose God's universe. The spiritual body is, nevertheless, a material body and must have a material habitation. Christ's resurrection body could be *touched* and *handled,* and consequently supposed a local habitation for its residence. Elijah and Enoch disappeared from earth in their human bodies (as also did those saints who rose when Christ came from the grave): changed no doubt from corruptible to incorruptible, from mortal to immortal. All the saints shall have such bodies as Christ and these trans-

lated saints possess, and as the angels possess; and must consequently hereafter occupy a material world for their eternal habitation.   And why should we search among the stars for a world more likely to become their habitation?   Or why should we try to persuade ourselves that any world that rolls around in its orbit, in obedience to the sovereign will, should be a more suitable locality for such a residence than their own native-born earth?   As far, at least, as strong probabilities go for proof, we can feel little difficulty in assuming,

3. That this earth of ours is the more probable, and, as far as we can form a judgment in the matter, the most proper place for the future residence and beatification of the saints.   It is their native home.   They were born—twice born, here.   They are bound here by every tie of consanguinity and relationship.   All their associations of childhood, youth and manhood are here. Here they have rejoiced and here they have wept.   Here sinned and here repented, and here found forgiveness in the atoning blood. And above all, as rendering earth the dearest spot in all the universe, this world of all others was honored as the birthplace of our blessed Immanuel, God with us.   Here he was cradled in the manger.   The dust of our earth was consecrated by his sacred feet; and it was over the hills and through the valleys of man's earthly habitations that our blessed Lord went about doing good —ministering to human wants and healing human infirmities.   It was here, as a man, among men, that he taught the way of life, that he brought life and immortality to light.   And above all, it was here that he bore his cross up the hill of Calvary, and there breathed out his life upon the accursed tree.   Calvary has a history in the records of every saint, which no other spot in all the universe can by any possibility have.   It is consecrated by an act with which is associated all his hopes of eternal life.   It is consecrated by the blood which alone can wash away his sin.

No other world has a Calvary—no other world a spot so dear as Calvary. The CROSS is the great centre of hope, and affection, and adoration of the whole company of the redeemed. Why then transfer it from its native place on Calvary? Why think to erect it on some other globe? It belongs to this earth, and we see not why it should ever be removed hence.

4. But we may establish the same strong probability from another point. The entire history of our world indicates such a destiny. Our world is a *growth*—rather a *development*. From the moment of its earliest history, when it came from the hand of creative power, without "form and void," to the present moment, it has been a continual progress—a progress which has already occupied an indefinite and unknown series of ages to accomplish, but which yet seems to give no indications of soon reaching its consummation.

The first glimpse we have of our world, as an entity of history, was that of an unsightly mass of matter; without beauty, form or utility, incapable of producing or sustaining either vegetable or animal life, and containing neither soil, mineral or precious stone. It was but a confused mass of raw material, out of which creative skill and wisdom and power should form all the endless varieties of things, animate and inanimate, which now bless and beautify the earth. Step by step the work proceeds. What the Bible, in the first chapter of Genesis, includes in the simple term *creation*, seems to comprehend the work of not less than six indefinitely long periods, in which each successive step was a decided advance on the preceding.

The first grand period saw the confused and unsightly mass separate into land and water. The sea and fountains of water were formed, and the dry land appeared. Rocks, minerals, metals, and a soil were made; and an atmosphere was spread about the globe, and the light made to appear. Then follows an age in which a series of chemical changes, internal convulsions, and external revolutions so far advance that the earth gives existence to vegetable life, or life in its lowest type ; the conditions for the production and support of animal life not yet existing. But ages roll on. The needful changes take place, and animal life, first in its lower grades, appears : fishes swim in the waters, and fowls sport in the air. And as we make one more mighty stride on the wings of time, we behold the fields rejoicing in their sporting tenants—the cattle on a thousand hills—all the higher orders of life have taken possession of the fields and the groves, and they luxuriate in the bounty of their maker's hand.

All this had been but preparatory to the creation of, and the establishing in his position as lord over this lower creation, the creature MAN. This was indeed a new era in the history of our world. The most marked that had yet transpired. All before had been preparatory to this. And even this, we shall see, was little more than preparatory to what should follow.

From this point we descend the mighty stream of human affairs, tracing the progress of man, and of the world which was built for his theatre of action, widening and deepening in the advancement of knowledge and science and civilization, and more especially in the ever onward and upward developments of religion, in the accomplishment of the purposes of mercy through the ever blessed atonement, till we find ourselves at length in the broad sea of the Millennial glory. And then, by another stride, more grand, more glorious than all before, man becomes the inhabitant of the New Jerusalem, renovated, exalted, glorified.

And shall we here be told that this humanity, which was born here, developed, expanded, and, up to this point, by a sure and glorious gradation, risen to a condition indicated by the Millennial reign of peace and righteousness, shall seek some far-off place of final rest—shall we be told that the " meek " shall no longer " inherit the earth "—that the " righteous " shall *not* " dwell therein *forever*," but shall be transplanted to some distant, unknown world for their final glorification? Why should we seek any other resting-place for the saints? Is not the earth a fitting place ?—at least, is it incurably unfitted to be man's final rest, and the place of his future blessedness and glory? This brings me to remark again,

5. That, sin and its ravages excepted, *this earth is a fit abode for the saints in glory*—good enough, pleasant enough, and withal, probably large enough. Sin aside, and this earth would at once become one perfect and perpetual EDEN. And what does the most refined taste, and cultivated mind, and exalted piety crave more? In Eden man's holy nature found its fulness. And can heaven grant more?

Suppose for a moment that sin were no more—that time, talent, wealth, influence, office, social position and habits, pleasures and pastimes, were all engaged on the side of God and religion, and what would the world at once become? What physically, what intellectually, and what morally?

The *physical* transformation which should follow the annihilation of sin would alone do much to make our earth a heaven. Suppose for a moment that all the wealth, skill and enterprise which are now perverted in the service of sin, to be devoted to physical improvements of the earth—to the construction of roads, bridges, railways, aqueducts—to the erection of commodious dwellings, churches, and public edifices for all the purposes of a high state of civilization and Christianity—to the ornamenting and high cultivation of fields, gardens and groves. If the wealth, now worse than wasted in wars, in intemperance, in hurtful amusements, in vicious habits, were devoted to such purposes as I have indicated, and to kindred objects, which contribute to the real aggrandizement and happiness of a people, what a perfect Paradise our earth in a very little while would become!   And if we add to the present stinted quota of industry and skill, which are now devoted to the real aggrandizement and well-being of the race all the time, industry, enterprise and skill which now go to demonize man, and cover the earth with deformities and barrenness, the earth would be but one beautiful and happy Eden.*   All its deformities would disappear; its barren deserts would be made fruitful fields.   Its worse than useless, its offensive, disease-engendering swamps and morasses would become productive grounds, or ornamental and useful groves.   Valleys would be exalted, rough places be made smooth; rocky cliffs, and deep ravines, and sterile heaths, all by the hand of skillful industry, be converted into fields of beauty and luxuriance.   Rocks and barren sands, and many a substance at present useless, if not a positive nuisance, would become the materials for the construction of useful and ornamental works.

As an illustration, I may refer to what I saw a few days since. In passing along the streets of one of the beautiful and romantic towns on the Hudson, I stopped before an inclosure of peculiar elegance and beauty.   In the centre rose a superb mansion, around which taste and skill and labor had spread graceful slopes and lovely greens, and flowers and fruits and trees of every foliage: and all inclosed by a high and thick wall, which was itself among the objects not the least to be admired.

On expressing admiration of the lovely spot, how much nature,

* Since writing the above, a visit to the Central Park in New York, has quite cherished the idea here advanced. Already enough has there been done in overcoming the deformities of nature and converting them into beauties, to illustrate what money, labor, skill and taste can do to "subdue" the earth, and make it what I have supposed. But the Park is but *begun*. When it shall be *finished*, what an illustration shall we then have; and, untainted by sin, what will it lack of being a Paradise?

Is the supposition, then, extravagant, that if the time, and the hundreds of millions of money, the skill and taste now squandered in idleness, vice, crime and hurtful amusements—in war, intemperance, or smoked away in tobacco fumes, were annually expended to beautify the earth, and make all its waste places fruitful fields, the earth would, after a few years, become the Eden we have supposed?

as well as art, had done for it, my friend replied that *nature* had lavished nothing on it.   It was, he said, a few years ago, but a barren, uncouth, rocky hill—good for nothing.   The beautiful stones that now formed the walls of the inclosure, the terraces and the walks, were once huge piles of unsightly rocks which deformed the spot.   All told what money, taste, skill and persevering industry can do—how the wilderness is made glad for them, and the desert to rejoice and blossom as the rose.

Nothing but the application of *more* wealth, skill and labor, and on a broader scale, is requistite, to produce greater and yet greater physical transformations, till the whole earth shall be converted into one great Eden, beautiful and luxuriant in all that can please the eye or gratify the taste—a Paradise in which the voice of God shall again hold sweet converse with men, and heaven and earth shall meet.

Were mind, skill, mental power generally devoted to the real advancement and happiness of man, what a change would it at once work in all human affairs!   How sad the perversion of the intellectual powers of man!   What adroitness, skill and shrewdness have in all ages been employed in the perpetuation of mischief!   Now suppose only that the mighty intellect of the world, in its most highly improved condition, were made wholly subservient to the best interests of man, and to the honor of God, and what in point of comeliness would earth lack to be a heaven?

The great mind of the world once consecrated to the welfare of man, and the great *heart* of the world sanctified, there would everywhere be good-will to man and glory to God in the highest. Sin would no longer alienate man from man—would not desolate by wars, or curse by intemperance, or any hurtful vice—would no longer monopolize wealth, industry and mind.   Suppose all the ravages of sin removed, and what more would we ask or wish for as heaven?

But, essentially, it matters little to us *where* heaven is.   The important points are, what is heaven? and have we a passport thither? and more than all, have we a fitness for that high and holy place?   Where God is, is heaven.   Where holiness pervades all hearts, and controls the whole inner man, there is heaven. Where the Lord Jesus Christ is, our blessed Immanuel, our intercessor and High Priest, our Prophet and King, there is heaven. Be it earth, our birthplace and home; or be it any other province of God's great Empire, it matters little.   All worlds are but the many mansions in our Father's house.   And where is our Father's house, and our Father's heart, there will we be at home, and be happy.

It may be pleasant, though not essential to hope and happiness, to contemplate this earth as our future home, and the scene of future blessedness.   But let it be the great endeavor of life, our unceasing prayer to God—the most earnest heart's desire, that we may have part and lot in Christ, so that where he shall be, there we may be also.

CHAPTER XXII.

Objection: that this earth is not large enough for the future residence of all earth's redeemed—Spiritual bodies; their locomotive powers—The employments of Heaven—Sin the great evil.

HAVING, as we believe, made out the strong probability that this earth, renovated and purified, shall become the final resting-place of the saints, where they shall rejoice in their God forever, it only remains to meet the only plausible objection to such a supposition: which is,

That this earth *is not large enough* for the future abode of all earth's redeemed.

The objection may not be so formidable as it at first appears. If it be directed against the *dimensions* of the earth, on the ground that it is too insignificant a globe to be allowed the honor of being the future abode of the saints, our answer is, that it was *not* esteemed too insignificant to be the theatre of the most august transaction that, probably, ever transpired in the whole universe: the Advent and Incarnation, the sufferings and death of the only begotten Son of God: not too insignificant for the grandest display of the eternal Godhead.

But if the objection be that the superficial area of this globe is too small for the habitation and enjoyment of that great multitude which no man can number, we shall present a few considerations which may obviate the objection.

And, first, we do not know how large an area will be needed. The redeemed shall be a "great multitude;" but does that determine that they shall be more than may find habitation on this globe? Especially may we demur when we bring into the account what shall then be the character of their residence, the character of their employments and wants; and more especially the nature and character of the inhabitants themselves. Not only, as we have supposed, shall the entire surface of the earth become habitable, and shall, under the full benediction of heaven, bring forth, almost spontaneously, like Eden, and in the greatest abundance, but two other circumstances may quite modify our calculations here.

The first is, that the inhabitants of heaven, wherever heaven may be, are possessed of *spiritual bodies*. Such bodies will doubtless require much less sustenance and space for habitation, than our present gross bodies; and consequently a much greater population may then occupy the earth. Yet the earth in its present condition, that is, subjected as at present to the curse, is capable, if all improved and subjected to the skill and industry of a careful cultivation, as even now it might be, is probably capable of sustaining at least ten times its present population. What then shall it be capable of sustaining in its renovated condition, when there shall be no vast fruitless deserts, no barren rocks, or inaccessible mountains, or sterile wastes? and especially if, literally, "*there shall be no sea?*" What countless millions the earth might then sustain!

But are we sure that we need, in our calculations, to make provisions for more than the earth at present would sustain, if its surface were fully occupied and its resources fully developed; or at most more than, in its renovated state, the earth would sustain? Suppose, as is the very common belief, that the earth shall exist nearly as it has and does still exist, for six thousand years from its creation, and then that it shall have a Millennium, or a Sabbatic period of a thousand years; and then shall follow the perfect, the heavenly and eternal state, when men shall cease to marry and be given in marriage, and *increase from natural generation shall cease*; and how multitudinous may we suppose the heavenly state would be? We are told it shall be a great multitude which no man can number. That is only saying the number shall be very great. May we not make, at least, a vague estimate here? No age ever numbered so many evangelical Christians as the present. Yet probably there are not above twelve millions of the true followers of the Lamb now living, and the sixty centuries, or one hundred and eighty generations that are passed, have not averaged one-third that number. Allow an average of four millions; and the number of all the saints that have lived and that now live, would amount to seven hundred and thirty two millions, or a number not exceeding three-fourths the present population of the globe; or one fifteenth of what we have supposed the earth capable of sustaining in its present disabled condition.

Suppose, again, that the majority of the race shall be saved during the thirty generations of the Millennium, say 500,000,000 each generation of thirty-three years; or 1,500,000,000 each century. We should then have, at the close of the one thousand years, an aggregate of only 15,000,000,000 of Millennial-born Christians, or only once and a half the number we have supposed the earth capable of supporting in its present condition. Surely then —though we add to this number all the true saints that have ever lived—it will not be deemed extravagant, that the *renovated* earth should sustain twice or thrice that number; at least a number greater than the most enlarged charity dare hope will people the abodes of the blessed.

We must not here overlook the fact that, not only shall the renovated earth produce vastly more than at present, but not a few substances not yet appropriated and still regarded as of little or no use, shall be appropriated for food, apparel, and a thousand purposes of comfort and convenience. We have already witnessed enough in this direction to warrant the inference that there is probably not a plant, shrub or tree, not a mineral, metal or substance of any sort, which human skill and ingenuity shall not appropriate to the use of man.

The other circumstance which may further relieve a difficulty any one may feel that this earth is too small to serve as the future abode of the righteous, is the fact that the redeemed will *not be confined to a local habitation.* They will be like the angels, capable of soaring from world to world; and at all times, no doubt, vast multitudes will be abroad from their earthly home, on errands of mercy, or excursions of duty in the service of the King, or for the purpose of gaining a knowledge of God's works and ways, and admiring, wondering, worshiping, and enjoying the wonderful displays of the Divine wisdom, power and goodness. Such an instance have we in the case of Moses and Elias on the Mount of Transfiguration. And such missions are probably not infrequent to the habitations of men. Departed spirits, the spirits of just men made perfect, may be the surest messages of mercy, of peace and consolation to them who dwell afar off in other provinces of God's great Empire. Multitudes may be abroad upon these errands of love. As in a great city, after the citizens have become numerous, and wealthy and intelligent and enterprising, and more especially as they become overtly benevolent, and their hearts enlarged, and their hands open in an expansive philanthropy, a great multitude would be dispersed abroad, either on business, or in the pursuit of knowledge or pleasure, or in the discharge of duties of love and charity. And many would *reside* abroad. In like manner it shall be, when this whole world shall become the city of our God, the New Jerusalem come down from heaven—heaven come down to earth: or rather earth made a heaven. Going out from this point as their birthplace and homestead, the whole universe shall be the broad field of research and investigation, of adoration and praise, of thanksgiving and perpetual joy.

Though in accordance with our calculations in respect to the populousness of the heavenly abode, we feel no need of such a surmise, yet, in the nature of the case, we can see the strong probability that the redeemed will be endowed with locomotive powers that shall measurably annihilate distances, so that a visit to other and far distant worlds, shall be but a pleasure and pastime. The universe will now become the boundless area for the study of God's works, and for wonder and worship amidst his glories. The earth once renovated, loyal to its King, and glorified, will no longer be an alien and outcast in the great family of worlds, but shall be restored to its moral orbit, and be brought near again to the great moral centre of the universe, to God the Father and Fountain of all. And, reinstated in the great fraternity, its blissful inhabitants shall mingle in sweet and living concord, passing and repassing from world to world, as the inmates of loving households, happy to meet and mingle in all the harmonies of love and friendship.

While, therefore, we may look for the home and the locality of the redeemed on this earth, their native home and locality, we may, at any given time, calculate that multitudes of the redeemed themselves will be wandering, loving, learning and adoring in as many different worlds as there are stars that shine in the firmament.

But our extended answer to the above objection may, with many, give rise to another objection not the less offensive, if less formidable. It is that spiritual bodies should receive, if not require, food. It will be perceived that I have reasoned on the supposition that the inhabitants of the spirit world (as some are partial to designate heaven) will not be altogether relieved from the pleasure, if from the necessity, of food. I do not know that we need to be careful to avoid such an inference. If such shall be the condition of the earth, under the full benediction of heaven, as to make a due supply of food no more than a pleasure or pastime—at least, that its preparation shall be relieved of all drudgery and grossness and be but a pleasant labor—the pleasure-engendering exercise of the bodily powers and of the mind, we cannot perceive the objection felt by many on this score. Angels eat; as we have evidence in their visits to Abraham and Lot. The Lord Jesus Christ took food and ate, when he appeared to his disciples in his risen and spiritual body. And I can see no ground and feel no necessity for the supposition that the blessed, in this respect, shall not, at least in a measure, be subjected to the same condition of life as at present. We assert nothing, and only feel it incumbent on us to show that, if the supposition be allowed, how even this condition may be met, on the theory that this earth shall be the residence of the finally blessed.

Again, I may remark that, as another argument to sustain our supposition, we see nothing like *exhaustion*, in the resources and capabilities of the earth, that would seem to imply its destiny is nearly accomplished. While, on the other hand, we see it in all respects fitted and furnished for purposes which seem no more than to have begun to be answered in its present destiny, or any destiny likely to be accomplished in the present probationary state of man. Vast deserts, unreclaimed—wilds, rocks, mountains, but useless deformities—exhaustless mineral resources kept in reserve for untold ages: these are some of the things that constrain us to look to some vast future to explain the present.

Or I might derive another argument from the *progressive history of our earth* as analogous to the progressive character, condition and destiny of man. We believe in the indefinite and, in human parlance, the infinite progression of man. From his beginning man is eternal; and all the evidence on the subject goes to show that there is no limit to his progress—at least, no limit intellectually and morally, however it may be physically. The only obstacle to an indefinite progress and improvement, is sin and the multiplied mischiefs of sin. This once removed, and we see no other hindrance to man's eternal development in every thing godlike.

But the earth was made for man. It is his by divine right. And we have seen how it has gone on from step to step in progress and improvement, indicating no hindrance but sin and what belongs to sin, to a return to its perfect, or Eden state. If then this earth were made a fit abode for man and given him for his abode, who shall tell us that, after a little, man shall outlive his home, outgrow the paternal mansion—that the earth, made for man, given to man, and exactly fitted to his best interests and highest happiness, is unfitted to his future condition?

This material ball we call earth, has not suffered the ruins of sin so disastrously as man has. She suffers but physically. Sadly as man has suffered physically, he has suffered indefinitely more intellectually and morally. We may then have less concern that the restored earth shall be a fit place for the future man, than that the restored man shall be fitted to inhabit the renovated earth. In either case we need have no concern. Sin once removed and man becomes a fit inhabitant of Paradise, and earth becomes a Paradise.

But I will not pursue the subject. It is a matter of pleasant, though not of vital interest, as I have said, to know *where heaven is*. The question of paramount and vital interest relates to our own fitness for heaven. Sin, we see, has done the mischief, whether in its effects on the earth, or on our own souls. The only essential question then is, how shall we escape the curse, the disgrace and the eternal ruin of sin? Blessed be God, there is a way of escape. A voice from heaven, clear, sweet, melodious as angels sing, proclaims, " Behold, the Lamb of God that taketh away the sin of the world."

In conclusion, I remark,

1. The supposition presented is fitted to give a *definiteness* to our views of heaven, seeming to connect it more intimately with the present life. Who has not at times experienced a sense of partially painful indefiniteness at the thought of dwelling, as a disembodied spirit in some far-off planet, among scenes unknown before, and in a mode of life perfectly untried? Be it that Christ shall be there—that holiness and happiness shall pervade the place —that angels shall be our companions, and the spirits of just men made perfect shall welcome us to joys unspeakable and full of glory: yet are we not creatures of habit and association? and are not these constituent parts of our nature which shall go with us into our future existence? If so, we seem to see how the natural dread of dying, the idea of a final separation from all the loved scenes of earth, meets a solace in the dark hour of death. The disembodied spirit shall return; be gathered again to the bosom of its loved body, now made incorruptible and immortal; and there again and forever regale itself amidst the hills and vales, along the rills and rivers, among the fields and groves of its once loved and its now doubly loved earth.

Many indeed are the pleasant associations connected with the idea that this earth shall be our future, eternal home. It is the scene of our joys, and no less of our sufferings. All our loved relationships are here, and all the ties of sympathy and love. Here we have sinned, here met a Saviour and found a pardon.

Here is our *home*. And is not the thought delightful that the emancipated soul, purified, exalted, glorified, shall return to its former home and find it renovated, beautified and all glorious for his reception—his home from which he shall go no more out forever!

2. Our subject gives us some idea what shall be *the employments and pursuits* of heaven. We might say, in a word, they shall be what they were in Eden. Our innocent progenitors were not idle admirers of the wonderful works of God. They did more than sing and praise and adore. They cared for the garden, and were lords of all the creatures God had made. And, aside from the toils, the drudgeries, the burdens and perplexities induced by sin, their employments did not differ essentially from ours. The pursuits of knowledge in the study of God's works, the admiration and enjoyment of God in all his ways as well as his works; toil as a pastime; and the various services of praise and worship, filled up the happy days and years (perchance) of the blessed pair. So shall it be in heaven.

3. The view we have taken attaches a new and a higher interest to this earth. This at present marred, soiled, polluted world of ours was, as it came from the hand of its Creator, a perfect model of perfection. As God surveyed the work of his hands, the earth and all pertaining thereunto, he pronounced all to be "good." It was beautiful in the eyes of infinite Perfection. And so it shall be in the "restitution of all things." All shall be restored to their pristine beauty and perfection. Now we see so much of its waste and deformity that we deem the earth only fit for burning. What a delightful interest, then, attaches to its glorious regeneration, and restoration to the high and holy purposes for which God originally made it!

4. Nor does the view taken necessarily detract aught from the sacredness of heaven, nor lessen the *motives* to reach after it. It is the *character* of heaven with which we are the most deeply

concerned, and the richness of the reward there to be realized. Without these the place is nothing.   Where God and holiness and unfailing felicity are, there is heaven.   We detract nothing from its sanctity, then, when we locate it on the earth.   Nor do we lessen the *motives* to reach after heaven and seek it as a supreme and lasting good.   I have shown that, for earth-born souls, no other world can possibly present so many attractions, or can have so many pleasing associations to render it a desirable habitation for the blessed, as this earth.   Such a heaven will be doubly dear, as it will be but *going home.*

5. Finally, we are again most vividly reminded of the *exceeding evil of sin,* and of the extreme preciousness of the gracious interposition of Christ.   It is sin that has marred the beauty of our world, that has covered it with deformities, deserts and desolations, that has laid it waste by war, pestilence and disease, that has cursed it with violence, superstition and crime.   It is sin that has made man vile, hateful and corrupt.   All natural evil, as well as all the moral evil which afflicts our world, is alike the progeny of sin.   It is sin that converted a once happy Paradise into pandemonium; and changed those once noble, happy beings who inhabited Eden into a race " whose mouth is full of cursing and bitterness," and " there is no fear of God before their eyes." And no less vividly are we reminded of the exceeding preciousness of Christ.   He comes to restore the ruins of the fall—to reinstate man in the image of his God—to take away the curse under which the " whole creation groaneth and travaileth in pain together until now "—to make earth again an Eden, where the will of God shall be done as it is in heaven—when God shall once more survey the workmanship of his hands in the lower world, and pronounce all to be " good."